PROGYMNASMATA

Society of Biblical Literature

Writings from the Greco-Roman World

John T. Fitzgerald, General Editor

Number 10

PROGYMNASMATA
Greek Textbooks of Prose Composition
and Rhetoric

Volume Editor
D. A. Russell

Progymnasmata

Greek Textbooks of Prose Composition and Rhetoric

Translated with Introductions and Notes by

George A. Kennedy

Society of Biblical Literature
Atlanta

PROGYMNASMATA
Greek Textbooks of Prose Composition and Rhetoric

Library of Congress Cataloging-in-Publication Data

Progymnasmata : Greek textbooks of prose composition and rhetoric / translated with introductions and notes by George A. Kennedy.
     p. cm. — (Writings from the Greco-Roman world ; v. 10)
Includes bibliographical references and index.
Text in English and Greek.
ISBN 1-58983-061-X (alk. paper)
    1. Greek language—Composition and exercises—Early works to 1800. 2. Rhetoric—Early works to 1800. I. Kennedy, George Alexander, 1928– II. Series.

PA257.P76 2003
808´.0481—dc21   2002155099

03 04 05 06 07 08 09 10   5 4 3 2 1

The book is printed in the United States of America
on recycled, acid-free paper.

Table of Contents

Introduction

Students of classical, medieval, and early modern literature, and of the history of education, need a knowledge of the system of teaching prose composition and elementary rhetoric practiced in European schools from the Hellenistic period until early modern times. This is described in detail in four Greek treatises that were written in the time of the Roman empire and studied throughout the Byzantine period. They are by, or attributed to Theon, Hermogenes, Aphthonius, and Nicolaus. The only Latin account of the exercises from the classical period is in Quintilian's *Education of the Orator* (1.9; 2.4; 10.5), written about A.D. 94, but a Latin version of the Greek handbook attributed to Hermogenes was made by Priscian about A.D. 500, preserved with his extensive works on grammar, and given some use in medieval schools. In the Renaissance Rudolph Agricola, Joannes Maria Catanaeus, and others made Latin versions of the handbook of Aphthonius and an English adaptation of this was published by Richard Rainolde in 1563. These texts were the common basis for teaching composition in western Europe for several centuries.

The curriculum described in these works, featuring a series of set exercises of increasing difficulty, was the source of facility in written and oral expression for many persons and training for speech in public life. In addition, the compositions inculcated cultural values, as well as understanding of conventional literary forms for those who entered on literature as a career or as an elegant pastime. In classical, medieval, and renaissance literature, fable, narrative, chreia, ecphrasis, comparison, speech in character, and other progymnasmatic forms were often combined in different ways to create epics, dramas, histories, and the genres of lyric poetry. As such, they are comparable to structural features of classical architecture that were artistically utilized in the great public buildings of the Greco-Roman period and were revived in the Renaissance in the West. Not only the secular literature of the Greeks and Romans, but the writings of early Christians beginning with the gospels and continuing through the patristic age, and of some Jewish writers as well, were molded by the habits of thinking and writing learned in schools.

The handbooks of progymnasmata may also interest modern

teachers of composition, for they present a sequence of assignments in reading, writing, and speaking which gradually increase in difficulty and in maturity of thought from simple story-telling to argumentation, combined with study of literary models. As such, the exercises were certainly effective in providing students for centuries with verbal skills that many students in our time seem less often to develop. Because the exercises were so completely structured, furnishing the student with lists of things to say on many subjects, they are open to the criticism that they tended to indoctrinate students in traditional values and inhibit individual creativity. Only Theon, among writers on progymnasmata, suggests that students might be asked to write about their own experiences—something that did not again become a subject of elementary composition until the romantic period. Nevertheless, it would be unfair to characterize the traditional exercises as inhibiting all criticism of traditional values. Indeed, a major feature of the exercises was stress on learning refutation or rebuttal: how to take a traditional tale, narrative, or thesis and argue against it. If anything, the exercises may have tended to encourage the idea that there was an equal amount to be said on two sides of any issue, a skill practiced at a later stage of education in dialectical debate. Although the period of the greatest use of progymnasmata, the time of the Roman empire, was often an age in which freedom of speech was limited, philosophical skepticism also flourished in the schools of the time, and the political context of the exercises looked back nostalgically to the time of democratic Athens.

"Pro-gymnasmata" means "preliminary exercises," preliminary that is to the practice of declamation in the schools of rhetoric, which boys usually began between the age of twelve and fifteen. The progymnasmata were assigned by Greek grammarians to students after they had learned to read and write as preparation for declamation and were continued in rhetorical schools as written exercises even after declamation had begun. Roman grammarians used similar exercises in Latin, preparing students for declamation. Although Quintilian favored the continuation of written exercises as part of the curriculum in rhetoric, most Roman rhetoricians seem to have given attention exclusively to declamation. The exercises were completed in written form and then often read aloud to the teacher or class; even in the rhetorical schools students usually wrote out their speeches before delivering them, but readers of the handbooks in this volume will note the consistent emphasis on speaking.

Until the fifth century B.C., so far as we know, Greek schools made no attempt to teach composition to students. Boys and some girls learned to read aloud and copy out canonical texts, especially the Homeric poems, and they memorized poetry and performed it orally on festive occasions. The wandering teachers known as "sophists," of whom Gorgias and Protagoras are probably the most famous because of their roles in dialogues of Plato, gave speeches which adolescents and young adults transcribed, studied, and imitated to gain facility in argument and style. In Plato's *Phaedrus* we meet a young man who is studying a speech attributed to Lysias, which he reads to Socrates. In the school of Isocrates in the fourth century the master read his own writings to his students, assigned them subjects for composition, and criticized their work. A course of elementary exercises in composition probably developed in schools in the fourth century. The term *progymnasmata* first appears in chapter 28 (1436a25) of the rhetorical handbook known as the *Rhetoric for Alexander,* probably written by Anaximenes of Lampsacus in the third quarter of the fourth century and preserved with the works of Aristotle. The author says that if students understand the forms and styles of composition as practiced in progymnasmata, they will have a plentiful supply of material for writing and speaking. Aristotle did not discuss preliminary exercises in his treatise *On Rhetoric,* or elsewhere in his voluminous writings so far as we know, but he does discuss rhetorical forms which later appear among the exercises, including fable, maxim, narrative, encomion, vivid description, and thesis.

During the Hellenistic period exercises in composition probably began to approximate the forms known from later writers. Both grammarians and rhetoricians doubtless made contributions, and development was parallel to the growing popularity of declamation in rhetorical schools. Although the earliest Latin rhetorical treatises, Cicero's *On Invention* and the anonymous *Rhetoric for Herennius,* do not directly discuss exercises in composition, there are some passages which seem to reflect knowledge of them. *On Invention* (1.27) and *Rhetoric for Herennius* (1.12) both allude to narrative as an exercise, and they associate "common-place" with denunciation of vice (*On Inv.* 2.77; *For Her.* 2.9), its usual subject among progymnasmata. In addition, in *Rhetoric for Herennius* (4.56–57) there is a description of how to develop the thought in a maxim. Suetonius, writing many years later about education in the second and early first centuries before Christ, reports that Romans practiced exercises in "problems," paraphrase, address, and characterization (*On Grammarians* 4), and elsewhere he mentions narration, translation, common-place, fable, thesis, refutation, and confirmation (*On Rhetoricians* 1). He says these exercises "evolved little by little," but gives no specific dates.

The earliest extended account of compositional exercises is the Greek treatise by Theon, which probably dates from the first century after Christ. Unlike the other handbooks it is addressed to teachers rather than to students and contains chapters on pedagogy. A short handbook attributed to Hermogenes of Tarsus, a famous rhetorician of the second century after Christ, is preserved separately from his genuine writings and may not be his work. The most influential handbook proved to be that by Aphthonius, a student of the great sophist Libanius in Antioch in the second half of the fourth century of the Christian era. Many progymnasmatic compositions from late antiquity and the Byzantine period survive. Best known are those attributed to Libanius, some of which were often included in the renaissance textbooks. Aphthonius' account of the exercises, each with a brief example, was combined with rhetorical treatises on stasis theory and style by Hermogenes to create the standard rhetorical compendium (the "Hermogenic corpus") of late antiquity and the Byzantine period. Commentaries on Aphthonius' *Progymnasmata* were compiled by John of Sardis in the ninth century, John Doxapatres in the eleventh century, and others. Theon's handbook, although less well known, was translated into Armenian and an Armenian handbook of composition, ultimately based on Aphthonius' account, also exists. A fourth handbook of composition is the work of Nicolaus of Myra, who taught rhetoric in Constantinople in the third quarter of the fifth century. He draws on the handbooks attributed to Theon and Hermogenes but not on that by Aphthonius. Portions of a handbook by Sopater, either the well-known sophist of the fourth century or another person with the same name, are quoted by John of Sardis. Brief references in late Greek and Byzantine writers indicate that many other Greek handbooks of progymnasmata once existed, and there was doubtless also an oral tradition among teachers, who adapted whatever seemed useful without acknowledging its source. A reference in the first paragraph of Theon's work to other treatments of the subject indicates that a variety of textbooks already existed in his time. Among later authors to whom progymnasmatic treatises, now lost, are attributed are Harpocration, Minucianus, and Paul of Tyre in the second century, and Epiphanius, Onasimus, Ulpian, and Siricius from the third or fourth century.[1] For an account of the continua-

[1] For lost progymnasmatic handbooks and what survives of Sopater's work, see Rabe's edition of Aphthonius, pp. 52–70.

tion of progymnasmata in the Byzantine period, see Herbert
Hunger, *Die hochsprachliche profane Literatur der Byzantiner*
(*Handbuch der Altertumswissenschaft* 12.5), vol. 1, pp. 92–120 (Munich: Beck, 1978). English translations of examples of chreias by a
variety of late classical and Byzantine rhetoricians can be found in
volume 2 of Hock and O'Neil's *The Chreia* (2002).

There is some variation in the number, names, and sequence of
the exercises among the extant works, and Nicolaus and John of
Sardis comment on what was apparently vigorous controversy
among teachers about the right order to follow in teaching. John
cites critics whom he calls "eristical sophists." They apparently
criticized the exercises generally, perhaps, like some Roman rhetoricians, favoring exclusive attention to declamation in the schools.

Table 1
Order of Treatment of Progymnasmata in Extant Treatises

Exercise	Theon	Hermogenes	Aphthonius	Nicolaus
Mythos, Fable	2	1	1	1
Diêgêma, diêgêsis, Narrative, narration	3	2	2	2
Khreia, Chreia, anecdote	1	3	3	3
Gnômê, Maxim	1[2]	4	4	4
Anaskeuê, Refutation	3	5	5	5
Kataskeuê, Confirmation	3[3]	5	6	5
Topos,[4] *Koinos topos,* Topic, Common-place	4	6	7	6
Enkômion, Encomion	7	7	8	7
Psogos, Invective	7	-	9	7
Synkrisis, Comparison	8	8	10	8
Ethopoeia, prosôpopoeia, Characterization, Personification	6	9	11	9
Ekphrasis, Ecphrasis, description	5	10	12	10
Thesis, Thesis, proposition	9	11	13	11
Nomos, Law	10	12	14	12

[2] Treated as a form of the chreia.
[3] Refutation and confirmation are discussed by Theon in connection with
narrative.
[4] Used only by Theon.

A NOTE ON THE TRANSLATION

Words in parentheses in the translations are additions or explanations by the translator.

The term *hypothesis* occurs frequently in the progymnasmata and, at the risk of some confusion to readers, has been retained in the translation. The word usually refers to themes of declamation on judicial or deliberative subjects, occasionally also epideictic, as practiced in schools of rhetoric. These themes identified specific laws and circumstances or historical individuals and contexts on which rhetoricians and their students composed and delivered complete speeches. *Hypotheses* differ from *theses* in that a *thesis*, which is one of the progymnasmatic forms, deals with a proposition without specifying persons and circumstances and was not required to have all the conventional parts of a complete *hypothesis*.

The hyphenated word "common-place" has been adopted in order to distinguish *koinos topos,* one of the progymnasmatic forms, from other meanings of "commonplace."

As in the translator's versions of other Greek rhetorical works, a semi-colon is regularly used before "for" to indicate the presence of an enthymeme: i.e., a minor premise or an example in support of a proposition.

For a list of 725 fable themes in the Aesopic tradition, see the appendix to the Loeb Classical Library volume of Babrius and Phaedrus, edited and translated by B. E. Perry, Cambridge: Harvard University Press, 1965.

BIBLIOGRAPHY

This list includes general resources for study of classical rhetoric and works cited in footnotes by author and short-title. Additional books and articles are fully identified when cited in the notes.

Allinson, Francis G., tr., *Menander: The Principal Fragments*. Loeb Classical Library. Cambridge: Harvard University Press, 1930.

Burtt, J. O., tr., *Minor Attic Orators*, vol. 2. Loeb Classical Library. Cambridge: Harvard University Press, 1954.

Butts, James R., *The "Progymnasmata" of Theon: A New Text with Translation and Commentary*. Dissertation, Claremont Graduate School, 1986.

Diels-Kranz: Hermann Diels and Walther Kranz, eds., *Die Fragmente der Vorsokratiker*, 7th ed. 3 vols. Berlin: Weidmann, 1951–54.

Dilts and Kennedy: Mervin R. Dilts and George A. Kennedy, eds.,

*Two Greek Rhetorical Treatises from the Roman Empire: Intro-
duction, Text, & Translation of the Arts of Rhetoric Attributed to
Anonymous Seguerianus and to Apsines of Gadara.* Mnemosyne
Supplement 168. Leiden: Brill, 1997.

Edmonds, J. M., tr., *Elegy and Iambus.* Loeb Classical Library.
Cambridge: Harvard University Press, 1931.

Felten, Joseph, ed., *Nicolai Progymnasmata.* Leipzig: Teubner, 1913.

Foerster, Richard, ed., *Libanii Opera*, 12 vols. 1903–22; rpt.,
Hildesheim: Olms, 1963.

Gangloff, Anne, "Myths, fables, et rhétorique à l'époque imperi-
ale," *Rhetorica* 20 (2002) 25–56.

Giannantoni, Gabriele, ed., *Socraticorum Reliquiae*, 4 vols. Rome:
Bibliopolis, 1983–85.

Heath, Malcolm, tr., *Hermogenes On Issues.* Oxford: Clarendon
Press, 1995.

Hock and O'Neil: Ronald F. Hock and Edward N. O'Neil, eds., *The
Chreia in Ancient Rhetoric*: Volume I. *The Progymnasmata.* Atlanta: Scholars Press, 1986; Volume II. *The Chreia and Ancient
Rhetoric: Classroom Exercises.* Atlanta: Society of Biblical Literature, 2002.

Jacoby, Felix, ed., *Die Fragmente der Griechischen Historiker*,
3 Parts. Leiden: Brill, 1923–63.

Kaibel, G., ed., *Comicorum Graecorum Fragmenta.* Berlin: Weidmann, 1890.

Kennedy, George A., *Greek Rhetoric Under Christian Emperors.*
Princeton University Press, 1983.

————, *A New History of Classical Rhetoric.* Princeton University
Press, 1994.

Kock, Theodor, ed., *Comicorum Atticorum Fragmenta.* 3 vols.
Leipzig: Teubner, 1880–1888.

Lausberg, Heinrich, *Handbook of Literary Rhetoric: A Foundation
for Literary Study*, translated by Matthew T. Bliss et al. Leiden:
Brill, 1998.

Martin, Josef, *Antike Rhetorik: Technik und Methode.* Munich:
Beck, 1974.

Matsen, Patricia P., Philip Rollinson, and Marion Sousa, eds.,
Readings from Classical Rhetoric. Carbondale: Southern Illinois
University Press, 1990.

Morgan, Teresa, *Literate Education in the Hellenistic and Roman
Worlds.* Cambridge University Press, 1998.

Nauck, Augustus, ed., *Tragicorum Graecorum Fragmenta.* 2nd ed.,
Leipzig: Teubner, 1889.

Page, Denys, ed., *Poetae Melici Graeci*. Oxford: Clarendon Press, 1962.

Patillon, Michel, *La Théorie du discours chez Hermogène le rhéteur*. Paris: Les Belles Lettres, 1988.

Patillon, Michel, and Giancarlo Bolognesi, eds., *Aelius Théon: Progymnasmata*. Edition Budé. Paris: Les Belles Lettres, 1997.

Porter, Stanley F., ed., *Handbook of Classical Rhetoric in the Hellenistic Age, 330 B.C.–A.D. 400*. Leiden: Brill, 1997.

Rabe, Hugo, ed., *Aphthonii Progymnasmata*. Leipzig: Teubner, 1926.

———, ed., *Hermogenis Opera*. Leipzig; Teubner, 1913; reprinted, 1969.

———, ed., *Ioannis Sardiani Commentarium in Aphthonii Progymnasmata*. Leipzig; Teubner, 1928.

———, ed. *Prolegomenon Sylloge*. Leipzig: Teubner, 1931.

Radermacher, Ludwig, ed., "Artium Scriptores (Reste der voraristotelischen Rhetorik," *Sitzungsberichte* der Oesterreichische Akademie der Wissenschaften, Philosophische-historische Klasse, 227, 3. Vienna: Rudolf M. Rohrer, 1951.

Spengel, Leonardus, ed., *Rhetores Graeci*. 3 vols., Leipzig: Teubner, 1854–56. Vol. 1, pt. 2, reedited by Caspar Hammer. Leipzig: Teubner, 1894.

van Dijk, Gert-Jan, *AINOI, LOGOS, MYTHOI: Fables in Archaic, Classical, and Hellenistic Greek Literature, with a study of the Theory and Terminology of the Genre*. Mnemosyne Supplement 166. Leiden: Brill, 1997.

Walz, Christian, ed., *Rhetores Graeci*. 9 volumes. London and elsewhere, 1832–36; reprinted, Osnabrück: Zeller, 1968.

West. M. L., ed., *Iambi et Elegi Graeci*. 2 vols., Oxford: Clarendon Press, 1972.

Wooten, Cecil, tr., *Hermogenes On Types of Style*. Chapel Hill: University of North Carolina Press, 1987.

Acknowledgments

In revising this work, I am particularly indebted to Professor D. A. Russell for numerous corrections and suggestions based on a lifetime of experience with later Greek texts. In addition, D. M. Schenkeveld, Malcolm Heath, and Edwin Carawan have provided welcome corrections and suggestions. For remaining faults I am myself responsible.

Pagination of Theon's Text

References by scholars to Theon's text ordinarily make use of page numbers in volume 2 of Spengel's *Rhetores Graeci*. Modern editors, however, have rearranged the order of the chapters and are followed in this respect in the translation. The result is that a passage may be difficult to find on the basis of its Spengel number. A collation of Spengel pages and pages in this translation is therefore provided here.

Spengel Pages	Pages in the Translation	Spengel Pages	Pages in the Translation
59–72	3–15	109–115	50–55
72–96	23–42	115–118	47–49
96–105	15–23	118–119	45–47
106–109	42–45	120–130	55–64

Chapter I

The *Exercises* of Aelius Theon

The author of this treatise is identified in the manuscripts simply as Theon. The tenth-century Byzantine encyclopedia, Suda, has an entry for Aelius Theon of Alexandria, identifying him as author of a treatise on progymnasmata as well as works on rhetoric and commentaries on Xenophon, Isocrates, and Demosthenes. Certainty is impossible, but this Aelius Theon of Alexandria is the leading candidate for author of this work.[1] When he lived can only be approximately determined. The latest authors to whom he refers are (ch. 11) Theodorus of Gadara and (ch. 14) Dionysius of Halicarnassus, indicating he was writing no earlier than the late first century B.C. Quintilian cites the views of a certain Theon on stasis theory (3.6.48) and of "Theon the Stoic" on figures of speech (9.3.76).[2] If either of these references is to the author of the progymnasmata, he must have been active earlier than the publication of Quintilian's Institutio Oratoria in A.D. 95. Thus the treatise may have been written at almost any time in the first century after Christ. It is the consensus of scholarly opinion that it is, in any event, the earliest surviving work on exercises in composition, certainly written sometime between the Augustan period and the flowering of the Second Sophistic in the second century after Christ, and it shows the system of instruction still in a stage of experiment and development. The Attic writers of the fifth and fourth centuries are regarded as the classic models for imitation by students, a development of the first century B.C., but included among them are the historians Theopompus, Philistus, and Ephorus, largely ignored by later rhetoricians. Theon seems to have a special interest in Thucydides, which may be a reflection of Thucydideanism in the Augustan period. On the other hand, there is no mention of Aelius Aristeides, who by the end of the second century had come to be regarded as an equal to the classical writers of the distant past and is cited in the work attributed to Hermogenes.

---

[1] See W. Stegemann in Pauly-Wissowa's *Realencyclopädie* V.A.2, coll. 2036–37.

[2] There are possible indications of Stoicism in the work; e.g., the distinction between *erotêsis* and *pysma* in the discussion of the chreia, a distinction which Diogenes Laertius 7.66 attributes to the Stoics. On other possible Stoic influences, see G. Reichel, *Quaestiones Progymnasmaticae* (Leipzig; Teubner, 1909) pp. 23–30.

Sometime in later antiquity Theon's work was edited, and the order of the chapters was rearranged to make it conform more closely to the system of exercises described in the handbook of Aphthonius, the most commonly used work on progymnasmata in late antiquity. This edited text is what has been preserved in Greek manuscripts, of which at least seven survive. The earliest, Laurentianus plut. 55.10, dates from the thirteenth century. The manuscripts include a few scholia, chiefly consisting of quotations from John of Sardis's commentary on Aphthonius that are relevant to Theon's discussion. John, probably writing in the early ninth century, cites Theon's treatise specifically in several passages and borrows from it without acknowledgement in others. Later commentaries on Aphthonius by John Doxapatres, Maximus Planudes, and an anonymous writer preserve material that originated with Theon but do not identify the source.[3] The Greek text was first printed in 1520 at Rome in the edition of Angelo Barbato and again, accompanied by Libanius' examples of progymnasmata and Latin translations, in the edition of Ioachim Camerarius in Basel in 1541, which was intended for use in schools. Another early edition, with Latin translation, and including Quintilian 2.4 and the treatise by Aphthonius, was published by Daniel Heinsius in 1626. The work is also found with progymnasmata by Libanius in the Praeludia Oratoria *of Frédéric Morel (1606–7).*

Two manuscripts in classical Armenian, copied in the seventeenth century from lost earlier versions, preserve the original order of the text as well as five and a half chapters at the end of the work where the Greek is lost; they also assist correction of the Greek text in some passages.

The term "progymnasma" occurs once in Theon's text (below, p. 5), but he prefers the simpler terms "gymnasma" or "gymnasia," while nevertheless making it clear that he regards the exercises as "preliminary" to the declamation of rhetorical hypotheses. The first few exercises he discusses are intended for quite elementary students of composition in grammar schools. This is especially clear from the pattern practice in grammatical inflection given by recasting a chreia through changes of number and case, a valuable exercise for elementary students. More-advanced exercises, especially those in refutation and confirmation, prepare the student for argumentation in declamation. Probably Theon, like some other Greek teachers and unlike Roman practice, taught both grammar and rhetoric. His work is, however, addressed to teachers, not to students. Alone among the Greek authors of progymnasmata he describes classroom methods consisting of oral reading, lis-

---

[3] See Patillon's edition of Theon, pp. cxx–cxxiv and 113–20.

tening, memorizing, paraphrasing, elaborating, and contradicting what has been read.

The translation published here was initially made from the text printed in Leonard Spengel's Rhetores Graeci, *vol. 2, pp. 59–130, for long the only text available to scholars. Numbers in brackets in the translation refer to pages in Spengel's edition, which remain the standard form of reference to the text. Subsequently, the translation was revised to incorporate some suggestions in the text, and especially restoration of the original chapter order, made by James R. Butts in his 1987 PhD dissertation at the Claremont Graduate School, which includes an English translation and notes. It was revised a second time after the publication of what is now the best edition of the text, that by Michel Patillon in the Budé series, the first edition to incorporate evidence for the text from the Armenian version.*

[vol. 2, p. 59 Spengel]   I. PREFACE

The ancient rhetoricians, and especially those who have become famous,[4] did not think one should come to rhetoric at all before grasping philosophy to some extent and being filled with the greatness of mind that comes from this source. Now, however, most students are so far from appreciating such studies that they rush into public speaking without even getting a knowledge of what are called general studies;[5] and what is most boorish of all, they proceed to debate judicial and deliberative hypotheses[6] without having been practiced in the proper way—as the proverb says, "learning pottery-making by starting with a big jar."[7] Let others write about whatever else is needed by one who is going to practice rhetoric. I shall now try to give an account of what it is necessary to know before undertaking the treatment of hypotheses in order to be properly trained, not that others have not written about these matters, but hoping that I too can contribute no little benefit to those intending to speak in public. We[8] have not only invented some additions to the exercises (*gymnasmata*) as described by others, but also we have tried to give a definition of each, so that, when asked what each of them is, one

---

[4] E.g., Isocrates, Plato, and Aristotle, perhaps also Theophrastus and others.

[5] *Enkyklia mathêmata*: grammar, rhetoric, dialectic, arithmetic, geometry, astronomy, and music, or other similar subjects.

[6] Themes of declamation; a speech.

[7] Cf. Plato, *Gorgias* 514e and *Laches* 187b.

[8] Like Aristotle and many teachers, ancient and modern, Theon often uses the first person plural of himself; beginning in the next paragraph he will also use it to include students.

can say, for example, that *mythos* is "fictitious discourse imaging truth"; and we have made clear their differences from each other, and we have included starting points (*aphormai*)[9] for each of the compositions, and we have further shown how one might make use of each most carefully.

[60]   There is no secret about how these exercises are very useful for those acquiring the faculty of rhetoric. One who has expressed a **diêgêsis** (narration) and a **mythos** (fable) in a fine and varied way will also compose a history well and what is specifically called "narrative" (*diêgêma*) in hypotheses[10]—historical writing is nothing other than a combination of narrations—and one who can refute or confirm these is not far behind those speaking hypotheses, for everything that we do in judicial hypotheses is there as well: first, there is prooemion and narrative; then we try to meet each of the things said in the narrative and fable and to put each to a test; next we take thought how we shall best arrange each of the epicheiremes,[11] and we amplify and disparage and do other things that would be too long to mention here. Surely the exercise in the form of the **khreia** (or anecdote) not only creates a certain faculty of speech but also good character while we are being exercised in the moral sayings of the wise. What is called **topos** (common-place) and **ekphrasis** (description) have very clear benefit, since the ancients have used these everywhere, all historical writers using ecphrasis very frequently and orators using common-place. And **prosôpopoeia** (personification) is not only an historical exercise[12] but applicable also to oratory and dialogue and poetry,[13] and is most advantageous in everyday life and in our conversations with each other, and (understanding of it) is most useful in study of prose writings. Thus, we praise Homer first because of his ability to attribute the right words to each of the characters he introduces, but we find fault with Euripides because his Hecuba philosophizes inopportunely.[14] Furthermore, the exercise of **synkrisis** (comparison)

----

    [9] This term appears repeatedly in Theon's treatise. It refers to the resources, materials, or topics for discussion useful in composition.

    [10] Contrary to what Theon says, *diêgêsis* is the usual technical term for a "narration" as part of a speech; cf. Aristotle, *Rhetoric* 3.16, Anonymous Seguerianus, ch. 2, and Apsines, ch. 3. *Diêgêma* becomes the more common word for the exercise in narrative; cf. the usage in Hermogenes and Aphthonius.

    [11] I.e., the arguments.

    [12] I.e., offering practice in the composition of speeches, a regular feature of ancient historiography.

    [13] I.e., to all genres in which characters are imagined as speaking.

    [14] E.g., her speeches in *Hecuba* 251–95, 585–628, and 786–845.

is useful in judicial speeches when we compare **[61]** either wrongs
to wrongs or good deeds to good deeds, and similarly in encomia
when we contrast good deeds. The advantage (of practice in comparison) for deliberative speeches is also very clear, for speeches of
advisers are concerned with which policy is preferable. What would
one say about **thesis**? It differs not at all from hypothesis except
that it lacks specific persons and place and time and manner and
cause; for example, the thesis whether it is appropriate for those
who are besieged to send an army abroad and the hypothesis
whether it is appropriate for the Athenians when besieged by the
Peloponnesians to send an army to Sicily. Similarly, attack on and
defense of **nomoi** (laws) is not the least part of an hypothesis. The
finest Demosthenic speeches are those in which there is a question
about a law or decree; I mean *On the Crown* and *Against Androtion*
and *Against Timocrates* and *Against Leptines* and *Against Aristocrates*. It made little difference that Aristocrates introduced a decree
rather than a law. I am not overlooking **enkômion**, which is a
species of hypothesis. There are in fact three species of hypothesis:
encomiastic, which the Aristotelians called epideictic,[15] dicanic (judicial), and symbouleutic (deliberative). Since we have become accustomed often to assign the writing of encomia even to young students, I have placed it among the preliminary exercises
(*progymnasmata*) and for the present have deferred an accurate
technical description of it to some appropriate place,[16] while here
limiting my teaching to a rather simple account.

*After this list of exercises and indication of the utility of each,
Theon turns to a brief description of pedagogical methods, which is a
unique feature of his handbook. He will return to the subject in chapters 13–17.*

Anagnôsis (reading aloud), as one of the older authorities
said—I think it was Apollonius of Rhodes[17]—is the nourishment of
style; for we imitate most beautifully when our mind has been

[15] In *Rhetoric* 1.9.33 Aristotle defines encomion as a subdivision of epideictic
concerned with praise of deeds.
[16] Whether Theon ever wrote a full discussion of encomia is unknown. Perhaps it would have included discussion of praise of kings, officials, and festivals,
not envisioned in school exercises; cf. D. A. Russell, "The Panegyrists and Their
Teachers," in *The Propaganda of Power*, ed. by Mary Whitby (Leiden: Brill, 1998),
p. 26.
[17] Probably not the famous poet but the rhetorician Apollonius Molon with
whom Cicero studied; cf. *Brutus* 312 and 316.

stamped by beautiful examples. And who would not take pleasure in *akroasis* (hearing a work read aloud), **[62]** readily taking in what has been created by the toil of others? But just as it is no help to those wanting to paint to look at the works of Apelles and Protogenes and Antiphilus unless they themselves put their hand to painting, so neither the words of older writers nor the multitude of their thoughts nor their purity of language nor harmonious composition nor urbanity of sound nor, in a word, any of the beauties in rhetoric, are useful to those who are going to engage in rhetoric unless each student exercises himself every day in writing.

Despite what some say or have thought, *paraphrasis* (paraphrase) is not without utility.[18] The argument of opponents is that once something has been well said it cannot be done a second time, but those who say this are far from hitting on what is right. Thought is not moved by any one thing in only one way so as to express the idea (*phantasia*) that has occurred to it in a similar form, but it is stirred in a number of different ways, and sometimes we are making a declaration, sometimes asking a question, sometimes making an inquiry,[19] sometimes beseeching, and sometimes expressing our thought in some other way. There is nothing to prevent what is imagined from being expressed equally well in all these ways. There is evidence of this in paraphrase by a poet of his own thoughts elsewhere or paraphrase by another poet and in the orators and historians, and, in brief, all ancient writers seem to have used paraphrase in the best possible way, rephrasing not only their own writings but those of each other. While Homer says (*Odyssey* 18.136–37), "Such is the mind of men who live on earth / As the father of men and gods grants it for the day," Archilochus,[20] rephrasing the lines, says, "Such, Glaucus, son of Leptines, is the mind / Of mortal men as Zeus brings it for the day." And again, Homer has spoken of the capture of a city in this way (*Iliad* 9.593–94): **[63]** "They kill the men, and fire levels the city, / And some lead off children and others deep-zoned women." Demosthenes (19.65) adapts it thus, "When we were on our way to Delphi, necessarily we saw all these things: houses destroyed, walls thrown down, a place deserted by those in the prime of life, few women and children, and pitiful old men." Aeschines (3.157) treats it thus: "Look at their dis-

[18] The opponents of paraphrase are unknown. Quintilian (1.9.2 and 10.5.5) recommends the practice.
[19] In ch. 3, below, Theon explains that a question (*erôtêsis*) can be answered yes or no, whereas an inquiry (*pysma*) requires a longer response.
[20] Frag. 131, ed. West.

asters in your imagination and think you are seeing their city captured, the throwing down of walls, burning of houses, temples
robbed, women and children led into slavery, old men, old women
learning late to forget liberty." Furthermore, Thucydides (2.45)
says, "There is envy in rivalry with the living, but one who no
longer stands in the way has been honored with unchallenged good
will"; and Theopompus,[21] "For I know that many look upon the living with ill-will, but they abandon their envy of the dead through
the number of years"; and Demosthenes (18.315), "Who among all
of us does not know that some envy, greater or smaller, exists for all
the living, but not even one of their enemies hates the dead." Indeed, Philistus[22] in his history of Sicily borrowed almost the whole
account of the war with Athens from Thucydides, and Demosthenes in his speech *Against Meidias* borrowed from speeches about
wanton violence by Lysias and Lycurgus and passages from Isaeus'
speeches against the violence of Diocles.[23] You may also find in
Isocrates' *Panegyricus* some things from Lysias' *Epitaphius* and
Olympicus. Not only this, but Demosthenes often paraphrases himself, not **[64]** only transferring things he said in one speech to another, but even in a single speech the same things are constantly repeated,[24] but this escapes the notice of the hearers because of the
variation of the style (*hermêneia*). In *Against Meidias* (§37) he says,
"Who of you does not know that the cause of many such things
happening is that those who do wrong are not punished, and that
the only way to prevent someone from being outraged in the future
is for one caught doing so always to pay the appropriate penalty?"
And in *Against Aristocrates* (§99)—the same passage occurs in
Against Androtion (§7)—he says, "If something has not been done
in accordance with the laws, and you, Aristocrates, imitated the act,
you would not for that reason be justly acquitted; on the contrary,
it is much more a reason for you to be convicted. For just as if someone had been convicted for that act, you would not have introduced
your decree, so if you are now convicted, another will be deterred."
In the *Philippics* he repeated the same things again and again, and
in *Against Leptines* there are no few places where he said that it is
not right for benefactors to be deprived of what was given them. In

[21] Theopompus, fourth-century B.C. historian; frag. 395, ed. Jacoby.
[22] Fourth-century B.C. author of a history of Sicily, now lost; number 556 in
Jacoby, vol. 3.
[23] None of these speeches has survived.
[24] Cf., e.g., Galen Rowe, "The Many Facets of *Hybris* in Demosthenes'
Against Meidias," *American Journal of Philology* 114 (1993): 397–406.

On the Crown, the idea is scattered through the whole speech that it is not right to make an accusation on the basis of the outcome of actions but on consideration of each of the policies. Who does not know that the ransoming of the prisoners is repeatedly discussed in *On the False Embassy* (§§166, 168–73, 222–23, 229–30)?

Surely *exergasia* (elaboration) is also useful in many other contexts, and especially in second speeches in trials. And *antirrhêsis* (contradiction) is useful in replies.

The introductory chapter concludes with an outline of the order in which the exercises will be discussed, which is also the order in which they should be undertaken by students.

We shall employ the following sequence in discussion of the exercises themselves. We begin, first, with the chreia;[25] for this is short and easily remembered. Then comes fable and narration, except for their refutation and proof; **[65]** for that seems in some way to come after the others.[26] It is agreed by all that the function of an orator is to demonstrate what is in doubt and to amplify what has been demonstrated. Demonstrative argument, therefore, both by nature and practice, comes first and amplification follows. It is necessary, (for example,) first to prove that someone is a traitor and then to arouse the feelings of the hearers at the greatness of the crime of treason. But although we said that, by nature, demonstration comes before amplification, in exercises the opposite is true. Easier things should be learned before more difficult ones, and it is easier to amplify what is clear than to demonstrate what is unclear. Thus, when we begin ourselves to form arguments [and refute or confirm them][27] out of our own resources, we shall start with the commonplace, followed by the ecphrasis, next the prosopopoeia, then we practice encomia, then syncrisis; these deal with things generally agreed to and there is nothing to be said on the opposite side of the case. After describing them, we shall provide training in the contentious exercises. The first of these is refutation of chreias, then of Aesopic fables and historical and mythical narratives, then of the-

[25] The Greek text begins with the myth and narrative but these chapters include reference to previous discussion of chreia; apparently the original order of the text was altered by an editor to accord with that other handbooks; cf. Hock and O'Neil, pp. 65–66. The original order is preserved in the Armenian version and has been followed here.

[26] Theon, however, does refer to refutation and proof in the chapters on the earlier exercises, beginning with the chreia.

[27] This phrase should probably be deleted; "confirm" is not in the Armenian text according to Patillon.

ses, and finally of laws. We shall make use of reading and listening and paraphrasing from the beginning, and of elaboration and even more contradiction when we have attained some facility.

2. ON THE EDUCATION OF THE YOUNG,
IN WHICH SOMETHING IS ALSO SAID ABOUT THE USE OF
PRELIMINARY EXERCISES BY THE ANCIENTS.

First of all, the teacher should collect good examples of each exercise from ancient **[66]** prose works[28] and assign them to the young to be learned by heart; for example, the kind of chreia found in the first book of Plato's *Republic* (329C): "Someone once went up to the poet Sophocles and said, 'How are you managing, Sophocles, in matters aphrodisial? Are you still able to have intercourse with women?' And he replied, 'Hush, man. I have escaped these things most gladly, like a slave running away from a mad and savage master.'" An example of a fable is the story of the flute player in Herodotus (1.141) and the stories of the horse <and stag>[29] in Philistus, in the first and in the second book respectively,[30] and in the twentieth book of Theopompus' *Philippica* the one about war and hybris, which Philip recounts to the ambassadors of the Chalcidians,[31] and Xenophon's story of the dog and the sheep in the second book of the *Memorabilia* (2.7.13–14).

The best examples of narration of the mythical sort would be those by Plato in the second book of the *Republic* (2.359b–60a) on the ring of Gyges and in the *Symposium* (203b–c) about the birth of Eros and about those in the underworld in the *Phaedo* (107d–8c) <and in the *Gorgias* (523a–24a)>[32] and in the tenth book of the *Republic* (10.614a–21b), and in the eighth book of Theopompus' *Philippica*[33] the story of Silenus. Of the factual sort, (the best examples would be) the one about Cylon in Herodotus (5.71) and in Thucydides (1.126) and about Amphilochus, son of Amphiarus, in the third[34] book of Thucydides (2.68), and about Cleobis and Biton

---

[28] By "ancient" Theon means Attic writings by philosophers, historians, and orators of the fifth and fourth centuries B.C.

[29] Added by Patillon from the Armenian version.

[30] Philistus, frag. 6, ed. Jacoby.

[31] Theopompus, frag. 127, ed. Jacoby; cf. Babrius, *Fables* 70.

[32] Added by Patillon from the Armenian version.

[33] Theopompus, frag. 74–75, ed. Jacoby.

[34] Butts (p. 174) suggests that differences in book references from our standard texts are not necessarily errors and that Theon's text of Thucydides was differently divided.

in the first book of Herodotus (1.31). Ephorus in his seventh book[35] and Philistus in his first[36] have the story of Daedalus' arrival at the court of Cocalus, king of the Sicanians. Also, you will find in Demosthenes' speech *On the False Embassy* (§§192–95) a plain and elegant narrative about the Olympian games held by Philip after the capture of Olynthus.[37]

There are also in ancient writers refutations and proofs of chreias and maxims and **[67]** assertions and such like. And clearly, into this kind of composition will fit what is said by Ephorus in the fifth book of his *Histories* against the assertions advanced by earlier writers about the Nile,[38] and refutations of mythical narratives in the second book of Herodotus about the fictions of the Greeks— how the Egyptians attempted to sacrifice Heracles to Zeus when he was visiting them but he slaughtered countless numbers of them instead (Herodotus 2.45); and in the first book of Ephorus about the fifty daughters of Thespius, with whom they say Heracles had sexual intercourse, all at the same time, when they were virgins;[39] and about Aristodemus, how he died when struck by lightning.[40] Some refutations and confirmations of factual narratives can also be taken from Herodotus, such as that in the fourth book (4.42–45) about how the whole earth is divided into three parts, one called Europe, one Libya, and one Asia; and from the first book of Thucydides (1.20) about the assassination of Hipparchus by Harmodius and Aristogeiton and those with them. There are still more examples to be taken from other historians: from the first book of Ephorus about the division of the Peloponnesus at the return of the children of Heracles;[41] from the twenty-fifth book of Theopompus' *Philippica* that the Hellenic oath, which the Athenians say the Greeks swore against the barbarians before the battle at Plataea, is a fabrication, as is the compact of the Athenians against the king. All do not celebrate with one accord the battle that took place at Marathon, and as he says, "all the other things about which the city of Athenians brags and misleads the Greeks."[42]

[35] Ephorus, frag. 57, ed. Jacoby.
[36] Philistus, frag. 1, ed. Jacoby.
[37] Rather than an account of the games themselves, Demosthenes tells the story of a request made by Satyrus, a comic actor, of Philip at the banquet after the games.
[38] I.e., about its sources. Not included by Jacoby.
[39] Ephorus, frag. 13, ed. Jacoby.
[40] Ephorus, frag. 17, ed. Jacoby.
[41] Ephorus, frag. 18a, ed. Jacoby.
[42] Theopompus, frag. 153–54. ed. Jacoby.

Similarly, it is possible to find what we are calling a *topos* in the ancient writers, such as the Demosthenic example in *On the Crown* (61): "For among the Greeks, not just some but among all equally, **[68]** there was a crop of traitors and bribe-takers and men who were enemies of the gods," and so on. Furthermore, there is Lycurgus' denunciation of an adulterer in *Against Lycophron* and Hypereides' against courtesans in *Against Aristagoras*.[43] We shall cite similar examples in the discussion of *topoi* below.

There are many examples of ecphrasis among the ancient writers, such as the description of the plague in the second book of Thucydides (2.47–54) and of the siege of the Plataeans in the third book (3.21), and elsewhere of naval battles (e.g., 7.50–54 and 70–71) and cavalry battles (e.g., 7.84–85). In Plato's *Timaeus* (21e–25d) is a description of Saïs, and in the second book of Herodotus of the seven walls of Ecbatana.[44] But we also have in the ninth book of Theopompus' *Philippica*[45] an ecphrasis of the Vale of Tempe in Thessaly, between the two great mountains of Ossa and Olympus; through them flows the river Peneius, into which all the rivers in Thessaly empty. And in the eighth book of Philistus are descriptions of the preparations of Dionysius the Tyrant (of Syracuse) against the Carthaginians,[46] and the making of weapons and ships and machines of war, and in the eleventh book a description of his funeral procession and the colorful nature of his funeral pyre.[47]

What would be a better example of prosopopoeia than (speeches in) the poetry of Homer and the dialogues of Plato and other Socratics and the dramas of Menander? We have, too, the encomia by Isocrates,[48] and the funeral orations by Plato[49] and Thucydides (2.35–46) and Hypereides (Or. 6) and Lysias (Or. 2), and Theopompus' encomion of Philip and of Alexander,[50] and Xenophon's *Agesilaus*. There are also syncrises among the ancients, by Demosthenes in *Against Leptines* (71–74) when he wants to accord Conon higher esteem than Themistocles, and you will find also in Xenophon's *Symposium* (8.12) Socrates testifying to Callias that love of the soul **[69]** is better than love of the body.

[43] For what is known of these two speeches, see Burtt, pp. 148–51 and 584–85.
[44] The description is actually in Herodotus 1.98.
[45] Theopompus, frag. 78 and 80, ed. Jacoby; cf. Aelian, *Varia Historia* 3.1.
[46] Philistus, frag. 28, ed. Jacoby; cf. Diodorus Siculus 14.11–44.
[47] Philistus, frag.40, ed. Jacoby.
[48] I.e., his *Evagoras* and *Encomium of Helen*.
[49] The *Menexenus*.
[50] These works are known only from Theon. Theopompus' treatment of Philip in his historical writings was very unflattering.

Examples of the practice of theses can be taken from Aristotle and Theophrastus; for many books of theses are ascribed to them.[51] Some "thetic" headings have been spoken by orators,[52] and indeed whole speeches might be thought to be almost the same as a thesis, as *On the Wedding Presents* ascribed to Lysias and *On Abortion*. In the former, the question is whether gifts given a woman on her marriage should permanently belong to her;[53] in the latter whether the embryo in the womb is a human being and whether women have the right to abortions. Critics[54] say that these speeches are not by Lysias, but it is worthwhile for the young to be acquainted with them for practice. It is also possible to find in every speech the heading of a thesis; for example, in Demosthenes' *Against Onetor for Eviction* (30.35–37) as to whether confessions based on torture are valid, and in Aeschines' *Against Timarchus* (1.127–31) if rumors are true, and other examples elsewhere.

We shall have plentiful examples of refutation of laws from many works of the orators, and most fully in Demosthenes' speeches *Against Timocrates* and *Against Aristocrates* and *Against Leptines*, and examples of confirmations in others, including Lysias' *Against Diocles* in support of the law against orators.[55] Even if the ancients have not made use of all the forms we have described, since they composed their speeches for real contests rather than for exercise, nevertheless they exhibit all the application of such compositions.[56]

And that the ancients were not neglectful of paraphrase is clear from what was said a little earlier, and there are many passages in their works more elaborately treated by others. The Cylonian Pollution was more elaborated by Thucydides (1.126) than by Herodotus (5.71) and Ephorus, and Demosthenes more than Hypereides

[51] Cf. the lists of their works in Diogenes Laertius 5.22–26 and 49.
[52] "Headings" are arguments on major issues found in a speech, such as fact, legality, justice, etc. These can be treated in much the same way as a thesis.
[53] The gifts in question are from the groom at the time the bride first removes her veil and the issue is whether the gifts should revert to the husband on the divorce or death of the woman.
[54] Dionysius of Halicarnassus, Caecilius of Calacte, or other late Hellenistic critics. The speeches mentioned have not survived.
[55] These three speeches of Demosthenes are concerned with defense of laws or attack on proposed laws. Lysias' speech *Against Diocles* is lost but probably opposed giving orators immunity from prosecution; see J. G. Baiter and H. Sauppe, *Oratores Attici* (Zurich, 1850; reprinted Hildesheim: Olms, 1967) II, p. 185.
[56] I.e., speeches by Attic Orators (Lysias, Demosthenes, et al.) show how different compositional forms (narrative, ecphrasis, syncrisis, refutation, etc.) can be combined in a complete speech.

elaborated the confusion the Athenians experienced **[70]**, "when in the evening someone came reporting to the prytaneis that Elateia had been captured" (Dem. 18.284). When considering what has been better elaborated it is possible to compare histories and whole speeches to each other; for example, speeches of Demosthenes <*Against Conon*>⁵⁷ to those of Hypereides and Theopompus' *Hellenic History* to that of Xenophon.

Contradiction (*antirrhêsis*) can be found most in speeches where one person accuses and the other defends himself on the charges; for example, in Aeschines' *Against Ctesiphon* and Demosthenes' *On the Crown*, as well as in the speeches of each *On the False Embassy*. You could find examples also in the histories by Thucydides: in the first book the reply of the Corinthians to the Corcyreans (1.68–71) and in the third book the speeches of Diodotus and Cleon (3.37–48). In Plato too can be found both elaboration and contradiction on the matters under discussion. In the *Phaedrus*, after speaking on the same hypothesis as Lysias,⁵⁸ (Socrates) then argues against both his own and Lysias' speeches, and in the *Republic*, after a discussion about justice with Thrasymachus (book 1) in the company of Glaucon and Adeimantus, after this (in book 2) he begins his reply to the whole charge.

Now I have included these remarks, not thinking that all are useful to all beginners, but in order that we may know that training in exercises is absolutely useful not only to those who are going to practice rhetoric but also if one wishes to undertake the function of poets or historians or any other writers. These things are, as it were, the foundation of every kind (*idea*) of discourse, and depending on how one instills them in the mind of the young, necessarily the results make themselves felt in the same way later. Thus, in addition to what has been said, the teacher himself must compose some especially fine refutations and confirmations and assign them to the young to retell, **[71]** in order that, molded by what they have learned, they may be able to imitate. When the students are capable of writing, one should dictate to them the order of the headings and epicheiremes and point out the opportunity for digression and amplification and all other treatments, and one must make clear the moral character (*êthos*) inherent in the assignment (*problêma*). And one should show concern for the arrangement of the words, teaching all the ways students will avoid composing badly, especially

⁵⁷ Added by Patillon from the Armenian version.
⁵⁸ That the attentions of a non-lover are to be preferred to those of a lover.

(how to avoid) metrical and rhythmical style, like most of the writings of the orator Hegesias and the so-called Asian orators,[59] and some things of Epicurus, the sort of thing he writes somewhere to Idomeneus: "Oh you who have since youth thought all my impressions sweet," and of those circulated as by him—we still do not find them in his collected works—: "Tell me, Polyaenus, how may I rejoice, how may I be delighted, how may there be great joy for me?"[60] Such things are completely blamable and clearly demonstrate faulty composition, but it is excusable when someone falls occasionally into those meters which have similarity to prose, the iambic for example;[61] all prose writers unintentionally fall into this kind of rhythm because of its similarity to prose. In his treatise *On Style*, where he is speaking against using rhythmical language, right at the beginning Ephorus has written a line of verse: "Again shall I remark about the use of meter."[62] One should no less aim at decorum and not directly lay bare shameful things but cover them over discreetly, as Aeschines (2.88), while attacking Demosthenes for an unmentionable vice, says that his body is not clean, not even the part from which his voice comes.

In addition, the style (*hermêneia*) must be clear (*saphês*) and vivid (*enargês*); for the need is not only to express a thought but also to make what is said dwell [72] in the mind of the hearers, so that what is said by Homer (*Odyssey* 2.146) happens: "I shall speak a word easily and place it in mind."

The making of corrections (by the teacher) in the early stages of study is not aimed at the removal of all mistakes but at correction of a few of the most conspicuous in such a way that the young man may not be discouraged and lose hope about future progress. In this process, let the one making corrections explain why the mistake occurred and how it is possible to compose in a better way. It seems much more helpful to assign to the young to write on some of the

[59] On the debased style of Hegesias, cf. Dionysius of Halicarnassus, *On Composition* 4 (p. 19 ed. Usener-Radermacher); on Asianism, see the Introduction to Dionysius' *On the Ancient Orators*.

[60] The Greek text is corrupt. The translation here is based on Patillon's reconstruction from the Armenian version, which may also be corrupt since it does not seem characterized by rhythmical regularity. These two quotations are known only from Theon. Epicurus was notorious for his crabbed style; cf. Cicero, *De Finibus* 1.14; Dionysius, *On Composition* 24 (p. 122 ed. Usener-Radermacher). The criticism here, however, is directed against the way the Greek seems to fall into lyric verse.

[61] Cf. Aristotle, *Poetics* 1449a25.

[62] Ephorus, *On Style*, frag. 6, ed. Jacoby; the line can be read as a scazon.

problems already elaborated by the ancients—for example, a topos or narration or ecphrasis or encomion or thesis or something of the sort—and afterward to have them examine these sources in order that they may acquire confidence if they have written similarly, and if not that they may have the ancients as correctors.

Since we are not all naturally gifted in every way, and some are lacking in the passions but are more successful in conveying character and some are the opposite, others deficient in both but better at developing enthymemes, we should try to augment natural advantages and fill in deficiencies with amplifications in order that we may be able not only to speak on great subjects well, as Aeschines did, and small ones as Lysias did, but have preparation for both, as did Demosthenes. In all cases one should also try to learn the appropriate delivery in each form of speech.

3. (SPENGEL 5.) ON CHREIA

See Hock and O'Neil, The Chreia in Ancient Rhetoric, *vol. 1, pp. 63–112, and Morgan,* Literate Education, *pp. 185–88. Chreias quoted by Theon are cited elsewhere, often attributed to different sources, and occur in variants; see the Catalogue in Hock and O'Neil, vol. 1, pp. 302–41.*

[96]   A chreia[63] (*khreia*) is a brief saying or action making a point, attributed to some specified person or something corresponding to a person, and maxim (*gnômê*) and reminiscence (*apomnêmoneuma*) are connected with it. Every brief maxim attributed to a person creates a chreia. A reminiscence is an action or a saying useful for life. The maxim, however, differs from the chreia in four ways: the chreia is always attributed to a person, the maxim not always; the chreia sometimes states a universal, sometimes a particular, the maxim only a universal; furthermore, sometimes the chreia is a pleasantry not useful for life, the maxim is always about something **[97]** useful in life; fourth, the chreia is an action or a saying, the maxim is only a saying. The reminiscence is distinguished from the chreia in two ways: the chreia is brief, the reminiscence is sometimes extended, and the chreia is attributed to a particular person, while the reminiscence is also remembered for its own sake. A chreia is given that name *par excellence*, because more than the other (exercises) it is useful (*khreiôdês*) for many situations in life, just as we have grown accustomed to call Homer "the poet" because of his excellence, although there are many poets.

---

[63] Or anecdote.

The most general categories of the chreia are three: some are verbal (*logikai*), some describe an action (*praktikai*), some mixed. Verbal are those that have their authority through words, without action; for example, "Diogenes the philosopher, when asked by someone how to become famous, replied that it was by thinking least about fame."[64] There are two species of verbal chreias, declarative (*apophantikon*) and responsive (*apokritikon*). Of the declarative, some are statements volunteered by the speaker; for example, "Isocrates the sophist used to say that those of his students with natural ability were children of gods." Others relate to a circumstance; for example, "Diogenes, the Cynic philosopher, seeing a rich young man who was uneducated, said 'He is dirt plated with silver.'" Here Diogenes did not make a simple statement but one based on what he saw. In addition, there are four species of responsive chreias: in response to a question; in response to an inquiry; giving a cause for the answer to a question; and what is called "apocritical," having the same name as the genus. A question (*erôtêsis*) differs from an inquiry (*pysma*) in that in response to a question it is necessary only to agree or disagree— for example, to toss or nod the head, or answer "yes" or "no"—while an inquiry demands a longer answer.[65] Thus, a reply to a question is, for example, "Pittacus of Mitylene, when asked if anyone escapes the gods' notice when doing wrong, said 'No, not even in contemplating it.'" **[98]** Anything added after the negative is superfluous, since the response is sufficient when he has made a denial. A pysmatic chreia is, for example, the following: "Theano, the Pythagorean philosopher,[66] having been asked by someone how soon after sexual intercourse with a husband may a woman go to the Thesmophoreion, replied, 'From her own husband, immediately, from somebody else's, never.'" Those giving a cause for the answer to a question are those that, apart from the answer to the question, include some cause or advice or something of the sort; for example, "Socrates, having been asked if the king of the Persians seemed to him to be happy, said, 'I cannot say, for I cannot know the state of his education.'"[67] Apocritic

---

[64] For this and subsequent references to Diogenes, with parallels, see *Socraticorum Reliquiae* V.B.388, ed. Giannantoni.

[65] The distinction was made by the Stoics; cf. Diogenes Laertius 7.66 and Butts, p. 231. The Greeks indicated "no" by tossing the head up and back rather than by shaking it from side to side.

[66] She is variously described as Pythagoras' wife, student, or wife of his student Brotinus; extant works attributed to her are regarded as spurious.

[67] Cf. Plato, *Gorgias* 470e.

chreias are those not in answer to a question or inquiry but in response to some statement; for example, "Once, when Diogenes was eating his lunch in the market place and invited Plato to join him, Plato said, 'Diogenes, how pleasant your lack of pretension would be if it were not pretentious!' " Diogenes was not asking Plato about anything nor was he inquiring of him, but he simply invites him to lunch, which is neither. There is, besides these, also another species of chreia falling into the verbal category and called "double." A double chreia is one having statements by two persons where either statement makes a chreia by one person; for example, "Alexander, the king of Macedon, stood over Diogenes when he was sleeping and said, 'A man who is a counselor should not sleep all night' (*Iliad* 2.24), and Diogenes replied (with *Iliad* 2.25), 'A man to whom the people have been entrusted and who has many cares.' "[68] In this case, there would have been a chreia even without the addition of the answer.

Chreias are actional (*praktikai*) when they reveal some meaning without speech, and some of these are active, some passive. Active ones describe some action; for example, "When Diogenes the Cynic philosopher saw **[99]** a boy eating fancy food, he beat his pedagogue with his staff."[69] Passive are those signifying something experienced; for example, "Didymon[70] the flute player, taken in adultery, was hung by his name."[71] Mixed chreias are those that partake of both the verbal and the actional but have the meaning in the action; for example, "Pythagoras the philosopher, having been asked how long is the life of men, going up onto the roof, peeped out briefly, by this making clear that life was short." And further, "A Laconian, when someone asked him where the Lacedaimonians set the limits of their land, showed his spear."

These then are the species of chreias. Some are expressed as gnomic sayings, some as logical demonstrations, some as a jest, some as a syllogism, some as an enthymeme, some with an example, some as a prayer, some with a sign, some as tropes, some as a wish, some with metalepsis, and others are composed of any combination of the ways just mentioned.

[68] Cf. Epictetus 3.22.92. Diogenes' point was that he was not a ruler.
[69] Cf. Libanius, *Progymnasmata* 1.2.
[70] Reading *Didymôn* with Lana and Butts (pp. 232–35) for the *Didymus* of the mss; cf. Diogenes Laertius 6.51.
[71] I.e., hung from *didymoi*, "the twins," = his testicles, as an appropriate punishment.

A chreia as a gnomic saying is, for example, "Bion the sophist said that love of money is the mother city of all evil."[72]

As a logical demonstration, for example, "Isocrates the orator used to advise his acquaintances to honor teachers ahead of parents; for the latter have been only the cause of living but teachers are the cause of living well." Isocrates expressed his statement with a logical reason.

As a jest, for example, "When Olympias learned that her son Alexander was proclaiming himself the child of Zeus, she said 'Will he not stop slandering me to Hera?' "[73]

Syllogistically, for example, "When Diogenes the philosopher saw a young man adorning his person excessively, he said 'If you are doing it to attract husbands, you are making a mistake; if for wives, you are doing wrong.' "

Enthymematically, for example, "When his acquaintance Apollodorus said to him, 'The Athenians have unjustly condemned you to death,' Socrates broke into a laugh and said, 'Were you wanting them to do so justly?' " [100] We need to add a proposition that it is better to be condemned unjustly than justly, which seems to have been omitted in the chreia but is potentially clear.[74]

With an example, as when Alexander, king of the Macedonians, being urged by his friends to amass money, said, "But even Croesus didn't gain much from it."

In the form of a wish, for example, "Damon the athletic trainer had swollen feet; when his shoes were stolen, he said. 'I hope they fit the thief!' "[75]

By using a sign, for example, "When Alexander, the king of the Macedonians, was asked by someone where he kept his treasures, 'Here,' he said, pointing to his friends."

As a trope (i.e., metaphor), for example, "Plato the philosopher used to say that the sprouts of virtue grow with sweat and toil."

With ambiguity, for example, "Isocrates the orator, when a boy

[72] The chreia is variously attributed to Bion the Borysthenite (philosopher, fl. 300 B.C.), Bias (one of the proverbial Seven Wisemen of early Greece), Diogenes, and others; cf. Hock and O'Neil, vol. 1, p. 337.

[73] Patillon here reports additional words in the Armenian version which he translates "et de me porter atteinte dans mes parties intimes." There may be some corruption in the Armenian text.

[74] This reflects the view of an enthymeme as a statement in which one premise is omitted.

[75] Attributed by Plutarch (*Moralia* 16d) to a cripple named Damonides and by Athenaeus (8.338a) to Dorion, a crippled musician at the court of Philip of Macedon; cf. Hock and O'Neil, vol. 1, p. 310.

was being enrolled as a student with him and the person who was enrolling him asked what he needed to have, said, 'A tablet *kainou* and a pencil *kainou*.' " It is ambiguous whether he means a tablet "and a mind" (*kai nou*) and a pencil "and a mind" or a new (*kainou*) tablet and new pencil.

There is metalepsis whenever, in answering, someone changes what is said to something other than what is being asked; for example, "Pyrrhus the king of the Epirotes, when some people at a drinking party asked whether the flute player Antigennidas or Satyrus was the better, said, 'To me, the general Polysperchon (is better).' "[76]

The combined form is not unclear, because it often occurs; for the gnomic can be melded into the jesting, or the use of a sign combined with an example, or ambiguity with metalepsis, or, simply put, there can be a combination of all the other forms, two or more being taken together into one chreia; for example, "Diogenes the Cynic philosopher, seeing a young man born from adultery who was throwing stones in the marketplace, told the youth to stop, 'Lest out of ignorance [101] you hit your father.' "[77] The answer includes at one and the same time a sign and a jest.

Chreias are practiced by restatement, grammatical inflection, comment, and contradiction, and we expand and compress the chreia, and in addition (at a later stage in study) we refute and confirm. Practice by restatement is self-evident; for we try to express the assigned chreia, as best we can, with the same words (as in the version given us) or with others in the clearest way.

Inflection takes many forms;[78] for we change the person in the chreia into all three numbers[79] and do this in several ways: (expressing it as) one person speaking about one or two or more; and conversely two speaking about one and two and more, and also plural persons speaking about one and two and more. If the chreia is that Isocrates the orator said that those with natural ability are the children of the gods, we inflect it as one person speaking of one other by saying, "Isocrates the orator said that the student with nat-

---

[76] Pyrrhus apparently dismissed the question as trivial.

[77] Cf. Diogenes Laertius 6.62.

[78] For elementary students of Greek, a highly inflected language, practice in grammatical inflection was important. Thus they were asked to restate a chreia in a variety of grammatical forms, even though the results might seem artificial. More advanced students could skip this exercise and practice elaborating, condensing, refuting, or confirming chreias; cf. the remarks of Nicolaus, ch. 4, below.

[79] Singular, dual, and plural.

ural ability was a child of gods"; and as two of two, that "The twin orators Isocrates said the twin students with natural ability are children of gods"; and as plural of plural, that "The orators Isocrates said the students with natural ability are children of gods." From these examples it is evident how we shall inflect the other forms; for (the original statements) are changed into the five grammatical cases. But since some chreias report sayings, some actions, and some a mixture of both of these, and since there are in turn other species of these, in each of these we shall try to teach inflection on the basis of an example.

The nominative presents no difficulty; for each of the chreias is customarily presented in that case. We practice the genitive as follows. If the chreia is a saying, we shall add to it that the saying "has become memorable," or "The story is remembered of X saying. . . ." The former is appropriately added after the statement [102] of the whole chreia; for example, "The saying of Isocrates, remarking (genitive) that those students with natural ability are children of gods, has become memorable." The second phrase can be in the middle or in the beginning of the statement; for example, "Pittacus the Mitylenean's saying, upon being asked if anyone escapes notice of the gods when doing wrong, is remembered: 'Not even if contemplating it.'" "The story is remembered" well fits all chreias about a saying except for a volunteered statement; for that use "The saying of X . . . has become memorable." If the chreia describes an action, and if that is passive, one should add, "The experience of X . . . has become memorable"; if it is active, "The action of X . . . has become memorable," and similarly in the case of a mixed chreia. Each of these, of course, ought to be put at the end of the chreias; for example, "Of Didymon the flute player, having been taken in adultery and hung by his 'name,' the experience is memorable," and "Of Diogenes the Cynic philosopher, seeing a boy eating fancy food and beating his pedagogue with his staff, the action is memorable."[80] In the dative case, in all chreias except the passive, we shall add "It seemed to X," or "It appeared to X," or "It occurred to X," or "It came to X," or something of that sort; for example, "To Diogenes the Cynic philosopher, seeing a rich young man who was uneducated, it seemed right to say, 'He is dirt plated with silver.'" In the case of a passive chreia, we add "It happened

[80] From the Armenian version Patillon adds here, "Of a Laconian, when someone asked where Lacedaimonians set the limits of their land, the action of showing his spear is memorable."

to X"; for example, "To Didymus the flute player, being taken in adultery, it happened that he was hanged from his 'name.' " In the accusative we shall generally add to every chreia, "They say," or "It is said;"[81] for example, Diogenes (accusative) the Cynic philosopher, on seeing a rich young man who was uneducated, they say to have said, 'He is dirt plated with silver.' " The vocative is clear; for we address the remark to the person to whom the chreia is attributed as though present with us; for example, "O Diogenes, Cynic philosopher, on seeing a rich young man **[103]** who was uneducated, did you say 'He is dirt plated with silver?' "

We can add a comment (*epiphônein*), appropriately and briefly approving what is said in the chreia, to the effect that it is true or noble or beneficial, or that other famous men have thought the same; for example, "Euripides the poet said the mind of each of us is a god."[82] We shall comment from the point of view of truth as follows: "For the mind of each is truly a god in regard to the benefits it brings by exhorting us and keeping us from loss." A comment from that of the noble is, for example, "It is noble for each one to think god is not in gold or silver but in himself." From that of the beneficial, the following: ". . . in order that we might not have ease of doing wrong by thinking that punishment lies far off." From the witness of the famous, whenever we say that a wise man or lawgiver or poet or some other renowned person agrees with the saying; for example, in the chreia just mentioned we shall say (*Odyssey* 18.136–37), "For such is the mind of men who live on the earth / As the father of men and gods grants for a day."

We contradict chreias from their contraries; for example, against Isocrates' saying that teachers ought to be honored above parents because the latter provided us with life, but teachers with living well. In opposition, we say that it would not be possible to live well if parents had not provided us with life. One should, however, understand that it is not possible to contradict every chreia, since many are said well and are in no way faulty, just as it is not possible to praise all, because the absurdity of some is immediately obvious.

We expand the chreia whenever we lengthen the questions and answers in it, and the action or suffering, if any. We compress by doing the opposite. For example, this chreia is brief: "Epaminon-

---

[81] The chreia is thus recast in indirect discourse with subject accusative and verb infinitive.

[82] Euripides, frag. 1108, ed. Nauck; sometimes attributed to Menander or other poets.

das, dying childless, said to his friends, **[104]** 'I leave two daughters,
the victory at Leuctra and that at Mantinea.' " We expand it as follows: "Epaminadas, the general of the Thebans, was, you should
know, a great man in peacetime, but when war with Lacedaimonians came to his fatherland he demonstrated many shining deeds of
greatness. When serving as Boeotarch at Leuctra, he defeated the
enemy; and conducting a campaign and contending on behalf of his
country, he died at Mantinea. When he had been wounded and his
life was coming to an end, while his friends were bewailing many
things, including that he was dying childless, breaking into a smile,
he said, 'Cease your weeping, my friends, for I have left you two immortal daughters: two victories of my country over Lacedaimonians, one at Leuctra, the elder, the younger just begotten by me at
Mantinea.' "

One should refute chreias on the ground of their being unclear,
pleonastic, deficient, impossible, incredible, false, inexpedient, useless, or shameful. Unclear, as if we say that Isocrates did not clearly
define what the boy enrolled with him needed for rhetoric. And
similarly, the chreia about Didymon the flute player; for it is not
clear to all what it means to be "hung by his name." A chreia is
refutable from pleonasm when something is said which can be removed while, none the less, the chreia remains complete; for example, "Socrates the philosopher, when asked if the king of the Persians seemed to him to be happy, said, 'I cannot say; for I cannot
know what kind of education he had.' " The chreia uses unnecessary words, not only in answering the question but also in giving the
reason for the answer and not waiting to see if a second question
was asked. This was not characteristic of Socrates the man, who
was a dialectician.[83] It is refutable from being deficient whenever we
show, (for example,) that Demosthenes did not rightly say that rhetoric was a matter of delivery;[84] **[105]** for we need many other things
for rhetoric. Refutable from the impossible, as if we say against
Isocrates that it is not possible for men to be born from gods, not
even if they have good natural abilities. From the incredible, that it
is not probable that Antisthenes, being Attic, on coming from
Athens to Lacedaimon would say that he came from the women's

[83] In dialectical exercises, questions were supposed to be answerable by "yes"
or "no."

[84] A "deficient" version of the anecdote that Demosthenes, when asked what
was most important in rhetoric, replied "Delivery," and asked what was second,
replied "Delivery," and asked what was third, replied "Delivery"; cf. Pseudo-
Plutarch, *Lives of the Ten Orators* 845d.

apartments to the men's. From the false, that Bion did not truth-
fully say that love of money was the mother city of all evil; for intemperance is more so. From the inexpedient, "It is harmful that
Simonides advises playing in life and being serious about nothing at
all."[85] From the useless, for example, "What was said would seem to
be of no use in life." From the shameful, whenever we show that the
chreia is shameful and reproachable; for example, "A man from
Sybaris, seeing how toilful was the life of Lacedamonians, said
there was no wonder that they did not hesitate to die in wars; for
death was better than such a way of life." He created a statement of
a soft and unmanly sort. One should refute from these topics, and
one should provide arguments against each part of the chreia, beginning with the first, using whatever topics are possible. But do
not forget that it is not possible to argue from all topics in all
chreias. We shall, of course, follow the same order of epicheiremes
as we have given of topics,[86] and the topics would be the same for
both refutation and confirmation of maxims. The more accomplished students can appropriately get their starting points (for
refutation and confirmation of chreias) from what we are going to
describe in regard to theses.

The prooemion should not be of a sort to fit other chreias but
should be unique to the one under discussion. This would be the
right procedure in a chreia and a fable and all other exercises whenever we take the starting points of the prooemion from one or two
of the chief parts. After the prooemion **[106]** one should state the
chreia, then next the supporting arguments. One should here also
use whatever amplification and digression and characterization is
possible.

4. (SPENGEL 3.) ON FABLE

See Morgan, Literate Education, *pp. 221–23; Gangloff,* "Mythes,"
pp. 26–32.

[72]   A fable (*mythos*) is a fictitious story giving an image of
truth, but one should know that the present consideration is not
about all fables but about those in which, after stating the fable, we
add the meaning of which it is an image; sometimes, of course, we
bring in the fables after having stated the meaning. **[73]** Fables are
called Aesopic and Libyan or Sybaritic, and Phrygian and Cilician

[85] Simonides, frag. 646, ed. Page.
[86] I.e., the unclear, the pleonastic, the deficient, the impossible, etc., as listed
above.

and Carian, Egyptian, and Cyprian, but there is only one difference among them: the specific kind of each is indicated at the beginning;[87] for example, "Aesop said," or a Libyan man or one from Sybaris or a Cyprian woman "said," and similarly in the other cases. If there is no addition to specify the genre, we commonly call such a fable "Aesopic." Those who say that some involve mute beasts, others human beings, some are impossible, others capable of being true, seem to me to make a silly distinction. All the specific features are found in all those mentioned. Aesopic is not applied as a general term because Aesop was the first inventor of fables—Homer and Hesiod and Archilochus and some others, prior to Aesop,[88] seem to have known them, and moreover Connis the Cilician and Thurus the Sybarite and Cybissus of Libya are mentioned by some as fablemakers—but because Aesop used fables to a greater extent and cleverly, in the same way that a meter is called Aristophanic and Sapphic and Alcaic or something else from different writers, not because these poets alone or first invented the meters but because they most used them. Some of the ancient poets call fables *ainoi*, some *mythoi*. Prose writers most often call them *logoi* rather than *mythoi*[89] and thus refer to Aesop as a *logopoios*, and Plato, in a dialogue on the soul,[90] sometimes uses the word *mythos*, elsewhere *logos*. A *mythos* is said to be a certain kind of *logos* since the ancients said that "to speak" was *mytheisthai*.[91] It is called *ainos* because it also provides some *parainesis* ("advice"). The whole **[74]** point is useful instruction. Now, however, some call riddles *ainoi*.

As an exercise, *mythos* is treated in a variety of ways, for we state the fable and inflect its grammatical form and weave it into a narrative, and we expand it and compress it. It is possible also to add some explanation to it, or if this is prefixed, an appropriate fable can be adapted. In addition, we refute it and confirm it.

We have made clear the nature of the original statement in the account of the chreia, but in fables the style should be simpler and natural, and in so far as possible artless and clear. Thus, one should first learn by heart those fables that are expressed in this way by the ancients. When a fable is being told as a whole, it is also useful for

[87] There are no differences in content, structure, or style, only in the source that is named.

[88] According to Herodotus (2.134), Aesop was a slave on Samos in the early sixth century B.C.

[89] Cf. Herodotus 2.134; on terms for fables, see van Dijk, Part I, section 3.

[90] Cf., e.g., *Phaedo* 60c–d.

[91] In the *Iliad* and other early poetry *mytheisthai* often means "to speak."

the learner to become accustomed to make an elegant beginning in the middle of the story, as Hesiod does (*Works and Days* 203): "Thus said the hawk to the nightingale with speckled neck." From what is added (line 210), "He is a fool who tries to withstand the stronger," it is clear that a nightingale was quarreling with a hawk and then the hawk became annoyed and seized her and spoke these words.

Fables should be inflected, like the chreia, in different grammatical numbers and oblique cases,[92] and one should give special attention to the accusative cases, because that is the way the ancients told most of the myths,[93] and very rightly, as Aristotle says; for they do not relate myths in their own person but they attribute them to antiquity in order to excuse the fact that they seem to be saying what is impossible.[94] The original grammatical construction must not always be maintained as though by some necessary law, but one should introduce some things and use a mixture (of constructions); for example, start with one case and change in what follows to another, for this variety is very pleasing.[95] **[75]** An example is the myth by Phaedo the Socratic in his (dialogue) *Zopyrus*,[96] for he begins in the accusative: "They say, Socrates, someone (accusative) to have given a lion cub as a present to the youngest son of the king." A little further on he changed the construction to direct discourse: "And, as I understand it, the lion, being brought up with the boy, still followed him wherever he went when he became a young man. As a result, the Persians said he loved the boy," and so on.

We weave in narrative in the following way. After having stated the fable, we bring in a narrative, or conversely we put the narrative first, the fable second; for example, having imagined that a camel who longed for horns was deprived even of his ears, after stating this first, we go on to the narrative as follows: "Croesus the Lydian seems to me to have suffered something similar to this camel," followed by the whole story about him.[97]

We expand a fable by lengthening the remarks of the characters

[92] E.g., "of hawks; to hawks; O hawk."

[93] I.e., in indirect discourse with subject accusative and verb in the infinitive.

[94] Aristotle discusses the use of fables in *Rhetoric* 2.20, but Theon's reference is to some other passage now lost.

[95] E.g., start with indirect discourse and move to direct discourse.

[96] Phaedo, frag. 11, in *Socraticorum Reliquiae* I, ed. Giannantoni; cf. Diogenes Laetius 2.105.

[97] Croesus' desire for Cappadocia led to the loss of his own kingdom, as described in Herodotus 1.71–91.

and by describing a river or something of that sort, and we condense by the opposite.

It is possible to provide a conclusion whenever, after the fable has been stated, we venture to bring in some gnomic statement fitting it.[98] For example, "a dog was carrying a piece of meat beside a river, and having seen his reflection in the water he thought it was another dog carrying a larger piece of meat. When he dropped what he had and jumped into the river to seize it, he disappeared under the water." We shall add the following comment: "You should note that often those hankering for greater things destroy themselves as well as losing what they have." There can be several conclusions (*epilogoi*) for one fable when we take a start from the contents of the fable, and conversely one conclusion when many fables reflect it. After proposing the simple meaning of the conclusion, we shall assign the young to imagine a fable **[76]** suitable to the material at hand. They will be able to do this readily when their minds have been filled with many fables, having taken some from ancient writings, having only heard others, and having invented some by themselves.

We shall refute and confirm as follows. Since even the fable-maker himself acknowledges that what he writes is false and impossible, though plausible and useful, one should refute by showing that what he says is implausible and not beneficial, and one should confirm in the opposite way. These are the most general headings under which the particulars fall.[99]

Now the prooemion should be appropriate to the fable.[100] After the prooemion one should usually set out the fable, but sometimes it can be left out, just as in an hypothesis a narration is not always necessary. Then one should change to the argument and refute each of the things said separately, beginning with the first, and trying to find a supply of things to say in reply to each part of the fable on each topic. Epicheiremes should be taken from the following topics: the unclear, the implausible, the inappropriate, the deficient, the redundant, the unfamiliar, the inconsistent, the disordered, the inexpedient, the unlike, the false.

[98] I.e., when we state the moral.
[99] E.g., it may be improbable that a dog would drop a bone on seeing its reflection in water (the particular), but the myth presents a generalized moral: the danger of losing what one has by trying to get something more
[100] In contrast to the kind of epideictic prooemion favored by some sophists, in which the prooemion may have only a tangential relation to the main theme; cf. Aristotle, *Rhetoric* 3.14.1–2.

Lack of clarity results either from one word or from many; from one when it is contrary to the usual meaning or is homonymous, from many when what is said can be taken in several ways unless something is added or taken away; for example, "I made you a slave being free"; for it is unclear (in the Greek) whether he made someone free instead of a slave or a slave instead of free. Something more detailed about clarity will be said a little later in the discussion of narrative.

The implausible is what is capable of happening or being said **[77]** but whether it (actually) happened or was said is incredible, either because of the person to whom the action or saying is attributed, or because of the place where something is said to have happened or been said, or because of the time at which something is said to have happened or been said, or because of the manner of the action or saying, or because of the reason given for these same things, since we say that it is not probable that such a person would have done or said this at this place or at this time or in this way or for this reason. The same can be said for what is not appropriate.

There is omission or redundancy when some of the things that could be said are omitted, or something non-essential is mentioned,[101] whether a person, thing, time, place, manner, reason or anything of the sort.

The unfamiliar is something said contrary to commonly believed history or common assumptions; for example, if someone should say that human beings were not formed by Prometheus but by some other one of the gods, or called an ass wise or a fox stupid.

The topic from the inconsistent is what is used when we show that the writer of the fable contradicts himself. This should not be used at the beginning but when we are refuting something in the middle or at the end and then show it to be opposed to what has been said earlier.

We shall argue on the basis of the order when complaining that what should have been said first in the fable is not stated in the first lines and what should be in the conclusion is elsewhere; and generally in regard to each part however we can, that it is not said in the appropriate order.

The topic of the inexpedient, which we shall use mostly in refutation of the conclusion, is surely clear.[102] The topics of the unlike and the false are only refutative of the conclusion. (We argue) from

---

[101] Accepting the interpretation of Butts, p. 273.
[102] I.e., arguing that the moral is inexpedient or not beneficial.

the unlike when the incidents in the fable are not at all or not in all ways concordant with the conclusion, and [78] from the false when the result does not at all follow as the writer claims, (for example, a claim) that those hankering after more are deprived of what they have; for this is not always true. And we shall make confirmations from the opposite topics.

Whenever the refutations and confirmations are numerous and strong there must be a recapitulation, but when they are few and weak one should not add a recapitulation. Here we shall use ridicule and amplification and diminution, and digressions and characterizations and, simply stated, all the forms of speech; for as we said, this exercise differs little from a judicial hypothesis. The same topics are useful also for the refutation and confirmation of narratives.

5. (SPENGEL 4.) ON NARRATIVE

Narrative (*diêgêma*) is language descriptive of things that have happened or as though they had happened.[103] Elements (*stoikheia*) of narration (*diêgêsis*) are six: the person (*prosôpon*),[104] whether that be one or many; and the action done by the person; and the place where the action was done; and the time at which it was done; and the manner of the action; and sixth, the cause of these things. Since these are the most comprehensive elements from which it is composed, a complete narration (*diêgêsis*) consists of all of them and of things related to them and one lacking any of these is deficient.

The properties of the person are origin (*genos*), nature, training, disposition, age, fortune, morality, action, speech, (manner of) death, and what followed death. Those of the action are great or small, dangerous or not dangerous, possible or impossible, easy or difficult, necessary or unnecessary, advantageous or not advantageous, just or unjust, honorable or dishonorable. To time belong what has gone by, what is present, what is going to be; what was first or second and so on; or what [79] is appropriate to life in our time, what in ancient times; in all cases, the dates people have set in public or private life;[105] then whether in winter or spring, summer or

---

[103] I.e., a narrative does not need to be factually true. John of Sardis (pp. 15–16, ed. Rabe; see below) points out that there are many things in the orators that are not true but are regarded as true on the basis of the reputation of the persons who report them.

[104] Or "the agent."

[105] This refers to the chronology of actions by the calendar, appointed times for public or private duties, including payment of debts, observance of sacrifices, and the like.

autumn, during the night or by day, whether the action took place during a meeting of the assembly or during a procession or festival; and whether at weddings or a reception of friends or in time of grief or any such circumstance of life. To place belong size, distance, near a city or town, whether the place was sacred or unhallowed, owned or someone else's, deserted or inhabited, strong or insecure, flat or mountainous, dry or wet, barren or wooded, and all similar things. To manner belong unwillingly or willingly,[106] and each of these is divided into three things: the unwilling into done by ignorance, accident, and necessity; the willing into whether something was done by force or secretly or by deceit. To the cause of actions belong whether it was done to acquire good things or for the sake of escape from an evil, or from friendship or because of a wife or for children or out of the passions: anger, love, hate, envy, pity, inebriation, and things like these.

"Virtues" (*aretai*) of a narration are three: clarity, conciseness, credibility.[107] Best of all, if it is possible, the narration should have all these virtues. If it should be impossible for conciseness not somehow to be counter to clarity and credibility, one should aim at what is more pressing; for example, if the subject is of a difficult nature, one should go for clarity and credibility; if, on the other hand, the subject is simple and not complicated, aim at conciseness and credibility. One should always keep to what is credible in the narration, for this is its most special feature. If it does not have credibility, the more clear and concise it is, all the more unconvincing it seems to the hearers. And if the subject is naturally believable, one should sometimes use conciseness, <sometimes clarity, but less in refutations),>[108] sometimes also brevity, **[80]** but mostly in confirmations and things that make the matter under discussion persuasive. Furthermore, one should narrate very briefly things that are going to distress the hearers, as Homer does (*Iliad* 18.20): "Patroclus lies dead." One should, on the other hand, dwell at greater length on pleasant-sounding things, as the same poet makes Odysseus narrate his adventures to the story-loving Phaeacians with much detail and leisure (*Odyssey* 9–12).

The narration becomes clear from two sources: from the subjects that are described and from the style of the description of the

[106] Cf. Aristotle, *Rhetoric* 1.10.7–8.
[107] This doctrine was taught by most later Greek rhetoricians. According to Quintilian (4.2.31), it originated in the school of Isocrates.
[108] Added by Patillon from the Armenian version.

subjects. It becomes clear from the subjects whenever the things being said, unlike those in dialectic and geometry, do not depart from common understanding, or whenever one does not narrate many things together but brings each to its completion. Some critics[109] blame Thucydides for not doing this. Since he divides his history into summers and winters he is often forced to switch to another event that happened in the same season before the whole of an incident is ended; then he narrates the rest of the subject as done during another winter or summer. Sometimes he needed even three and four seasons until he came to the end of the subject that he was describing from the beginning, always taking up again the events that happened in each season as begun in the first account, so that, taken together, the facts are unclear and hard to remember. One should also guard against confusing the times and order of events, as well as saying the same thing twice. For nothing else confuses the thought more than this.

One should, moreover, avoid inserting long digressions in the middle of a narration. It is not necessary simply to avoid all digression, as Philistus does, for they give the hearer's mind a rest, but one should avoid such a lengthy digression that it distracts the thought of the hearers and results in the need for a reminder of what has been said earlier, [81] as in Theopompus' *Philippica*. We find there two or three or more whole histories in the form of digressions where there is nothing about Philip and not even the name of any Macedonian.[110] Narration becomes unclear by omission of what ought necessarily to have been mentioned and by an allegorical account of disguised events.

As for style, in aiming at clarity one should avoid poetic and coined words and tropes and archaisms and foreign words and homonyms. Poeticisms are words that need exegesis such as *krêgyon* (for "good, useful"), *atherizein* ("to make light of"),[111] *marnasthai* (for "to do battle"), and such like. Coined words (*pepoiêmena*) are, for example, *kelados, konabos, kelaruzei*,[112] and such like. Tropes are like the line, "Broad-browed Zeus grants a wooden wall to the Tri-

[109] Cf., e.g., Dionysius of Halicarnassus, *Thucydides* 9.

[110] On Theopompus' digressions, mostly geographical, see Gordon S. Shrimpton, *Theopompus the Historian* (Montreal: McGill-Queen's University Press, 1991), pp. 72–101.

[111] A Homeric word; for the correction, see Butts, p. 373. The mss. read *allerizein* which is unknown. Patillon conjectured *alegizein*, "not to be distressed."

[112] These words are "coined" in the literal sense of onomatopoetic; they echo the sound of their meanings: "rushing, clashing, gushes," respectively.

togenes (Athena)."¹¹³ With this trope the Pythian oracle signified to the Athenians to leave their city, go aboard their ships, and use them as a "wall." Archaisms are words that were once in common use but are now abandoned, as Demosthenes says in *Against Aristocrates* (§33) about the law of Dracon, "not to maltreat or amerce (*apoinan*); for the ancients called fining 'amercement.' " Foreign words are those native to some but not usual to others, as if one calls the *limên* (harbor) a "marketplace" (*agora*), as do the Thessalians, or a boy-friend *kleinos* ("famous") instead of *erômenos* ("beloved"), like the Cretans. A homonym is a single word pronounced in the same way but with different significations, like *pais* ("boy"); for it means a son and a young child and a slave.

What is called an "amphiboly" by the dialecticians makes the expression obscure because of the confusion between an undivided and divided word, as in the phrase "Let an *aulêtris* ("flute-girl") that has fallen **[82]** be 'public.' "¹¹⁴ It means one thing when the word *aulêtris* is taken as a whole and undivided, another when divided: "Let an *aulê tris* ("a hall thrice") fallen be public property." Furthermore, (the expression is ambiguous) when it is unclear what some part of a word belongs to; for example, Heracles fights *ouken-taurois*. This has two meanings, that Heracles does not at all (*oukhi*) fight with centaurs or that he fights not among (*ouk en*) bulls.¹¹⁵ Similarly, an expression becomes unclear when it is not evident to what some signifying portion refers; for example (*Iliad* 2.270), "And they though distressed at him sweetly laughed." For it is am-biguous whether they are distressed at Thersites, which is false, or at the launching of the ships. And again (*Iliad* 2.547–48), "The peo-ple of great Erechtheus, whom once Athene / Nurtured, Zeus' daughter, and the grain-giving land bore." It is unclear whether he is saying the people or Erechtheus were nurtured by Athene and born from the land. Because of this kind of ambiguity, the books of Heraclitus the philosopher are obscure, whether he overdoes it on purpose or even out of ignorance.¹¹⁶ One should also avoid hyper-bata¹¹⁷ like many in Thucydides, although we do not completely re-ject all kinds of hyperbaton; for it makes expression varied without

---

¹¹³ Herodotus 7.141. There are several etymologies of *tritogenês* as an epithet of Athene.

¹¹⁴ I.e, regarded as a prostitute. On amphibolies, see C. Atherton, *The Stoics on Ambiguity* (Cambridge Univ. Pr., 1993), pp. 184–88.

¹¹⁵ Or possibly "not among Taurians," as suggested by Butts, p. 307.

¹¹⁶ Cf. Aristotle, *Rhetoric* 3.5.6.

¹¹⁷ Placing words out of their normal order in a sentence.

becoming inartistic. Do not stick digressive phrases or clauses in the middle of sentences, especially not long ones; for clauses whose apodosis follows closely do not trouble listeners. And, of course, leaving out some words is contrary to clarity. One should also avoid using the same grammatical case when different people are involved; for it becomes ambiguous to what person they are to be attributed, especially in the use of the accusative, which alone of the cases is where many people think ambiguity occurs. There is an example in Demosthenes' speech *Against Meidias* (§71): "It is common knowledge that Euaeon (accusative), the brother (accusative) of Leodamus, **[83]** Boeotus (accusative), killed at a banquet." It is unclear whether Euaion killed Boeotus or, what is false, Boeotus killed Euaeon, and whether the brother of Leodamas is Euaeon or Boeotus. There can be ambiguity also in the nominative case, as in the first book of Herodotus:[118] "They are also Egyptians Colchians"; for it is unclear whether the Egyptians are Colchians or the opposite, the Colchians are Egyptians. The same thing occurs in the genitive and dative: "Colchians being Egyptians" and "to Colchians being Egyptians." It is unambiguous in the accusative and clear in the other cases that the style becomes no longer ambiguous by addition of articles: "They are Egyptians, the Colchians"; for it has become clear that he is speaking about the Colchians, saying that they are Egyptians.[119]

In the same way, the narration is concise from what is said and how it is said. Conciseness is language signifying the most important of the facts, not adding what is not necessary nor omitting what is necessary to the subject and the style. Conciseness arises from the contents when we do not combine many things together, do not mix them in with other things, and when we leave out what seems to be assumed; when we do not begin too far back in time and do not lavish words on incidentals, as do those who acquire the habit of narrating events subsequent to those in the case. In historical writing it is perhaps appropriate to spin things out and to begin far back and to explain some of the things that seem incidental, but in speaking a narration one ought to look to the chief point of the whole subject that he has set out, bringing into the narration only things that complement this. For example, speaking about Cylon, if one is composing a history of him it is appropriate to say from what an-

[118] In our texts, Herodotus 2.104.
[119] In Greek grammar, the presence of the article can indicate a subject, its absence a predicate.

cestors he descended and from what father and mother and many
other things, the event in which he competed at Olympia and what
victories he earned, **[84]** and to give the dates of his victories, but
in speaking a narrative (*diêgêma*) about him, as Herodotus (1.71)
and Thucydides (1.126) did when each undertook to speak of the
Cylonian pollution, it is right not to raise such questions about
him.[120] Among principles of word choice, one should avoid using
synonyms; for words having the same meaning make the sentence
needlessly long; compare Demosthenes in the *Second Olynthiac*
(§1): "It is altogether like some superhuman and divine beneficence." And do not use a phrase instead of a word; for example, "he
departed this life" rather than "he died," and things like that. Furthermore, things that can be supplied (by the hearer) should be altogether eliminated by one who wants to compose concisely, and
one should use simple words rather than compounds, and shorter
ones rather than longer ones whenever they signify the same thing.
But there is need for care, lest from desire for conciseness one fall
into an idiosyncrasy or obscurity without realizing it.

In order for the narration to be credible one should employ
styles that are natural for the speakers and suitable for the subjects
and the places and the occasions: in the case of the subjects, those
that are probable and follow from each other. One should briefly
add the causes of things to the narration and say what is incredible
in a believable way, and, simply put, it is suitable to aim at what is
appropriate to the speaker and to the other elements of the narration in content and in style. Our example will be the narrative
(*diêgêma*) about Plataeans and Thebans in the beginning of the second book of Thucydides (2.2–6). It was probable that the Thebans,
always differing with the Plataeans and knowing that there would
be war, would want to forestall them by seizing Plataea in time of
peace; that they laid plans to seize the city on a moonless night
rather than openly, and in addition **[85]** arranged for some Plataeans to open the gates to them, no guard having been stationed
because of the treaty; and that the traitors were acting out of private hatred for some of their fellow-citizens whom they thought to
destroy when this happened, but they did not intend to betray the
Thebans.

[120] I.e., details of his ancestry and athletic victories are appropriate in biogra-
phy or epideictic; Herodotus and Thucydides mention him in passing because his
death at the hands of the Alcmaeonids was regarded as the source of a curse on
Athens. Both note that he was an Olympic victor but give no details.

It is credible that the Plataeans, realizing that their city had been suddenly captured by the enemy, thought, because of the dark, that many more had come in, and credible that they came to terms, but later, having realized that the (invaders) were not numerous, attacked them. The confusion of the Plataeans throwing spears at the Thebans, and the accompanying cries and laments of the women and slaves hitting the Thebans with stones and tiles, is most credible. The night had been very rainy and many of the Thebans, pursued through mud and darkness, were unable to escape from the city because of their unfamiliarity with the streets. It is credible too that someone fastened the gates with the spike of a javelin instead of using a bolt-pin in the beam, and the account of the woman giving an axe is very credible; for it was probable that a woman who lived near the deserted gate would have been frightened when she saw the enemy shut in the town, not expecting safety, and driven to madness in causing harm, whatever they could, but first of all to the nearby houses. I pass over the fact that it was like a woman to feel pity even for the enemy when they had been defeated.[121] Not to prolong the discussion, all the rest is similar.

The exercise of narrative is not uniform; as in fable the narrative is stated and inflected and interwoven and compressed and expanded. Furthermore, in the statement of it we alter the order of the headings, and in addition it is possible also to keep **[86]** the same order and to vary the expression in many ways. Moreover, while narrating it is possible to add a comment and to weave two or three narrations into the statement. In addition to all this, there is refuting and confirming.

Explanation of statement and inflection and combination, as well as of compression and expansion, has been given in the discussion of fables. We shall rearrange the order in five[122] ways. It is possible to begin in the middle and run back to the beginning, then to jump to the end, which Homer did in *Odyssey*. He began with the period when Odysseus was with Calypso, then went back to the beginning in an elegant arrangement; for he had Odysseus narrate each of his own adventures to the Phaeacians; then, after taking up the rest of the narration, he continued to the end at the point where

[121] Theon adds explanation of cause to Thucydides' incidental mention of the woman who gave the Thebans an axe. He fails to note, but perhaps assumes, the feature of the passage that most contributes to its rhetorical effectiveness, which is the selective use of vivid details.

[122] So Patillon from the Armenian; the Greek manuscripts read "many." Theon often identifies the number of things he lists.

Odysseus killed the suitors and made friends with their relatives. Also, Thucydides, after starting with the events about Epidamnus, went back to the fifty years before the war and then took up the Peloponnesian war.

But it is also possible to begin from the end and go to events in the middle and thus to come down to the beginning. Herodotus teaches us how to do this in the third book (3.1), where he says, "Cambyses sent a herald to Egypt to seek a daughter of Amasis (for a wife), and he made the request on the advice of an Egyptian man who blamed Amasis for having torn him from his wife and children and handed him over to the Persians." Then he narrates the reasons, explaining that the king of the Persians had requested whoever was the best eye doctor from the king of the Egyptians. The natural order of the narration would be first to mention the Persian king's ophthalmia and how he sent **[87]** to Egypt to request an eye doctor from the ruler there and the ruler sent this man. Then, because the doctor was distressed at having been sent away from his wife and children, he avenged himself on the one who sent him by advising the king of the Persians to demand a daughter from the king of the Egyptians, in order that the latter either might be displeased at giving the daughter or would arouse (Persian) enmity if he did not.[123] Furthermore, it is possible to begin with events in the middle, go to the end, and stop with things that happened first. Or, again, beginning from the end to go back to the beginning and stop in the middle, and also starting from the first events to change to the last and stop with those in the middle. So much for rearrangement of the order.

Since we are accustomed to setting out the facts sometimes as making a straightforward statement and sometimes as doing something more than making a factual statement, and sometimes in the form of questions,[124] and sometimes as things we seek to learn about, and sometimes as things about which we are in doubt, and sometimes as making a command, sometimes expressing a wish, and sometimes swearing to something, sometimes addressing the participants, sometimes advancing suppositions, sometimes using dialogue, it is possible to produce varied narrations in all these ways.

[123] In their translations, both Rawlinson and de Sélincourt rearranged the passage in a natural order.

[124] To be answered "yes" or "no"; cf. above, note 65. Theon here shows awareness of what are now called "speech acts"; cf. Dirk Schenkeveld, *Mnemosyne* 37 (1984) 291–353.

At the beginning of the second[125] book of his *Histories* Thucydides set out the following narrative in the manner of a straightforward statement: "A force of Thebans a little over three hundred in number made an armed entry during the first watch of the night into Plataea in Boeotia, a town in alliance with Athenians," and so on. If we want to suggest something more than a simple statement of facts, we shall speak as follows: "The arrival at Plataea of the Thebans was, it seems, the cause of great troubles for Athenians and Lacedaimonians and the allies on each side; for a force of Thebans a little over three hundred in number made an armed entry during the first watch into Plataea in Boeotia," **[88]** and then we append the rest of the narration.

If we want to treat this as a question, we shall do so as follows: "Is it really true that a force of Thebans a little over three hundred in number made an armed entry during the first watch into Plataea in Boeotia?" And continue in this interrogative way with the rest of the account.

If we want to treat it as an enquiry, (we shall ask,) "Who were the Theban men, a little more than three hundred in number, who made an armed entry during the first watch into Plataea in Boeotia?" And phrase the rest as an enquiry.

Raising doubts[126] and asking questions do not differ from each other in procedure, so we shall be satisfied with an example of one of them. If we ask a question or express doubt, we shall proclaim, "Is sleeplessness the most talkative thing of all?"[127] The speaker seems in doubt because, while a questioner seeks an answer, one in doubt does not quite do so but only addresses himself as at a loss.

If we want to treat it as a command, we shall do so as follows. At the end of the narration, after (describing) the destruction of those who entered Thebes, we shall introduce someone advising the Thebans or Plataeans as follows: "Come, O Plataeans, be worthy of your city and of your ancestors who contended with Persians and Mardonius, and of those who lie buried in your land. Show the Thebans that they do wrong in thinking you should harken to them and be slaves and in forcing those unwilling to do so, contrary to oaths and treaties, when, a little more than three hundred in number, they entered under arms during the first watch into our city, an

[125] In our texts, at 3.2.
[126] Butts's translation (p. 329), "rhetorical question," seems justified by the example, though the Greek (*epaporein*) normally means "to raise a doubt" or "to bring something into question."
[127] From Menander's lost play, *The Heiress;* cf. Allinson, p. 383.

ally of Athenians." Then we shall continue the rest as addressing
Plataeans. If we suppose the command to be addressed to the Thebans, we shall say, "Come, O Thebans, make clear how you are worthy of yourselves **[89]** and your ancestors and the rule you have over
all Boeotia, and show to the Plataeans that, though they are your
slaves, they have not only run away to the Athenians but also have
destroyed a little more than three hundred of your men who went
under arms about the first watch into Plataea, which belonged to
them." And we shall narrate the rest in this way. It is possible also
to create a command, if we suppose someone exhorting the Thebans before they made the entrance into Plataea, ordering them to
do what they did: "Come, O Thebans, so that a little more than
three hundred of you may go under arms about the first watch into
Plataea, which belongs to you but now is an ally of Athenians." And
we shall describe the rest, as far as possible, in this way.

If we express a wish, we shall say, "O that a force of Thebans,
a little more than three hundred in number, had never gone under
arms during the first watch into Plataea in Boeotia, an ally of Athenians," and continue the narrative to the end in the form of a wish.

The way the narration is produced in the form of an oath is clear
enough.[128] We excuse ourselves from describing the use of direct address since we have already given an example of the vocative in discussing the declension of grammatical cases (in a chreia). In advancing a supposition we shall say, "Let us suppose that men of Thebes,
a little more than three hundred, went under arms about the first
watch into Plataea in Boeotia, a ally of Athenians; and that Naucleides and those with him opened the gates, there being no guard stationed there because of the treaty," and the rest in the same way.

If we wish to use a dialogue form, we shall suppose some people talking with each other about what has been done, and one
teaching, the other learning, about the occurrences; for example,
(A.) "Often **[90]** in the past it occurred to me to ask you about what
happened to the Thebans and Plataeans at Plataea, and I would
gladly hear now if this is a good opportunity for you to give a narrative account." (B.) "By Zeus, it is a good opportunity, and I shall
tell you now if, as you say, you have a desire to hear about these
things. The Thebans, always at odds with the Plataeans, wanted to
seize hold of Plataea in peace time. A force of them, therefore, a little more than three hundred in number, went under arms about the
first watch into the city, an ally of Athenians." (A.) "How then did

[128] I.e., "I swear by the three hundred Thebans . . ."; cf. Dem. 18.208.

they easily escape notice, going in at night when the gates were shut and a guard posted?" (B.) "You slightly anticipated what I was going to say, that some men, Naucleides and those with him, opened the gates, there being no guard posted because of the peace," and so on. In the same way we shall continue asking and answering in accordance with the rules of dialogue.

Moreover, when stating the facts, sometimes we use the positive,[129] but it is possible (as an exercise) not only to use the positive but also to produce narrations in negative form. The positive form is the way we said Thucydides produced his narration; a negative version would be, for example, "Neither did a band of Thebans, a little more than three hundred in number, go under arms about the first watch into Plataea in Boeotia, an ally of Athenians, nor did Naucleides and those with him open the gates," and so on to the end.

There is another variation, called "asyndeton," when we omit the conjunctions uniting the words; for example, "A force of Thebans, a little more than three hundred in number, went under arms, about the first watch, into Plataea in Boeotia, an ally of Athenians; (*then omitting the conjunctions in Thucydides' version*) Naucleides and those with him opened the gates to them; they set their arms in the market place," **[91]** and what follows similarly. And in Demosthenes (18.69), "Amphipolia, Pydna, Potidaea, Halonnesus, I mention none of these." Or again (9.27), "But he has gone to the Hellespont, earlier he came to Ambracia, he holds Elis, a great city in Peloponnesus; recently he was plotting against Megara." It is possible to combine these changes with each other and to create a mixture from two or more, thus to state some of the narrative in the negative, some with asyndeton, some however one wants, in order to make the language varied.

To add a maxim to each part of the narration is called *epiphônein*. Such a thing is not appropriate in historical writing or in a political speech but belongs rather to the theater and the stage.[130] As a result, it is most common among such poets as Menander, who does it often and everywhere, including at the beginning of both *The Dardanian* and *The Drafting Officer:*[131]

[129] The Greek text adds "as Theon does in the dialogue." This may be a gloss, i.e., a note by a scribe, pointing out that in the dialogic treatment just above the positive is used; Butts, pp. 394–96, suggests that this paragraph and the next, unexpected in the context, may be a latter addition to the original text.

[130] Theon fails to recognize that the maxim can create an enthymeme and thus add credibility.

[131] See Allinson, *Menander,* p. 415.

Son of a poor man, reared beyond
The family's means, he was ashamed to see
His father having little. Being well brought up,
He yielded good fruit quickly.

The unnecessary last sentence only seeks applause in the theater. Of course, when it is smoothly mixed in and these gnomic statements escape notice, the narration does somehow become charming, as in the first book of Herodotus. There he is speaking about human life, saying how it is not steadfast but has many changes in its course; then, counting the number of days in human life as those in seventy years, he adds: "Of all these days one never brings anything alike to another." Then (Solon) moralizes in this way (Herodotus 1.32): **[92]** "Thus, Croesus, man is wholly accident." Or as Gyges says to Candaules (1.8): "Master, what you have said is not sound. Would you order my mistress to be seen naked? A woman puts off her modesty with her clothes." And admittedly there are examples to be found in the orators, not least in the most "political," Demosthenes, and in the most political of his speeches. In the *Second Olynthiac* (§§19–20), talking about Philip, he says he has around him "mimickers of laughter and poets of shameful songs," and those whom the city of Athens expelled as being too licentious, and that Philip's real nature escapes the notice of everyone because of his success in war. After that, he adds the moral: "Remarkable successes hide and overshadow such shameful doings." It is possible, conversely, to put the gnomic statement before the narration, similar to what we described in the case of a fable; for example in Menander's *The Honest Heiress*, "Is sleeplessness the most talkative thing of all?"[132] Then follows a narrative: "It wakes me up and brings me here / To talk about all my life from the beginning."

It is possible to weave narration into narration whenever we try to narrate two or three narrations at the same time. The followers of Isocrates practiced this much and Isocrates himself did it in the *Panegyricus* (54–55) as follows: "The children of Heracles came, and a little before them Adrastus, son of Talaus, being king of Argos. He was one of those who suffered misfortune in the expedition against Thebes," and so on. And again (*Panegyricus* 68; cf. *Panathenaicus* 193), "Since Greece was still weak, there came into **[93]** our land Thracians with Eumolpus, the son of Poseidon, and Scythians with Amazons, daughters of Ares, though not at the same time," and so on. So much for the variations of the ex-

[132] See Allinson, *Menander*, p. 353.

ercise [and that it is possible to practice with them also in fables].[133]

The following discussion of refutation and confirmation is treated as a separate chapter (numbered 6 by editors) in the manuscripts and in editions antedating that of Spengel.

As for refutation and proof, we said[134] that the same topics are useful as in fables, but in narratives the topics of the false and impossible are also fitting. Thucydides (1.20.2) uses this in refuting the claim that Hipparchus was tyrant when killed by the followers of Harmodius and Aristogeiton, and Herodotus (3.2) in opposing those stating that Cambyses was Egyptian on his mother's side. Now it is not always possible to apply all the topics in narratives, but if sometimes it is, we shall use the following order: first, the topic from the unclear in the ways that we mentioned in discussing clarity; second, we shall take the topic of the impossible, showing that the fact cannot be as the sources say, either because it is not at all natural or because the things described did not take place at the same time. An example is a reply to those saying that Heracles killed Busiris; for according to Hesiod, Busiris was eleven generations older than Heracles.[135] And all in all we shall have starting points in reply to many such things from the refutations of (stories about) Arion.[136] Then, if we suppose that the thing is possible, we would say that it is incredible. And if it is credible, we shall consider if it is false. But if it should seem true, we shall then ask if something is omitted or too much has been added; then whether the writer contradicts himself in the narration. In addition, we shall criticize the order of the headings, if the order has not been appropriate. If all these things have been expounded in an acceptable way, still one should show that what is said is inappropriate and not beneficial; **[94]** for there are some things which ought not to have been done, but which, having been done already, it is expedient to

---

[133] Spengel printed this sentence at the end of the chapter (p. 96 in his edition); Butts (pp. 346–47) restored it here, where it belongs, and regarded the second clause as a gloss.

[134] In the last sentence of chapter 4.

[135] Cf. Isocrates, *Busiris* 36–37. The extant works of Hesiod do not mention Busiris.

[136] Probably Theon is thinking of refutations of the story of Arion's rescue by a dolphin as told in Herodotus 1.24; see Antonio Milazzo, "Arione in Elio Teone," *Papers on Rhetoric*, ed. Lucia Calboli Montefusco (Bologna: CLUEB, 1993), I, pp. 53–59.

keep silent. For example, if someone said that Ajax the Locrian did the impious things to Athene he is said to have done and then was supposed to have died happily in old age, having suffered no harm at sea nor at home.[137] We shall easily have a supply of arguments if in each of the topics mentioned we use what are called the "elements" of which all action consists. These are, as we said earlier, person, action, place, time, manner, cause.[138]

For the sake of an example, let us give an account of the use of one topic, the incredible. If we are refuting a narration on the basis of its being incredible, we shall proceed as follows, showing that it is unbelievable of the person and that the action and place where the action allegedly took place are incredible, and similarly the time and manner and cause of the action. For example, in the case of Medea, arguing from the person, that it is incredible that a mother would harm her children, and from the action that it is not probable that she cut their throats; from the place, that she would not have killed them in Corinth where lived Jason, the father of the children; from the time, that it is incredible that she would have done it at this time when she, a foreign woman who had been thrown out by her husband, had been mistreated and Jason had acquired greater power by marrying Glauke, daughter of Creon, the king of the place; from the manner, that she would have tried to escape notice and would not have used a sword, but poison, especially since she was a sorcerer; from the cause, that it is unbelievable that she would have killed her children out of anger at her husband, for the misfortune would not have fallen on Jason alone but would have been common to herself, and all the more in that women are thought to be softer in bearing sufferings. Similarly in other **[95]** topics, we shall proceed through the elements in order, making use of what we can, and we shall confirm the truth from the opposite topics.

These same topics are suitable against mythical narrations told by the poets and historians about gods and heroes, as well as about creatures whose natural shape has changed, as some say of Pegasus and Erichthonius and Chimeras and Hippocentaurs and such like. Not only to refute such mythologies, but also to show how such a distorted story originated, is a matter for a more mature skill than

---

[137] In the cyclic epic, *The Sack of Ilium*, as summarized in Proculus' *Chrestomathy* 1, the "lesser" Ajax was said to have torn Cassandra away from the image of Athena at the fall of Troy. On Athena's hatred of him and his death at sea, cf. *Odyssey* 4.499–504.

[138] Cf. the beginning of this chapter.

most have. Herodotus did it in the second book (2.56–57) in the account of the "doves" that flew from Egypt; one came to Dodona,
the other to the shrine of Ammon. Criticizing the mythology, he
says that certain maidens from Egyptian Thebes were priestesses,
of whom one was sold as a slave to Dodona and one to the shrine of
Ammon, and since they spoke in a barbarous language and were in-
comprehensible to the local inhabitants, the story grew that they
were birds. Plato in *Phaedrus* (229b–30a), in rejecting the narrative
about Oreithyia and Boreus, says that a blast of the boreal wind
pushed Oreithyia down a nearby rock with Pharmacia, and thus she
was said to have been carried off by Boreas. Of course, Ephorus[139]
also uses this manner of speaking in his fourth book, saying that
Tityus, a lawless and violent man, was the master of Panopeus, and
because he was bestial by nature he was called "Snake," and those
who lived in ancient times around Phlegra, what is now known as
Pallene, were savages and temple robbers and cannibals—the so-
called "Giants" whom Heracles is said to have subdued after taking
Troy—, and because the few with Heracles prevailed over the Giants who were numerous and impious, **[96]** the circumstance of the
battle was thought by all to have been a deed of gods; and other
similar stories about Lycurgus, and Minos and Rhadamanthys, and
Zeus and the Couretes, and other mythological figures in Crete.
There is a whole book by Palaiphatus the Peripatetic, entitled *On
Incredulities,*[140] in which he refutes such things; for example, (he
says) that the first men seen riding on horseback were taken to be
Centaurs, and that Diomedes the Thracian, who spent all his
money on raising horses, was said to have been killed by his own
horses; and according to the same account Actaeon was killed by his
dogs, and Medea, anointing the gray hairs on the heads of men and
making them dark, was said to make the old young by cutting them
in pieces and cooking them in a cauldron; and things similar to
these.

6. (SPENGEL 7.) ON TOPOS

[106]   Topos[141] (*topos*) is language amplifying something that is
acknowledged to be either a fault or a brave deed. It is of two kinds:
one is an attack on those who have done evil deeds, for example, a

[139] Ephorus, frag. 31 and 34, ed. Jacoby.

[140] For a translation of what survives of this work, see Jacob Stern, *Palaepha-
tus: On Unbelievable Tales* (Wauconda, IL: Bolchazy-Carducci, 1996).

[141] Unlike other writers, Theon does not use the phrase *koinos topos,* "common-
place."

tyrant, traitor, murderer, profligate; the other in favor of those who
have done something good: for example, a tyrannicide, a hero, a
lawgiver.[142] Some topoi are single, some not; single ones are those
just mentioned; those not single are, for example, against a traitorous general, against a temple-robbing priest, against one who com-
mits an outrage at a festival or on holy ground, or on behalf of a
woman who has killed a tyrant. It is called a *topos* because starting
from it as a "place" we easily find arguments (*epikheiroumen*)
against those not admitting that they are in the wrong.[143] For this
reason some define it as a starting point for epicheiremes. An accusation against a violent attacker is common and undisputed and is
called a *topos,* and starting from that attack, as from a "place," we
easily have an abundance of things to say against a Conon or a Meidias.[144]

Topos differs from encomia and invectives in that the latter are
concerned with specific persons and include a demonstration, for
example, Isocrates' *Encomion of Helen* and an invective against Eu-
rybatus,[145] if there is one somewhere; whereas topoi are concerned
simply with their subjects and involve no demonstration, and because in encomia and invectives one must provide prooemia but in
topos the thought aims to be something that seems cut off and a
part of something else spoken earlier and like an epilogue, with expansion of **[107]** what has already been demonstrated. As a result,
one should begin as though other things have already been said, as
in Aeschines (1.190): "Do not think, men of Athens, that the beginnings of our misfortunes come from the gods; they come from
the licentiousness of men." And in Demosthenes (18.296): ". . . polluted men and flatterers and accursed, who have hacked off the
limbs of their country, having pledged freedom first to Philip, now
to Alexander, measuring happiness by their belly and shameful
parts." And again (19.259): "For a disease, Men of Athens, a dreadful disease has fallen on Greece, difficult to deal with and needing
much good luck and careful consideration from you." But many

[142] As the discussion indicates, however, the exercise of *topos* was largely limited to attacking a vice.
[143] Patillon inserted "not" from the Armenian version. The individuals attacked may not admit being in the wrong, but topos often assumes that they are
being denounced after proof of their guilty, as in a second speech in a trial; on second speeches see Nicolaus, pp. 150, 153 below; John of Sardis, pp. 203–4 below.
[144] Cf. Demosthenes 54 and 21, respectively.
[145] A proverbial name for a traitor, derived from the envoy sent by Croesus to
Cyrus; cf. Ephorus, frag. 58, ed. Jacoby and Demosthenes 18.24.

(teachers and students) already give thought to prooemia, and set out the subject as if giving a narration, and they add amplifications to the whole. In so doing, they probably gain something but they destroy the special feature of the exercise.

One should construct the argument from the moral choice made by those who have done the deeds and from the magnitude of the evil actions they perform and from what others suffer because of them and also from the return that they themselves get. If, as in a lawsuit, we wish to use prooemion and narrative, after the prooemion and the description of the crime we shall take up the proofs, first from the intent of the doer, (saying) that it was evil, and second from the thing with which the crime was concerned, that it is one of the most needed things; for example, that a thief is plotting for money, which is most needed by everybody, and it is for money that we work the soil and sail the sea and, in a word, that we do all the things in life in order to have money from which we can live. After this, (we shall argue) from what is implicit (in the act), (saying) that the crime is one thing in name but in truth **[108]** it includes many crimes; for example, adultery includes force and theft and bastardy and countless other things. Then from syncrisis, and this is threefold; for we compare what is charged to something greater or lesser or equal. When we make a comparison to something greater we amplify the lesser to show that it is equal to that; for example, that a thief does as much wrong as a temple robber because both are moved by the single desire of stealing and the thief would not hesitate to rob a temple if he had the opportunity nor would the temple robber hesitate to steal. When we make a comparison to the lesser we shall speak as follows: "If the thief is punished for taking men's money, how much the more will this man be punished for looting the possessions of the gods?" But when we put an equal beside an equal we shall say that if we do not allow one doing equal wrong to go scot-free, neither is it right to overlook this man's action. Then comes argument from opposites; for if a hero deserves honor, a traitor deserves punishment. Following this is argument from antecedents of the act; for example, against the temple robber, that prior to his impieties toward the gods it is likely that the temple robber dared to do many things against human beings and many things against the dead and omitted many of the customary honors to the gods, such as festivals, sacrifices, and prayers, and it is likely he often gave false oaths, and similar things. Then (we shall argue) from the result and what followed the act; for ex-

ample, after the robbery of the temple the holy places remain disordered, while the robber lavishes his loot on his own pleasures; and
that because of such wrong-doings there come on cities the wrath
of the gods and famines and pestilences, destruction of armies, and
all such things. Then from the irremediable nature of the act, that
what has been done cannot be set right. Then from the judgment of
lawgivers or poets or wise men by mentioning their opinions; for
example, that to them what has been done seems wicked and deserving punishment.

In addition to all this, **[109]** we shall create vividness (*diatypo-
sis*) whenever we describe the crime in the process of execution and
the suffering of the one wronged; for example, in denouncing a
murderer we shall vividly describe what kind of person committed
the murder, how brutally and without mercy, by his own hand,
when he, though a man, set on another human being, drawing his
sword and striking a blow, and if the blow happened not to be fatal,
inflicting one after the other, and how he was polluted with the
blood of the murdered man, and what cries the latter uttered, begging his assailant for mercy and calling for help, now to men, now
to the gods, and other such things.

In compound topoi it is also possible to employ the arguments
that have been mentioned, and we shall have an abundance of arguments from what is added to single topoi; for a traitor deserves
anger, but much more when he is a general; and things done beyond
expectation provide many starting points for discourse. Amplification of wrongs should derive from such things, and of praiseworthy
actions from their opposites.

7. (SPENGEL 11.) ON ECPHRASIS

[118]   Ecphrasis (*ekphrasis*) is descriptive language, bringing
what is portrayed clearly before the sight. There is ecphrasis of persons and events and places and periods of time. An instance of
ecphrasis of persons is, for example, the Homeric line (*Odyssey*
19.246, of Eurybates), "Round-shouldered, swarthy-skinned,
woolly-haired," and the lines about Thersites (*Iliad* 2.217–18), "He
was bandy-legged, lame in one foot, and his two shoulders /
Stooped over his chest," and so on. And in Herodotus, the appearance of the ibis (2.76) and the hippopotami (2.71) and crocodiles
(2.68) of the Egyptians. Ecphrasis of events includes, for example,
descriptions of war, peace, a storm, famine, plague, an earthquake;
of places, for example, meadows, shores, cities, islands, a desert, and

such like; of times, for example, spring, summer, a festival, and the like. There are also ecphrases of objects, such as implements and weapons and siege engines, describing how each was made, as the making of the arms (of Achilles) in Homer (*Iliad* 18.478–614), and in Thucydides the circumvallation of the Plataeans (3.21) and the preparation of a siege engine (4.100): "They sawed a great beam in two and hollowed it all out." And in the ninth book of Ctesias, for example, "The Lydians, just before dawn, looking from afar toward the acropolis and seeing the standards of the Persians on long wooden posts, turned in flight **[119]** since they thought the acropolis was full of Persians and had already been captured."[146] There can also be mixed ecphrasis, like the night battle described by Thucydides and Philistus;[147] for night is a time and battle an event.

This exercise shares a characteristic with what has been said earlier (about topos). In so far as neither is concerned with a particular and both are common and general they are alike, but they differ, first, in that topos is concerned with matters of moral choice, while ecphrasis is, for the most part, about lifeless things and those without choice; second, when describing things in a topos we add our own judgment, saying something is good or bad, but in ecphrasis there is only a plain description of the subject.[148]

When composing an ecphrasis we shall treat events both from the point of view of what has gone before, what was included within them, and what results from them; for example, in an ecphrasis of a war we shall first recount events before the war: the raising of armies, expenditures, fears, the countryside devastated, the sieges; then describe the wounds and the deaths and the grief, and in addition the capture and enslavement of some and the victory and trophies of the others. If, on the other hand, we are describing places or times or objects or persons, drawing on the narrative account of each we shall have starting points for what to say from the noble and the useful and the pleasant, as Homer did on the subject of the arms of Achilles, saying that they were beautiful and

---

[146] Frag. 688, ed. Jacoby. Ctesias was a Greek doctor at the Persian court at the end of the fifth century and author of a history of Persia, now lost.

[147] Cf. Thucydides, 2.2–5, 3.22, 7.44; Philistus incorporated material from Thucydides; cf. above, p. 7.

[148] Theon's examples of ecphrasis clearly include particulars (Thersites, the shield of Achilles, etc.), and in literature ecphrasis regularly includes subjective remarks on the beauty, greatness, or terror of what is described, as Theon notes below. In describing ecphrasis as not concerned with particulars he is probably thinking of descriptions of a storm, earthquake, spring, etc.

strong and remarkable to his fellow fighters to look at and objects of fear to the enemy.

The virtues of an ecphrasis are as follows: most of all, clarity and a vivid impression of all-but-seeing what is described; next, one should not recollect all useless details and should make the style reflect the subject, so that if what it describes is colorful, the word choice should be colorful, [120] but if it is rough or frightening or something like that, features of the style should not strike a discordant note with the nature of the subject.

Some authorities approve practicing ecphrases by refuting and confirming the descriptions composed by others, (arguing,) for example, that Herodotus gives a false account of the appearance of the ibis when he says that they are white-feathered except for the head and neck and tip of the tail, for actually the tail is entirely white. To us the critics seem to say nothing new beyond what we have said, since we believe such a species (of exercise) falls among refutations and confirmations of narrations.

8. (SPENGEL 10.) ON PROSOPOPOEIA

This chapter is unusual in that no illustrations of the exercise are cited from earlier literature. Theon uses "prosopopoeia" of any speech in character and is apparently unaware of the distinction between "prosopopoeia," "ethopoeia," and "eidolopoeia" found in the later progymnastic treatises.

[115]   Personification (*prosôpopoeia*) is the introduction of a person to whom words are attributed that are suitable to the speaker and have an indisputable application to the subject discussed; for example, What words would a man say to his wife when leaving on a journey? Or a general to his soldiers in time of danger? Also when the persons are specified; for example, What words would Cyrus say when marching against the Massagetae? Or what would Datis say when he met the king after the battle of Marathon? Under this genus of exercise fall the species of consolations and exhortation and letter writing.[149]

First of all, then, one should have in mind what the personality of the speaker is like, and to whom the speech is addressed: the speaker's age, the occasion, the place, the social status of the speaker; also the general subject which the projected speeches are

---

[149] I.e., addresses at festivals, exhortations, and letters in which the writer imagines what a particular historical person would have said. The exercise provided preparation for declamations on political themes in the person of historical

going to discuss. Then one is ready to try to say appropriate words. Different ways of speaking belong to different ages of life, not the same to an older man and a younger one; the speech of a younger man will be mingled with simplicity and modesty, [116] that of an older man with knowledge and experience.[150] Different ways of speaking would also be fitting by *nature* for a woman and for a man, and *by status* for a slave and a free man, and *by activities* for a soldier and a farmer, and *by state of mind* for a lover and a temperate man, and *by their origin* the words of a Laconian, sparse and clear, differ from those of a man of Attica, which are voluble. We say that Herodotus often speaks like barbarians although writing in Greek because he imitates their ways of speaking. What is said is also affected by the places and occasions when it is said: speeches in a military camp are not the same as those in the assembly of the citizens, nor are those in peace and war the same, nor those by victors and vanquished; and whatever else applies to the persons speaking. And surely each subject has its appropriate form of expression. We become masters of this if we do not speak about great things vulgarly nor about small things loftily nor about paltry things solemnly nor about fearful things in a casual manner nor about shameful things rashly nor about pitiable things excessively, but give what is appropriate to each subject, aiming at what fits the speaker and his manner of speech and the time and his lot in life and each of the things mentioned above.

Now since the distinction among persons and subjects is a varied one—for we demand something or we exhort or we dissuade or we console or we seek forgiveness for what we have done, or do something else of this sort—it is necessary to mention the special materials for each of these.

In exhorting, then, we shall say that what we are urging is possible and easy and noble and appropriate; that it is beneficial, just, reverent—and the latter is of two sorts, either toward the gods or toward the dead—; that it is pleasant; that we are not the only ones doing it or the first; or that even if we are the [117] first, it is much better to be the beginners of noble deeds; and that when done it brings no regret. One should also mention any previous relationship

personages such as Demosthenes, as well as for composing speeches in works of history and in dramas. This passage and Nicolaus (below, p. 166) suggest that letter writing in character may have occasionally been practiced in schools. Imaginative, literary epistolography was a minor genre of the Second Sophistic; cf. extant examples by Alciphron, Aelian, Aristanetus, and Philostratus.

[150] For a somewhat different view, see Aristotle, *Rhetoric* 2.12–14.

of the exhorter to the person being exhorted, and if the latter at sometime was benefited by being persuaded. The same manner of treatment will be used if we are making some criticism,[151] but if dissuading we shall use the opposite arguments.

In consoling, we shall say that what has happened was unavoidable and common to all mankind and was unintentional; for sensible people are rather little distressed by unintentional actions. But if it happened intentionally, one should say that the person was the cause of what happened to himself; for because of self-love people are less distressed when they have experienced misfortunes through their own doings. One should say that there exists even a greater evil than this, which many others have suffered and borne calmly; in addition, that if in the short run it is painful, yet it is both noble and reputable; then, that it was useful and that nothing is to be gained from distress over what has been done. Expressing pity has great power for consolation, especially when someone is composing a speech for a bereavement; for those in distress are naturally resentful of those who think they have experienced nothing dreadful, and in addition to their pain it is possible for them to become angry at those consoling them, but they naturally accept consolations in a better spirit from those who join in their lamentations, as from relatives. Thus after the laments one should bring in words of admonishment.[152]

Whenever we seek forgiveness we shall have starting points from the following: first, that the action was unintentional, either through ignorance or chance or necessity; but if it was intentional, one should say that it was reverent, that it was customary, that it was useful. One should argue from whatever topics are possible; for all are not fitting to all the species of prosopopoeia.

This exercise is most receptive of characters and emotions. A simple treatment is sufficient at the introductory level **[118]** if the young are given practice in use of topics such as these, but for those who want to put their hands to prosopopoeia in a more accurate and complete way it is possible to make use of the materials for epicheiremes in theses, to be discussed by us a little later.

---

[151] Reading *aitiômetha,* as suggested to me by D. A. Russell.

[152] Numerous examples of Greek and Latin consolations survive, including famous works by Plutarch and Seneca. On conventions of the genre see Menander Rhetor 2.9, differing in some respects from what is suggested here.

9. (SPENGEL 8.) ON ENCOMION AND INVECTIVE

[109]   Encomion (*enkômion*) is language revealing the greatness of virtuous actions and other good qualities belonging to a particular person.[153] The term is now specifically applied to praise of living persons whereas praise of the dead is called an epitaphios and praise of the gods a hymn; but whether one praises the living or the dead or heroes or gods, the method of speaking is one and the same.[154] The term encomion derives from the ancient custom of eulogies of the gods at a revel (*kômos*) or game (*paidia*).[155]

Since good things especially are praised and some good things relate to the mind and character, others to the body, and some are external to us,[156] [110], clearly these would be the three large classes of things[157] from which we shall get an abundance of arguments for an encomion. External goods are, first, good birth, and that is twofold, either from the goodness of (a man's) city and tribe and constitution, or from ancestors and other relatives. Then there is education, friendship, reputation, official position, wealth, good children, a good death. Goods of the body are health, strength, beauty, and acuteness of sense. Important ethical virtues are goods of the mind and the actions resulting from these; for example, that a person is prudent, temperate, courageous, just, pious, generous, magnanimous, and the like. Fine actions are those praised after death—for people are wont to flatter the living—and conversely, actions praised when we are alive and yet overcoming the envy of many; for as Thucydides says, envy is in rivalry with the living.[158]

[153] The only earlier surviving discussions of encomion in Greek are those in Aristotle's *Rhetoric* 1.9.33 and *Rhetoric for Alexander* ch. 3. Theon's account has similarities to these discussions but is probably derived from intermediate sources.

[154] The encomia of Helen by Gorgias and by Isocrates celebrated the dead, but are not epitaphioi, which are specifically funeral orations. Aristotle uses *epitaphios* as a noun, referring to the famous speech by Pericles, *Rhetoric* 1.7.39. At the end of the chapter Theon briefly mentions praise of lifeless things. Aristotle (*Rhetoric* 1.9.2) mentions praise of animals and inanimate objects; encomia of trivialities such as bees and salt are mentioned by Isocrates (*Helen* 12), and encomia of cities became an important genre. Dio Chrysostom wrote an encomion of hair and Synesius an encomion of baldness, both extant.

[155] More accurately, *enkômion* derives from *kômos,* a song escorting home a victor in athletic games.

[156] These are the traditional "goods of mind, body and estate." Cicero, *Tusculan Disputations* 5.85, describes the classification as Peripatetic, but it is a commonplace of Hellenistic philosophy and rhetoric.

[157] Reading *genikôtera* or *genikôtata* with Patillon from the Armenian.

[158] Thucydides 2.45 and Demosthenes 18.315 on envy are quoted by Theon in ch. 1, above p. 7.

(Fine actions) are also those done for others rather than ourselves; and done for the sake of the honorable, not the expedient or the pleasant; and in which the toil is that of the doer but the benefit is common; and through which the populace experiences benefits and which are done for benefactors and even more for those who are dead; thus they are praised more than retributions and dangers on behalf of friends.

Actions are praised on the basis of the occasion and whether someone did them alone or was the first or when no one else acted, or did more than others or with few helpers or beyond what was characteristic of his age or contrary to expectation or with toils or because they were done very easily or quickly. One should include the judgment of the famous; (for example,) in praising Helen, that Theseus preferred her.[159] It is useful also to conjecture about the future on the basis of past events, as if one were to say about Alexander of Macedon, "What would he, who overthrew many great peoples, have done if he had lived a little longer?" And like Theopompus in the encomion of Philip, that if Philip wanted to continue the same practices, [111] "He will be king of all Europe."[160] It is not without utility also to make mention of those already honored, comparing their deeds to those of the persons being praised.

It is pleasant sometimes to draw a topic of praise from names and homonyms and nicknames, as long as this is not too vulgar and laughable. An example from names is that Demosthenes was "the people's strength" (*dêmou sthenos*); from homonymy when someone happens to have the same name as a famous man; and from nicknames, that Pericles was given the sobriquet of "Olympian" from the magnitude of his successes.

These then are the topics from which we shall argue, and we shall use them in the following way. Immediately after the prooemion we shall speak of good birth and other external and bodily goods, not arranging the account simply and in any random order[161] but in each case showing that the subject used the advantage prudently and as he ought, not mindlessly—for goods that result from chance rather than moral choice are the least source of praise—; for example, that in good fortune he was moderate and humane and

---

[159] Cf. Isocrates 10.18.

[160] Frag. 257, ed. Jacoby. Theopompus' encomion of Philip is unknown expect from Theon's references here and in ch. 2. In his historical works Theopompus showed hostility to Philip.

[161] Butts, p. 491, suggests "chronologically."

that he was just toward friends and exercised self-control in his bodily endowments.

If he has none of the previously mentioned goods, one should say that he was not brought low by his misfortunes nor unjust in poverty nor servile when in want, and that although coming from a small city he became illustrious, as did Odysseus and Democritus, and that he was not corrupted by being reared under a bad government but became the best of those around him, like Plato in the time of oligarchy. It is also praiseworthy if someone from a humble home becomes great, as did Socrates, the son of the midwife Phaenarete and the stone carver Sophroniscus. It is also worth admiring a workman or someone from the lower class who makes something good of himself, as they say Simon the leather worker and [112] Leontium the courtesan became philosophers.[162] For virtue shines brightest in misfortunes.

After this we shall take up actions and successes, not listing them as though we were giving a narrative—<for narrative is characteristic of historians>[163]—but arranging each under one of the virtues, then describing the deeds (that exemplify the virtue); for example, saying first that he was temperate and then adding immediately what he did temperately, and similarly with the other virtues. One should either not mention things said against the man—for these become a reminder of his mistakes—or disguise and hide them as much as possible, lest without knowing it we create an apology instead of an encomion; for "it is proper to compose a defense of those who are blamed for doing wrong but to praise those outstanding for some good quality" (Isocrates, *Helen* 15). Encomia of inanimate things such as honey, health, virtue, and the like we shall compose analogously from the same topics, arguing from whatever is possible. These are the sources of praise, and we shall derive blame[164] from the opposites.

10. (SPENGEL 9.) ON SYNCRISIS

Syncrisis (*synkrisis*) is language setting the better or the worse side by side. There are syncrises both of persons and of things. An ex-

---

[162] Meineke's conjecture *Simôna* for the *Hêrôna* of the mss. is, according to Patillon, confirmed by the Armenian version. Diogenes Laertius 2.122–23 says that Simon the shoemaker wrote personal reminiscences of Socrates. Leontium was a member of the school of Epicurus; cf. Cicero, *On the Nature of the Gods* 1.93.

[163] Added by Patillon from the Armenian.

[164] *Psexomen;* cf. *psogos* in the second paragraph of §11, "On Thesis," below.

ample involving persons is a comparison of Ajax and Odysseus, of things a comparison of wisdom and bravery. Since, however, we give preference to one of the persons by looking at their actions, and at anything else about them that is good, the method would be the same in both cases.[165]

First, let it be specified that syncrises are not comparisons of things having a great difference between them; for someone wondering whether Achilles or Thersites was braver would be laughable. Comparison should be of likes and where we are in doubt which **[113]** should be preferred because of no evident superiority of one to the other.[166]

Whenever we compare persons we shall first put side by side their good birth and education and the excellence of their offspring and the offices they have held and their reputation and the condition of their bodies and any other bodily and external good that we mentioned earlier in discussing encomia. After this we shall compare their actions, giving preference to those that are more beautiful and giving reasons why the good qualities (of one) are more numerous and greater (than those of the other) and more steadfast and more lasting, and preferring things that were done at a more crucial time <and brought great benefit from the doing>[167] and if they had not been done there would have been great harm, and giving preference to things done by choice rather than by necessity or chance, and things which few did more than what many did—for common and ordinary things are not very praiseworthy. (Actions are better) which we do with toil rather than easily and which we accomplish beyond (expectations of) our age and (apparent) ability more than when (such actions are ordinarily) possible. As we said in discussing encomia, we should either not mention hostile criticism or should do so as briefly as possible. It is appropriate only to disparage and scoff at slanders when brought by the opponent; for in this way a syncrisis will differ from an hypothesis.[168] In speaking an hypothesis, in addition to mentioning the specific successes of the subject, we shall also amplify any mistakes made by the opponents, but a syncrisis claims to identify simply the superiority of successful deeds.

[165] I.e., the method for comparing "things" is the same as that comparing persons.
[166] Opinion about this differed somewhat among different teachers; cf. Hermogenes, below, p. 84, Daniel Sheerin, "Rhetoric and Hermeneutic *Synkrisis* in Patristic Typology," *Nova & Vetera: Patristic Studies in Honor of Thomas Patrick Halton* (Washington: Catholic Univ. of America Press, 1998), pp. 22–39.
[167] Added by Patillon from the Armenian.
[168] I.e., a judicial declamation.

When we are comparing inanimate things it will probably seem
ludicrous to consider good birth or anything like that, but there is
nothing to prevent looking at some analogy to such things; for example, the inventors or nature of the things or the place where they
naturally grow, as if one said that health is the daughter of Apollo,
since that god is a healer, or that honey comes from heaven because
to many it seems to be a substance derived from dew, or, by Zeus,
that it comes from the best city, since the finest honey occurs in Attica [114], and other such things. Next, one must speak about the
advantages resulting from each of the things being compared. This
is the way, then, that we shall make comparisons of better things.
The procedure is the opposite whenever we seek to discover the
worse of two things to be avoided; for example, stupidity or pain.

One-to-one comparisons, then, would follow this method, but
we usually compare more than one thing to more than one in two
ways. One way is when we take extreme examples of the things
being compared and put these beside each other and in the comparison of these we think to find the whole genus (of one group) in
comparison with the whole genus (of the other). For example, if we
wanted to compare the genus of males to that of females (to find)
which of them is braver, by comparing the bravest man to the
bravest woman; whichever we find better, we would conclude that
the whole of that genus is better than the other. If, then, we wanted
to prefer the genus of males to that of females we shall compose as
follows. We shall propose that Themistocles was greater than the
genus of males in bravery and Artemisia[169] greater than the genus of
females; if then Themistocles was braver than Artemisia, the genus
of males is also braver than that of females. But if we wanted to
prefer the female genus we would propose Tomyris as the bravest
of women and Cyrus of men;[170] therefore, if Tomyris was braver
than Cyrus, the genus of females is also braver than that of men.

The second way is when, rather than comparing one or two of
the most outstanding to the most outstanding, we prefer that genus
in which there are more distinguished members; for example, if
there are more brave males than women, the genus of males is
braver than that of women. For if Tomyris the [115] Massagete or

[169] Queen of Caria, who led a contingent in Xerxes' invasion of Greece. At the
battle of Salamis Xerxes said of her, "My men have behaved like women and my
women like men" (Herodotus 8.88).
[170] Tomyris, Queen of the Massagetae, defeated the Persians in a battle in
which Cyrus was killed; cf. Herodotus 1.205–14.

Sparethra,[171] the wife of Amorges, king of the Sacae, is better than Cyrus, or by Zeus, even Semiramis,[172] wife of Zoroaster of Bactria, still one should not grant that the female is braver than the male, there being one or two very brave women but many, many males.

There are two ways of arranging these discourses: either we give an account separately of each of the things being compared, or combine them in one account, judging one better than the other, as Xenophon, when making a comparison in the *Symposium* (8.12–36), judges love of the soul superior to love of the body.

11. (SPENGEL 12.) ON THESIS

Discussion of practice in defending and refuting a thesis by Theon and other writers of progymnasmatic treatises shows how logical argumentation was taught at an introductory level, in contrast to the more sophisticated dialectic of the philosophical schools, described in Aristotle's Topics *and writings of Neoplatonists.*

[120]   Thesis[173] (*thesis*) is a verbal inquiry[174] admitting controversy without specifying any persons and circumstance; for example, whether one should marry, whether one should have children, whether the gods exist. Thesis differs from topos in that the latter is an amplification of some matter of agreement, while the former is concerned with something in doubt. Thus Hermagoras[175] called it "what is being judged" and Theodorus of Gadara called it "heading in hypothesis."[176] There is a difference also in the result because the end in thesis is to persuade, in topos to get retribution, and because a topos is spoken in a lawcourt, thesis in an assembly and a lecture room; moreover, judges are the hearers of a topos, of a thesis citizens in general, and they differ in many other ways. Thesis differs from prosopopoeia, because thesis does not reveal a personality but prosopopoeia does, because the latter is most often involved with the invention of words appropriate to the persons who

---

[171] Cf. Ctesias, frag. 3ff., ed. Jacoby.

[172] Queen of Assyria at the end of the ninth cent. B.C.; for legends about her see Diodorus Siculus 2.4–20.

[173] I.e., defense or refutation of a proposition.

[174] Reading *episkepsis logikē* with the Greek mss.

[175] Hermagoras of Temnos, rhetorician of the second century B.C. and father of stasis theory; cf. Dieter Matthes, "Hermagoras von Temnos," *Lustrum* 1958/3, esp. pp. 125–30.

[176] Theodorus (rhetorician of the third quarter of the first cent. B.C.), frag. 2, ed. Rosella Granatelli, *Apollodori Pergami ac Theodori Gadarei Testimonia et Fragment* (Rome: Bretschneider, 1991), p. 15.

are introduced. One does not compose speeches in the same way when simply considering whether one should have children and when introducing a father advising his son to beget a child.

We shall get prooemia of theses either from a maxim **[121]** supporting the thesis or from a proverb or a chreia or a useful saying or an historical report, or from encomion or invective (*psogos*) against the thing which is in question. There is no narration in theses; for there are no circumstances to explain, but (directly) after the prooemion we put the headings.

Since some theses are theoretical—where the inquiry is for the sake of understanding and knowledge; for example, whether the gods provide for the world—and some are practical—having reference to some action such as whether one should marry—, it is clear that the practical are more political and have a rhetorical character, while the theoretical are more appropriate for philosophers. None the less, it is possible for students of rhetoric to handle the latter by starting from topics for practical theses. Surely there is no difference if someone discusses (the practical question) whether one should marry, or the question whether one should marry or not, and (the theoretical question) whether marriage should be chosen or avoided. What is being explained is one and the same in all these cases.

Now the most general headings of practical theses are supported by argument from what is necessary and what is noble and what is beneficial and what is pleasant, and refuted from the opposites. We shall handle each thesis with whatever topics are possible; for as we indicated repeatedly, it is not possible to treat every problem from every starting point. There are also the following topics. First, that what is recommended in the thesis is possible, and second, that it is in accordance with nature and according to the common manners and customs of all mankind; for it is not a sufficient reason for doing something that it is possible unless it is in accordance with nature and custom. Third, that it is easy, and if it is not easy but is possible, that something is much more praiseworthy if it is not easy. Then, that we are not the only ones doing it but many others do also. Next, that we are not the first **[122]** and there have been many others before us, and even if we are the only ones or first, still it is better to be the initiator of fine deeds and being alone is more praiseworthy than acting with another. Then that it is appropriate. Then that it is just. Then that it is reverent; this is twofold, either pleasing to gods or to the dead. Next that it is necessary.

Then that it is honorable and that it is profitable and that it contributes to security and that it is the beginning of greater things; that it is pleasant, and that if it is not done it brings regret and it is hard to correct the omission.

From the opposite (we argue as follows): if the opposite should not be done, this should be done; and if the opposite is shameful, this is noble; and if that is inexpedient, this is beneficial; and if the opposite is unpleasant, this is pleasant. In the same way from the like; for if the like is preferable, this too is preferable. Similarly from the lesser and the greater and the part and the whole. Next, we shall argue from the end for which we choose the action; for if the end is preferable, what is productive of the end is preferable. After this from what is implicit; that many fine or beneficial or pleasant things are included with it. Then we shall argue from the antecedents and the concomitants and, third, from what will follow.

A more advanced student should include in each of the topics just mentioned the evidence of famous men, poets and statesmen and philosophers. Also, any histories that agree with what is being said, and one should not make mention of these things randomly or by chance,[177] but amplifying the examples, first from what has been done by an individual, private man, then by those in authority or a king, next by those in the city, and finally from what has been done in certain lands and by foreigners, but not **[123]** to the point of filling up the speech with histories and poems. One should refute by using the opposite topics.

We shall arrange the epicheiremes[178] in the same order as we did in the discussion of topoi, beginning from the first and continuing to the last. For the sake of illustration, let the first thesis be a practical one; for example, whether a wise man will engage in politics. In supporting the thesis that one should engage in politics, it should be said first that it is *possible* for a wise man to engage in politics. Second, that it is *in accordance with nature;* for example, that there is a polity even among animals and a leader of each herd, and that among barbarians and among Greeks and among the gods themselves—so it is said—the best always rule. Next, that it is also *easy* for a wise man to engage in politics; for having been trained in studies of human ethics, he will rule over men with graceful ease. Then, that even if it is not easy, one must, of course, regard the happiness

---

[177] Cf. above, n. 161, and Butts, p. 523.
[178] I.e., the argument supporting application of the topics.

of the city as more important than one's own labors. Next, that many of his fellow citizens are ready to help, and that he is *not the first,* since many wise men have engaged in politics: Pittacus, Solon, Lycurgus, Zaleucus, countless others. Then, that even if no wise man had engaged in politics in ancient or modern times, still, to be the *initiator* of fine deeds is more praiseworthy. After this, that engaging in politics is *appropriate* for a wise man; for who better than he will judge justly, and will advise what is beneficial, and will introduce laws and decrees, and will do these things without being bribed? In what action will he more demonstrate virtue and likeness to god? In addition, that it is *just* to render to the fatherland and the citizens and the ancestral gods repayment for the nurture and education they have given him. Then, that it is reverent and *pleasing to the gods* for human beings [124] to be well governed, and next that it is *sweet to the dead* for their descendants to be kept safe. Then, that it is *necessary* for the city to have someone giving thought for its future, and especially a good person; for without this a city could not survive. After this, that one becomes more *honored* by engaging in politics, even if he was heretofore unknown. Then, that he will conduct daily affairs more *profitably* from a financial point of view, and that he will most *safely* escape from sycophants and the envy of those plotting against him. Next, that for a wise man to engage in politics is the beginning and *start of greater and more beautiful things,* not only privately but in common, and that the pleasantest life is that of those who engage in politics. This almost naturally follows most of the aforesaid topics.

In addition to these arguments, (we can say) that a neglected government suffers a change for the worse that is hard to remedy, and one who has neglected government before it becomes bad experiences regret when it cannot be helped. Next, from *opposites;* for if acting against the fatherland is shameful, to participate in politics is good; if the former is not beneficial, the latter is; if the former is unpleasant, the latter is pleasant. And if something like to politics—let us say caring for the young—is noble and beneficial and pleasant, then engaging in politics is itself noble and beneficial and pleasant. We shall argue *from the lesser* as follows: If a good man must take care of one house, he must also care for a whole city. *From the greater,* if a good man should care for his nation, he should also care for one city. *From the part,* if a good man should introduce one law, or even one resolution, then he should also introduce a whole constitution. Or conversely, *from the whole,* if the wise man proposes a general constitution for humans, as Plato does in the *Republic,* it is right to engage in politics in one's own city. After this we shall discuss the happiness of the city both in peace and time of war, **[125]** and at any time at all, things which are the end of being well governed. Then *from what is implicit,* that in name and appearance engaging in politics will provide one benefit to the city but in fact there are many; for according to the school of Aristotle, it is necessary for the statesman to advise about war and peace, and about finances, and about defense of the land, and about imports and exports, and about legislation and other such things.[179]

Although it is possible to provide an example of topics preliminary to the action and at the same time as the action and after the action using the same thesis, it will be clearer to use another; for example, whether one should have children. After mentioning the wedding and all the necessary antecedents of having children, we shall praise parentage by showing that it is good and beneficial and pleasant; next, the things accompanying the conception of children, and after that the things that follow; for example, provision for our care and feeding in old age, and the successes and pleasures of having children, and similar things. From the opposites we shall have an abundance of arguments in refutation.

So much, then, for a practical thesis. Now let us try to go through one of the theoretical theses, starting from the same topics. We shall, however, not keep to the same order here as in practical theses but shall compose in whatever way seems best to fit the proposed problem. Probably it would be better to do the same also in practical theses. The order fits each problem when, mentioning the weaker and simpler epicheiremes first, then a little further on we take up the stronger and more complex arguments, and when we put the arguments for something in advance of the propositions which they support, and when **[126]** we slip weak arguments in between stronger ones, and whatever else is said in discussions of arrangement.[180]

Let us suppose we are inquiring whether the gods exercise a providential care for the world (*kosmos*). Here again we shall say that it is *possible* for the gods to provide for us and for them to be in no way diminished by concern for the world; then, that it is *easy* for a god to exercise foresight and involves no trouble; next, that he has

[179] Cf. Aristotle, *Rhetoric* 1.4.
[180] Cf., e.g., *Rhetoric for Herennius* 3.18.

daemons and heroes and other gods as helpers in this care; then, that all mankind, both Greeks and barbarians, have a *belief* about the gods as caring for us. A sign of this is that, otherwise, altars and temples and oracles would not have been erected on account of the benefits which individuals have experienced in time of famine or plague or war or something of the sort, by being relieved of these, nor would they have turned their mind to prophecy,[181] and especially when in the greatest danger. Next, that this is the *opinion of the wise*, for example, Plato, Aristotle, and Zeno;[182] then, that it is the *opinion of lawgivers;* for otherwise there would not be indictments for impiety. Then, that those believing the gods care for us are the *most honored*. <Then, that thinking the gods provide for us is *profitable*.>[183] Then, that believers pass their lives most *securely* and carefully in thinking that they are being observed in all the actions in life; and that people live most *pleasantly* who believe that they have the gods as protectors. After this, that since god is *just,* he would not permit those worshiping him to be uncared for. Then, that the *nature of the universe* gives evidence that all things have come to be with the god's care for the preservation of the world; for the seasons of the year take their changes at regular times, and rains and harvests recur in season, and the succession of the seasons too has been well crafted by nature for their continuance and preservation, as Xenophon makes clear in the *Memorabilia* (4.3.3–9). Then, that this care for the world is of all things *most fitting* for the god [127]; for it is not pious to say that the god is idle and inactive, or, by Zeus, that he is involved in the troublesome business that we are; because of being mortal and weak we necessarily toil. Then, that it is *necessary* for providence to exist; for if someone removed providence from the god he would remove also the conception of him we have, by which we comprehend his very existence; for it is because of the god's concern for us that we have belief in his being. Then, that the world would not have come into existence in the first place if there were no providence; for just as no house can come into being without a builder from the self-moved concurrence of the stones and bricks, nor a boat without a shipbuilder, <nor a cloak without a weaver,>[184] nor in general any things, insignificant or val-

---

[181] Reading *manteia* with Butts, p. 536, for Spengel's *panti*, "at all."

[182] Zeno of Citium (335–263 B.C.), founder of the Stoic philosophical school. The thesis here defended is especially identified with the Stoics. Note that the writer on figures cited by Quintilian (9.3.76) is called "Theon the Stoic."

[183] Added by Patillon from the Armenian.

[184] Added by Patillon from the Armenian but omitted in his French version.

ued, without the artisan for each, so it is laughable to say that the world, the fairest and most honored of all things that exist, has come to be without some finest and *most divine craftsman* and is the result of self-movement.[185]

After this are arguments from the *opposite,* that it is simple minded to believe the great order in the revolutions of the heavenly bodies occurs without some providence but is random and chance. Then, from *what is like,* that if it is not possible for a household to subsist well without a manager nor a ship without a pilot nor an army without a general nor a city without a statesman, neither can the world hold together without a foreseeing god. In addition, *from the part,* that if it is agreed that heroes and daemons and gods are seen exercising care throughout our cities, it follows that gods care for the whole world. Then *from what is implicit,* that although one belief is nominally being denied, in truth many are; for if there is no divine providence, neither can justice subsist nor reverence nor trust in oaths nor bravery nor temperance nor friendship nor gratitude nor, simply stated, any **[128]** other virtuous action, things which men of intelligence cannot do without. From the opposite topics we shall treat the other side of the question.

Since some theses are single, some compound—single, (for example,) whether one should marry, compound whether a king should marry—one should divide compound theses into each separate thesis in order to provide the proper arguments to each of the parts. And we shall compose amplifications and digressions as the parts of the thesis permit. Similarly, we shall make use of emotions and characterizations and exhortations and nearly all the kinds (*ideai*) of discourse. We shall introduce many circumstances of life and speak fitting words about each. For example, in considering whether one should marry, after a general and universal discussion applying to all mankind, from which we confirm or refute the obligation to marry, we shall continue with consideration of each way of life—for example, that of a farmer, a trader, a soldier, a rich man, a poor man, a king—and thus we shall have a great supply of things to say to make one thesis into many. We shall use the same starting points of epicheiremes for refutation and proof of maxims, as I said earlier.[186]

[185] The view of Epicureans.
[186] Cf. above, p. 23.

12. (SPENGEL 13.) ON LAW

Law (*nomos*) is a decision of a political nature by the people or by a leading man, regulating how all those in the city should live, not limited to a certain period of time.[187] Scrutiny of laws is two-fold; for either they are being introduced and proposed or they are already in effect. In the case of those being proposed, there is an evaluation whether the law should be ratified or not. Concerning those already in effect, debates take place in court by those pleading, not to abolish the laws entirely, but advancing on each side what is the more profitable interpretation, **[129]** and the speakers amplify what seems to have been written and conceal opposing interpretations.

Since our discussion now is about refutation and confirmation of a law, and especially laws that are being introduced, we must describe this. When laws are being introduced we either speak against them and rebut them or we speak for them and supply supporting evidence. After the prooemion we rebut from the following topics: from what is unclear, impossible, unnecessary, contradictory, unjust, unworthy, inexpedient, shameful.

Some lack of clarity occurs from pronunciation, which certain authorities call "from prosody,"[188] some from the meaning of a word, some from homonymy, some from polyonymy, which others call synonymy,[189] some from syntax, some from compounding and dividing words, some from pleonasm, some from ellipsis, some from inconsistency.

There is a problem from pronunciation whenever some similar words are used in the same order and it is possible to pronounce what has been written in two ways; for example, "Let a maid not wear gold ornaments, and if she does, *dêmosia estô* (let her/them be public property)." Here we are in doubt whether the maid is to become a public prostitute or the ornaments are to be confiscated, since it is possible for *dêmosia* to be pronounced with a short or long alpha.[190]

There is lack of clarity from the meaning of a word when what has been written is new or very archaic or foreign; for example,

[187] I.e., unlike a decree, it is of general application. Cf. the Platonic *Definitions* 415b8–9 and the last sentence of this chapter.
[188] Cf. e.g., Aristotle, *Sophistical Refutations* 166b1; Hermogenes, *On Stases* p. 41,15, ed. Rabe.
[189] "Synonymy" was primarily used of a feature of poetic style; cf. Aristotle, *Rhetoric* 3.2.7; Quintilian 8.3.16.
[190] If short, it is neuter plural and refers to the coins, if long it is feminine singular and refers to the maid.

podokakkê ("stocks") or *hêmedapê* ("native land"), and if one said *keramos* instead of *desmôtêrion* ("dungeon"), like the Cretans, as some interpret the line in Homer (about Ares, *Iliad* 5.387): "He was bound for thirteen months in a bronze *keramos*."[191]

There is lack of clarity from homonymy when one word signifies two, three, or even more things; for example, if someone writes "Let evidence not be taken from a *pais*." We shall then ask whether it means that a "child" is not to give evidence or a "son" on behalf of a father or a "slave" on behalf of a master. The one word "boys" means all these things.

[130]   From polyonymy, on the other hand, whenever only one thing is signified but many names are used for it; for example, "weapon, blade, sword, dirk." There is a lack of clarity when someone thinks there are as many signifieds as names.

And in syntax; for example, when Pittacus[192] said "to share, father and mother, equally"; for the statement is ambiguous as to whether the children are to share the possessions of the parents or the parents those of the children. And further, when a word in the middle of a sentence creates a different meaning when taken with what precedes or what follows it; for example, "Let a general victorious in war dedicate a statue of Ares, golden with a spear." Is a golden statue or golden spear meant?

Concerning combining and dividing—or as some[193] say concerning confusion between the divided and the undivided—; for example, the law ordering brothers and children to come to the settlement (of an estate). If this is taken as "divided" it means that first the brother, and if he is not alive, then the children are to be summoned, but it can be combined to mean they are to be called at the same time. Or again, "The false witness taken three times 1000 (drachmas) let him give"; for either it means that one detected thrice in giving false evidence should pay a 1000 or that if detected once he should give 3000 drachmas.

Lack of clarity occurs from pleonasm whenever it is possible to infer something more than what is written as potentially implied; for example, if someone issued a law that those on the mother's side should also inherit. The mother might claim that, if it called for those on the mother's side to inherit, all the more would it be calling for the mother herself to inherit.

[191] *Keramos* in most Greek dialects means an "earthen pot," but in Cretan refers to a dungeon.
[192] Democratic lawgiver in Mytilene, c. 600 B.C.
[193] Dialecticians; cf. above, p. 31.

Lack of clarity from ellipsis occurs in many ways; <either in omission of cause or person or necessity or manner or place or time or quality or quantity. Omission of cause,>[194] for example, "Let a father-beater's hands be cut off." (The law) omits to say whether if done in ignorance, or even for a good reason, or applies to all in general. There are many kinds of ellipsis in regard to a person; for persons certainly differ in nature and age and nearness of relation and fortune; for example, "The children of a traitor are to be killed," where it has not defined if this includes an adopted son or a female child. . . .

The Greek text of Theon's treatise ends abruptly at this point. For what originally followed we are dependent on the Armenian version as edited, with French translation, by Michel Patillon and Giancarlo Bolognesi. Reconstruction of the original is sometimes uncertain, and an English translation of a French translation of a reconstruction of a Greek text from an Armenian translation of it would be of dubious value for detailed interpretation. What follows is thus only a summary of what seem to have been the main points, with a few short passages translated from the French, as indicated in the notes. For more information readers should consult the fine edition of Patillon and Bolognesi.

[Page 99 Patillon]

Ellipsis of necessity: for example, a law providing that a person who has won the prize for bravery in battle three times necessarily ought not to be a soldier, but without explaining why this is necessary.[195]

Ellipsis of manner: for example, a law that specifies the execution of an adulterer but fails to specify the manner of execution.

Ellipsis of place: for example, a law approving erection of a statue of one who has won a prize for bravery without specifying where.

Ellipsis of time: for example, a law stating it is improper to begin to defend oneself with force but without specifying when it is proper.

Ellipsis of quality: for example, a law making money subject to tax but not specifying what kind of money (gold money? foreign money?).

[194] Added by Patillon from the Armenian.
[195] An argument for the law would be to give other soldiers a chance, but is that a necessity?

Ellipsis of quantity: for example, a law providing exemption from tax but not specifying the amount.

Obscurity derives from contradiction when a law contradicts itself. Some topics will not apply to laws invented for practice in the schools, but these should confirm as much as possible to actual usage.[196]

Next we shall ask if such legal provisions are possible. **[100 P]** "One shall not tell lies in the agora" is impossible to enforce in practice. A law might require an adulterer to lose his eyes, but if a blind man is caught in the act, how will one take away the sight of one who does not have it?

Next is whether the law is needed. One can say that it has not been proposed in view of some good or useful purpose but about things without importance and it is nothing more than one of those useless laws that one can ratify or not.

The topic of contradiction shows that a law is contrary to an existing law. In school exercises someone reads out the laws that are imagined to apply. These should not be thought of as the laws of Athens or any particular place. We shall try to show that the proposed law departs from universal usage. For example, one would object to a law denying a woman the right to make a valid will on the ground that it is contrary to universal practice.

Next, does the law apply equally to all or only to some (i.e., is it unjust?). If it gives preference to certain classes, it may be open to the objection of not distributing a public benefit to all; **[101 P]** or conversely, if it applies to all it may fail to take account of differences of condition. For example, a law providing that one who has inflicted blows and wounds will pay ten thousand drachmas or lose his civic rights. The penalty will not fall equally on rich and poor; the rich will pay a fine, the poor will lose their rights. Then, does the penalty set by the legislator fit the crime? The penalty can be too great—for example, death for killing an animal or slavery for having accepted benefits—or too little—a fine of a thousand drachmas for killing a man or an olive crown as a reward for bravery.[197]

Next, what is inexpedient. A law, for example, is inexpedient and dangerous that requires pulling down part of the city wall for a procession in honor of an Olympic victor. Next, that it is shameful;

---

[196] On real and fictitious laws as posited in the declamation of judicial themes (*controversiae*), see S. F. Bonner, *Roman Declamation in the Late Republic and Early Empire* (Berkeley: Univ. of California Press, 1949), pp. 84–132.

[197] An olive crown would be an appropriate prize in athletics, a gold crown for bravery in war.

for example, denying citizenship to publicans and artisans working with fire, or fining an adulterer a thousand drachmas, obliging him to choose between a big fine and lusts of the flesh.
[102 P] We support a law with topics opposite to these. In refutation and confirmation of laws we shall use the emotions and characterizations, then amplifications, digression, and all forms of discourse. These same topics will be used in arguing about decrees. A decree differs from a law in that it responds to an immediate need and its effect is limited in time.

Chapters 13–17 deal with pedagogical techniques for teaching composition as a preparation for more advanced rhetorical studies, such as declamation. Theon identified these techniques briefly in the first and second chapters of his works.

Note that imitation of classical models is a fundamental principle in Theon's teaching, as in that of Dionysius of Halicarnassus, Quintilian, and other teachers, both Greek and Latin, in the time of the Roman empire. Note also that the pedagogical devices described by Theon provide training in all five of the traditional parts of rhetoric: invention, arrangement, style, memory, and delivery.

13. READING ALOUD AND ITS OBJECT

Theon's account can be compared with Quintilian's discussion of reading aloud and explication of texts, (Institutio Oratoria 2.5). Quintilian says that reading was commonly supervised by assistant teachers in Greek rhetorical schools, since the rhetor in charge did not have time to listen to each student, and indicates that it was almost unknown in Latin rhetorical schools. He recommends requiring younger students of rhetoric to read aloud in class and says he had experimented with the exercise but had found it impracticable in his own school: tradition was against it and his students were mostly older ones who had come to study declamation with him. The practice of reading prose aloud in Greek rhetorical schools was a continuation of the reading of poetry in grammar schools.

"Reading (*anagnôsis*) is the enunciation of a written text in a loud and strong voice."[198] Young men should begin by reading aloud simple works by orators: speeches by Isocrates,[199] then (some)

---

[198] Patillon, p. 102. Reading thus provides valuable exercise in rhetorical delivery.

[199] One would expect Lysias to be mentioned first, since his speeches were almost universally regarded as the best models of the simple style, and many were quite short; perhaps the Armenian text is corrupt.

by Hypereides and Aeschines, then by Demosthenes. The teacher should explain that oratory is encomiastic or judicial—divided into private or public cases—or deliberative, and he should indicate the objective of each.[200]

The teacher is to give an explication of a work before it is read, identifying features of invention, arrangement, and style, a kind of brief course in rhetorical theory. Perhaps the student is to practice reading the speech in private; then he apparently reads the speech (or part of it?) aloud, probably to the class, as Quintilian recommends and as the next chapter might suggest, but perhaps sometimes individually to the teacher. Probably there will be occasional corrections and comments from the teacher during the reading. Theon's account, as reconstructed from the Armenian translation, omits description of practical details that we would like to know.

The teacher will describe the subject. He will set out the questions at issue, if the student has reached the stage of understanding stasis theory, and will list the arguments and describe the art of the speech for an advanced student. **[103 P]** He will instruct him about character types; for example, a sycophant as portrayed by Demosthenes (18.242), and will point out the uses of ethos and pathos, digressions, amplifications, diminutions, and other treatments, as well as styles of expression and uses of ornaments of style.

Reading of oratory is to be followed by reading of works on history, of which Theon distinguished six genres. He recommends reading Herodotus, Theopompus, Xenophon, Philistus, Ephorus, and Thucydides, but also mentions other historians, of whom Cimnus and Philias (if the names are correct) are totally unknown today.

Above all, we shall accustom the student to fit voice and gestures to the subject of the speech. It is this that actualizes the art of the speech. We shall present and imagine with the greatest care all that concerns an orator: his actions, credibility, age, and status; the place where the speech was delivered, the subject it treats, and everything that contributes to the feeling that the speech actually concerns us as we read it aloud. This is how the actor Polos[201] interpreted his roles, so well, they say, that he shed real tears on stage.

[200] According to Aristotle (*Rhetoric* 1.3), the honorable, the just, and the advantageous, respectively.
[201] Patillon suggests that this refers to Polus of Aegina, a famous actor in Athens in the late 4th cent. B.C.

There are several genres of historical writing. There is ge-
nealogical history, from which come lists of archons and ephors of
Athens and elsewhere and priestesses of Argos and kings of
Lacedaimon, **[104 P]** Macedonia, and Persia: such are the works of
Apollodorus of Athens, Acusilaus of Argos, and Hecataeus of
Miletus. Second, there is political history that allows us to follow
the succession of events such as revolts and wars; examples can be
found in Thucydides and Philistus. Then there is mythical history,
proposing legends of the heroes and the gods to our imagination.
The famous books of the *Tragôdoumena* of Asclepiades are a good
example. Other historians preserve memory of fine sayings; the
writings of Xenophon about Socrates are an example of the genre.
Biographical writing also belongs to this genre; for example, accounts of noble lives by Aristoxenus the musician and others by
Satyrus.[202] General historians inform us about countries, towns,
rivers, situations, nature, etc. Works by Cimnus, Philias, Philo-
stephanus, or Istrus are examples. Descriptions of constitutions,
such as those by Aristotle, also belong to this genre. Finally, there is
the more highly developed form of history, practiced by Herodotus
and many other historians, which combines features of all the genres just described.

We shall read Herodotus first, despite the fact that he covers so
much, because of his great simplicity of style. From his work we
shall move to Theopompus and Xenophon, then to Philistus and
Ephorus, and finally to Thucydides. Training will be the same as in
the case of reading the orators. **[105 P]** Avoid doing what some
teachers do, leaving aside the brilliance and sublimity in Thucydides, while cutting him down into an imitation full of obscurities and
stressing whatever is abstruse and difficult in his writing. Do not
imitate only one model but all the most famous of the ancients.
Thus we shall have copious, numerous, and varied resources on
which to draw. It is wrong to limit imitation to a single author; those
who imitate only Demosthenes become stiff, tiresome, and obscure,
and those who want to imitate only Lysias are thin, weak, and
clumsy. "When someone admires what is good in all and understands how to conform his thought to that, so that there exists in
him a kind of ideal model of style which each can mold in accordance with his own nature, he does not seem constrained to fix his
eyes on a single style, but he acquires, spontaneously for his per-

[202] Peripatetic biographer of the 3rd cent.; part of his *Life of Euripides* survives
on papyrus.

sonal use, a part of all these excellences."[203] Thus it is most useful to collect what has some beauty in all works, to recite this, and to recall it frequently while joining the appropriate delivery to the subject.[204]

14. LISTENING TO WHAT IS READ

There is no discussion of this subject in other rhetorical texts, but Plutarch's essay (in the Moralia), *"How a Young Man Ought to Listen to Poetry," has a number of similarities to what Theon recommends.*

"In listening (*akroasis*), the most important thing is to give frank and friendly attention to the speaker."[205] **[106 P]** Then the student should recall the subject of the writing, identify the main points and the arrangement, finally recall also the better passages. If at first he cannot recall the words or their arrangement, it is still useful for him to try, but not everything at once. Have him write it down at leisure. Begin with the prooemion, and then, after practicing with that for several days, continue to the narration, then move on to the arguments, two or three at a time.

Some younger orators acquired so good an ability by listening to famous orators that their works were attributed to the master. Theopompus, who had heard Demosthenes deliver his speech against Leptines, was inspired by the words of the orator in his own work. Some critics, including the great Dionysius of Halicarnassus, say that the speeches *Against Aristogeiton* are by one of Demosthenes' auditors rather than by himself. **[107 P]** One should not practice this exercise at every reading, but reserve it for important authors. To prevent students from choosing bad texts through ignorance, it should usually be the teachers who choose the daily exercise in listening.

If on a particular day nothing has been read aloud, it is useful for students to describe what they did in the recent past or what has happened to their friends or to describe some public event, such as a riot, a procession, a spectacle, or political agitation.[206] If they undertake such a composition, they will make good use not only of the

[203] Quoted from Patillon, p. 105. What he translates *matrise* ("model") perhaps represents Greek *kharaktêr*.

[204] Patillon, n. 535, suggests that this refers to word-for-word memorization of some texts, which the student can then deliver with appropriate voice and gesture.

[205] Patillon, p. 105.

[206] Theon's suggestion that students write essays about their own experiences ("What I did on my summer vacation") is unparalleled and surprising from an an-

words and phrases they have learned but also the facts and characterizations.

15. PARAPHRASE

*Theon's discussion of practice in paraphrase can be compared with
Quintilian's account,* Institutio Oratoria *10.5.4–11. Examples of exercises in paraphrase in Morgan,* Literate Education, *pp. 205–15.*

"Paraphrase (*paraphrasis*) consists of changing the form of expression while keeping the thoughts; it is also called metaphrase."[207]
There are four main kinds: variation in syntax, by addition, by subtraction, **[108 P]** and by substitution, plus combinations of these:

Syntactical paraphrase: we keep the same words but transpose
the parts, which offers numerous possibilities.[208]

By addition: we keep the original words and add to them; for example, Thucydides (1.142.1) said, "in war, opportunities are not
abiding," while Demosthenes (4.37) paraphrased this, "opportunities for action do not await our sloth and evasions."

By subtraction: speaking in an incomplete way, we drop many
of the elements of the original. (No example seems to have been offered.)

By substitution: we replace the original word with another; for
example, *pais* or *andrapodon* for *doulos* (slave), or the proper word
instead of a metaphor or a metaphor instead of the proper word, or
several words instead of one or one instead of several. **[109P]**

There are other ways of varying the content along the lines discussed in the chapter on narration; for example, recasting an asser-
tion as a question, a question as a potentiality, and similarly other
forms of expression that we mentioned.

*In a somewhat obscure passage Theon seems to describe two exer-
cises. In one exercise, the same person who has read a passage reflects upon the sense and then seeks to reproduce the passage, in so
far as possible keeping the words of the original in the original
order. In the second exercise, a speech of Lysias is read and then the
student tries to recast it in the style of Demosthenes, or conversely*

---

cient teacher. There would have been ample opportunity to describe riots, processions, spectacles, and political agitation in ancient Alexandria.

[207] Patillon, p. 107. Among the rather few occurrences of the term *metaphrasis*,
meaning "paraphrase," are Seneca, *Suasoriae* 1.12, and Plutarch, *Demosthenes* 8.2.

[208] Theon is thinking more of rearrangement of the order of words than of actual changes in syntax; cf. above, p. 63. Such syntactic paraphrases as changing a
clause into a genitive absolute would, perhaps, fall under "substitution."

a speech of Demosthenes in the style of Lysias, and similarly with other orators and historians.

We should not attempt to paraphrase everything, only what lends itself to a good restatement. For example, a thought like the following: "Although recognizing that it is legal to accept the gifts offered, **[110 P]** you indict as illegal the return of gratitude for them" (Demosthenes 18.119) might be paraphrased by a teacher as, "If you recognize that it is legal to accept the gifts offered, you cannot say that gratitude for them is illegal."

Begin with the simplest thing, for example, with exercise of memory, then pass to paraphrasing some argument in a speech, then to paraphrasing some part of the speech, either the prooemion or narration. Thus our young men will gradually become capable of paraphrasing a whole speech, which is the result of perfected ability.

The following two exercises, elaboration and contradiction, are to be practiced only by advanced students; cf. Theon's remarks at the end of chapter 2, above.

16. ELABORATION

"Elaboration (*exergasia*) is language that adds what is lacking in thought and expression."[209] What is "lacking" can be supplied by making clear what is obscure; by filling gaps in the language or content; by saying some things more strongly, or more believably, or more vividly, or more truly, or more wordily—each word repeating the same thing—, or more legally, or more beautifully, or more appropriately, or more opportunely, or making the subject pleasanter, or using a better arrangement or a style more ornate.

Consider the words about the Euboeans in Aeschines' *Against Ctesiphon* and Demosthenes' *On the Crown*. The Athenians had gone to their aid, even though the Euboeans had been the cause of wrong to them, and had **[111 P]** saved them and restored their cities (in 357 B.C.). Aeschines says (3.84): "You righteously and justly restored the cities themselves and their constitutions to those who had entrusted them to you, not thinking it right to remember your anger when they had put faith in you." And Demosthenes (18.100): "You, on the one hand, did a noble thing in saving the island, but it was a yet nobler thing by far, that when their lives and their cities were absolutely in your power, you gave them back, as it was right to do, to the very men who had offended against you, and made no reck-

[209] Patillon, p. 110.

oning, when such trust had been placed in you, of the wrongs which you had suffered." Because Demosthenes' version is heavier in sound (?),[210] Aeschines' version can seem in contrast solid, firm and simple, and because those who understand such things can perceive that Demosthenes repeats sounds, let us, when teaching, examine and discuss the details. Aeschines simplified in combining the good deeds into one; Demosthenes made them into two things, presenting separately the act of saving and the act of restoring, and at the same time he has amplified the second act with the addition of "a yet nobler thing by far." Moreover, Aeschines spoke of the state of mind in which the Athenians acted; Demosthenes described it more fully: "You, on the one hand, did a noble thing," brings credibility by adding "on the one hand."[211]

17. CONTRADICTION, OR COUNTER-STATEMENT

"Contradiction (*antirrhêsis*) is discourse that attacks the credibility of another discourse."[212] Try to show that the other discourse is obscure, impossible, **[112P]** incredible, deceitful, or inadequate in thought or expression; or, conversely, redundant or lacking vigor, or confused; or that the discourse is contradictory, or departs from what is legal, or is unseemly or inexpedient or inopportune; or that the speaker spoke as much against as for himself—what some call turning his argument against himself—, or that the rules of good arrangement are violated, or that the speech was ineffectively delivered.

First, invite the student to contradict the arguments, even those that seem difficult to attack, as a recent author has done in contradiction of Demosthenes (18.119): "Although recognizing that it is legal to accept the gifts offered, you indict as illegal showing gratitude for them." The critic has objected, "Yes, Demosthenes, for whoever wants can give, but he only receives who has the right to receive." Then gradually go on to contradict the whole argument, then to contradict the narration, and finally complete a contradiction of the whole.

Such are the exercises that are appropriately practiced before undertaking hypotheses.

[210] Cf. Patillon, p. 11: "d'une consonance plus lourde et offre un développement aux consonances plus marquées."

[211] According to Patillon, p. 171, n. 590, the Armenian translator understood *men* in the Greek as an affirmative, which he translates *assurément*. What Theon actually said is unclear, but probably he regarded the first clause in Demosthenes' statement as contributing to credibility.

[212] Patillon, p. 111.

Chapter II

The *Preliminary Exercises*
Attributed to Hermogenes

Hermogenes of Tarsus was a boy wonder as a declaimer in the time of Marcus Aurelius (A.D. 161–180) (see Philostratus, Lives of the Sophists 2.7) and has traditionally been identified as the author of treatises on stasis and on ideas of style which became part of an authoritative collection of rhetorical texts, used from late antiquity to the Renaissance. This short work on progymnasmata is also attributed to him but it has a different manuscript tradition from the other works and is of doubtful authenticity. John of Sardis, writing about A.D. 800, refers to it as by Hermogenes, but a scholiast (Rhetores Graeci VII p. 511, ed. Walz) *attributes it to the fourth-century sophist Libanius, and Priscian describes it as by Hermogenes or Libanius. It was not unusual for scribes to attribute works of unknown authorship to famous authorities in the field: other instances include attributions to Dionysius of Halicarnassus, Aelius Aristeides, and Cassius Longinus. Syrianus, an early commentator on Hermogenes, seems not to have known this work, and whoever created the Hermogenic corpus prefixed Aphthonius' account of progymnasmata to Hermogenes' genuine works, ignoring the treatise attributed to Hermogenes. This is the simplest of the accounts of preliminary exercises, little more than an abstract of previous handbooks. Its date of composition is uncertain, possibly in the third or fourth century. The author refers (p. 84, below) to Aelius Aristeides, the great orator of the second century, and Nicolaus, writing in the late fifth century, knew the work. Similarities to Aphthonius' work, dating from the late fourth century, probably derive from use of common sources.*

About A.D. 500 the Roman grammarian Priscian wrote a Latin handbook of progymnasmata largely based on this work. He called the exercises praeexercitamina, *made minor changes in content and added brief Latin illustrations from Terence, Sallust, Virgil, and Cicero. Priscian's work implies that the exercises were being taught in his time to Latin-speaking students; his handbook was preserved in manuscripts with his other works and had some use in the Middle Ages and later.*[1]

---

[1] See E. R. Curtius, *European Literature and the Latin Middle Ages*, trans. by W. R. Trask (Princeton University Press, 1953), p. 442; J. J. Murphy, *Rhetoric in*

An English translation of Priscian's version can be found in Miller,
Prosser, and Benson's Readings in Medieval Rhetoric, *pp. 52–68.*

The following translation is based on the edition of Hermogenes'
works by Hugo Rabe, pp. 1–27. There is a less literal translation by
Charles Sears Baldwin in his Medieval Rhetoric and Poetic *(New*
York: Macmillan, 1928), pp. 23–38. The text begins without any in-
troduction, but subsequently the author refers to an unidentified ad-
dressee in the second person singular, apparently a young man who is
undertaking a program of instruction in composition.

[p. 1 Rabe]   1. ON FABLE

See Gangloff, "Mythes," pp. 32–34.

Fable (*mythos*) is regarded as the first exercise to be assigned to
the young because it can bring their minds into harmony for the
better. In this way they (i.e., teachers of grammar) think to form
students while still tender. The ancients seem also to have used it,
Hesiod telling the fable of the nightingale (*Works and Days* 203) and
Archilochus that of the fox.[2] Fables are named after their inventors,
some being called Cyprian, some Libyan, some Sybaritic, but all
collectively **[2]** are called Aesopic because Aesop used fables in his
teaching.[3] They give some such sketch of it as follows. They think
it right for it to be fictitious, but in all cases to be useful for some
aspect of life. In addition, they want it to be plausible. How would
it become plausible? If we attribute appropriate things to the characters. For example, someone is arguing about beauty; let him be
represented as a peacock. Cleverness needs to be attributed to
someone; here a fox is appropriate. For imitators of the actions of
human beings, choose apes.

Sometimes fables need to be expanded, sometimes to be compressed. How would this be done? If we sometimes recount the
fable in a bare narrative, at other times invent speeches for the given
characters; thus, to make it clear to you by an example, "The apes
gathered **[3]** to deliberate about the need to found a city. Since it
seemed best to do so, they were about to begin work. An old ape restrained them, saying that they will be more easily caught if

---

the Middle Ages (University of California Press, 1974), p. 131, and Paul E. Prill,
"Rhetoric and Poetics in the Early Middle Ages," *Rhetorica* 5 (1987) 129–47; for
its later use, see D. L. Clark, "The Rise and Fall of Progymnasmata in Sixteenth
and Seventeenth Grammar Schools," *Speech Monographs* 19 (1952): 259–63.

[2] Frag. 86, p. 143, ed. Edmonds.
[3] See above, p. 24, n. 89.

hemmed in by walls." This is how you would tell the fable concisely, but if you wanted to expand it, proceed as follows: "The apes gathered to deliberate about building a city. One stepped forward and delivered a speech to the effect that they had need of a city: 'For you see,' he says, 'how happy men are by living in a city. Each of them has his house, and by coming together to an assembly and a theater all collectively delight their minds with all sorts of sights and sounds,' " and continue in this way, dwelling on each point and saying that the decree was passed; then fashion a speech also for the old ape.[4] So much for this.

They want the expression to avoid the use of periods and to be close to sweetness.[5] **[4]** The statement explaining the moral will sometimes be put before the fable, sometimes after it. Orators too seem (sometimes) to have used a fable in place of an example.[6]

2. ON NARRATIVE

The authorities want narrative (*diêgêma*) to be an exposition of something that has happened or as if it happened. Some place the chreia before the narrative.[7] A narrative (*diêgêma*) differs from a narration (*diêgêsis*) as a piece of poetry (*poiêma*) differs from a poetical work (*poiêsis*).[8] A *poiêma* and a *diêgêma* are concerned with one thing, a *poiêsis* and a *diêgêsis* with many; for example, the *Iliad* is a *poiêsis* and the *Odyssey* is a *poiêsis*, while the "Making of the Shield" (*Iliad* 18) and "Descent into the Underworld" (*Odyssey* 11) and "Killing the Suitors" (*Odyssey* 22) are *poiêmata*. Again, the *History* of Herodotus is a *diêgêsis*, as is that of Thucydides, but the story of Arion (Herodotus 1.23) or of Alcmeon (Thucydides 2.102) is a *diêgêma*.

They want there to be four species of narrative: one is mythical; one fictitious, which they also call dramatic, like those of the tragedians; one is historical; and one is political or private.[9] Our present account deals with the last.

---

[4] John of Sardis gives an example of such a speech in his ch. 11 on ethopoeia, translated below.

[5] *Glykytês*, or "sweetness," is one of Hermogenes' "ideas" of style; see Wooten, pp. 75–81.

[6] Cf. Aristotle, *Rhetoric* 2.20.

[7] E.g., Theon and Harpocration; cf. Doxapatres in Walz, ed., *Rhetores Graeci* I, p. 192,14.

[8] On these terms, common beginning in the Hellenistic period, see George A. Kennedy, ed., *Cambridge History of Literary Criticism, I: Classical Criticism* (Cambridge University Press, 1989), pp. 204, 211, 257, and 259–64.

[9] That is, it specifies persons and places as would the narration in a public or private judicial speech; Priscian calls this legal narrative.

The figures (*skhêmata*) of narratives are five: direct declarative,
[5] oblique (or indirect) declarative, interrogative, asyndetical,
comparative. Now direct declarative discourse is, for example,
"Medea was a daughter of Aeetes. She betrayed the Golden
Fleece." It is called "direct" because through the whole account, or
most of it, it keeps the nominative case. Oblique declarative discourse is, for example, "The story is that Medea, daughter of
Aeetes, was infatuated with Jason," and so on. It is called "oblique"
because it uses the other grammatical cases.[10] The interrogative figure is, for example, "What dreadful thing did Medea not do? Was
she not infatuated with Jason, and did she not betray the Golden
Fleece, and did she not kill her brother Apsyrtus?" And so on.
Asyndeton occurs, for example, in "Medea, the daughter of Aeetes,
was infatuated with Jason, betrayed the Golden Fleece, murdered
her brother Apsyrtus," and so on.[11] Comparative (narrative) is such
as, "Medea, the daughter of Aeetes, instead of showing self-control,
fell in love; and instead of guarding the Golden Fleece, betrayed it;
and instead of saving her brother Apsyrtus, murdered him." The
direct figure is appropriate for histories, for it is clearer; the oblique
is more appropriate [6] for trials;[12] the interrogative is suitable for
dialectical debate, the asyndetical for epilogues, for it is emotional.

3. ON CHREIA

A chreia (*khreia*) is a recollection (*apomnêmoneuma*) of a saying or
action or both, with a pointed meaning, usually for the sake of
something useful.

Some chreias are verbal, some actional, some are mixed. Verbal
(*logikai*) are those in which there is only a saying; for example,
"Plato said that the muses dwell in the souls of those naturally
clever." An example of the actional ones (*praktikai*) is, "Diogenes,
on seeing an undisciplined youth, beat his pedagogue." Mixed are
those having a combination of a saying and an action; for example,
"Diogenes, on seeing an undisciplined youth, beat his pedagogue
and said, 'Why did you teach him such things?'"

[10] I.e., the "oblique" cases: accusative, genitive, dative, or vocative. In the example given, the accusative is used in indirect discourse. Cf. Theon on practice in
inflection, above pp. 19–21.
[11] Asyndeton is the omission of conjunctions. Priscian calls this periodic narrative.
[12] This may be a mistake on the part of the author; in fact, narrations in judicial speeches are usually in direct discourse and aim at clarity, whereas narrative in
indirect discourse is largely found in the historians.

A chreia differs from a recollection (*apomnêmoneuma*)[13] most in length, for recollections may be rather long and a chreia must be short. It differs from a maxim (*gnômê*) in that the latter is a bald statement [7] while the chreia often takes the form of a question and answer, and again in that the chreia may describe an action while the maxim consists only of words, and again in that the chreia identifies a person who has acted or spoken while the maxim does not identify a speaker.

Much is said by the ancients about different kinds of chreia, (for example,) that some of them are declarative, some interrogative, some investigative.[14] But now let us come to the point, and this is the elaboration (*exergasia*). Let the elaboration be as follows: first, a brief encomion of the speaker or doer; then a paraphrase of the chreia; then the cause; for example, "Isocrates said that the root of education is bitter but its fruit is sweet." Praise: "Isocrates was wise," and you will slightly develop the topic (*khôrion*). Then the chreia, "He said this," and you will not state it in bare form but expand the statement. Then the cause, "For the greatest things are wont to succeed through toil, and when successful bring pleasure." Then by contrast, "Ordinary things need no toil and in the end [8] give no pleasure, but things of importance are the opposite." Then from a comparison, "For just as farmers need to reap fruits by working the soil, so also with speeches." Then from an example, "Demosthenes, by shutting himself up at home and working hard, later reaped the fruit in the form of crowns and testimonials." It is also possible to bring in a judgment; for example, "Hesiod said (*Works and Days* 289), 'The gods put sweat before virtue,' and another poet says,[15] 'The gods sell all good things to us for toils.'" At the end you will put an exhortation to the effect that one must be persuaded by the person who has said or done this. So much for now; you will get more complete teaching later.

4. ON MAXIM[16]

Maxim (*gnômê*) is a summary statement, in universal terms, dissuading or exhorting in regard to something, or making clear what a particular thing is. Dissuading, as in the following (*Iliad* 2.24), "A

[13] E.g., Xenophon's *Memorabilia of Socrates*. Just above the author has defined chreia as a concise recollection.

[14] Cf. Theon, above p. 16.

[15] Epicharmus (fifth century B.C. comic poet), frag. 287, ed. Kaibel.

[16] In Priscian's Latin version this is called *sententia*, and "sentence" was sometimes used as the English term for *gnômê* in the Renaissance and early modern period.

man who is a counselor should not sleep throughout the night"; exhorting, as in the following (Theognis 175), "One fleeing poverty,
Cyrnis, must throw himself / Into the yawning sea and down steep
crags." Or it may do neither of these things but explain **[9]** the nature of something; for example (Demosthenes 1.23), "Undeserved
success is for the unintelligent the beginning of thinking badly."

Furthermore, some maxims are true, some plausible, some simple, some compound, and some hyperbolic. An example of a true
one is, "It is not possible for anyone to lead a life without some
pain";[17] of a plausible one, "I never ask who a man is who enjoys
Bad company, knowing that Such he is as those with whom he likes
to be";[18] of a simple one, "Wealth can even make men benevo-
lent";[19] of a compound one (*Iliad* 2.204), "Many lords are not good,
let there be one lord"; and of a hyperbolic (*Odyssey* 18.130), "Earth
bears nothing frailer than man."

The elaboration is similar to that of the chreia, for it proceeds
by the following: brief encomion of the speaker, as in **[10]** chreias;
simple statement; statement of the cause; a contrast;[20] a comparison; an example; a judgment. For an example, consider the maxim,
"A man who is a counselor should not sleep throughout the night."
You will praise the speaker[21] briefly. Then give a simple statement
paraphrasing the maxim; for example, "It is not fitting for a man
proved in councils to sleep through the whole night." The cause: "A
leader should always be engaged in thought, but sleep takes away
counsel." For contrast, a private individual is the opposite of a king,
and sleep the opposite of waking. How then might one express it?
"If there is nothing wrong with a private individual's sleeping
through the whole night, clearly it is appropriate for a king to be
wide-awake." With comparison: "Just as pilots continue awake for
the common safety, so it is appropriate for leaders." With example:
"For Hector, by not sleeping during the night and taking thought,
sent Dolon as a spy to the ships."[22] The final topic is support from
a judgment. Let the end be an exhortation.

---

[17] Menander, frag. 411, ed. Koch.
[18] Euripides, *Phoenician Women,* frag. 812, ed. Nauck.
[19] Menander, frag. 19, ed. Koch.
[20] The manuscripts insert "an enthymeme," perhaps a gloss by a scribe.
[21] Probably Homer; the speaker in the context of *Iliad* 2.24 is a dream in the
likeness of Nestor.
[22] Cf. *Iliad* 10.299–330; but the expedition ends in disaster.

5. ON REFUTATION AND CONFIRMATION

[11]   Refutation (*anaskeuê*) is an overturning of something that has been proposed, and confirmation (*kataskeuê*) is the opposite. No attempt should be made to argue against or for things that are entirely false, like fables,[23] but clearly there is need to compose refutations and confirmations of things open to argument on either side.

You will refute by argument from what is unclear, implausible, impossible; from the inconsistent, also called the contrary; from what is inappropriate, and from what is not advantageous. From what is unclear; for example, "The time when Narcissus lived is unclear." From the implausible, "It was implausible that Arion would have wanted to sing when in trouble."[24] From the impossible; for example, "It was impossible for Arion to have been saved by a dolphin." From the inconsistent, also called the contrary, "To want to destroy the democracy would be contrary to wanting to save it." From the inappropriate, "It was inappropriate for Apollo, a god, to have sexual intercourse with a mortal woman." From what is not advantageous, when we say that nothing is gained from hearing these things. Confirmation is derived from the opposites.[25]

6. ON COMMON-PLACE

Topos, modified by *koinos,* ("common-place") is an amplification of something that is agreed, as though demonstrations had already [12] occurred; for we are no longer inquiring, (for example,) whether this person is a temple robber or a war hero but we amplify the fact as proved. It is called "common"-place because (what we say) applies to every temple robber or every war hero.

One must proceed as follows: first, by investigation of the opposite, then (stating) the action itself, then a comparison, then a maxim; then you will attack the past life (of the person) with conjectures on the basis of the present; then you will reject pity by use of what are called "final headings"[26] and will give a vivid sketch of the action. Prooemia will not occur in an obvious way in a topos but will be preserved to some extent; thus, in order that it may be clear

---

[23] Theon (above, p. 26) had envisioned the possible refutation of fables.

[24] Arion escaped from the pirates by singing and then jumping into the sea, where he was rescued by a dolphin; see Herodotus 1.24.

[25] Confirmation is discussed in chapter 11 on thesis.

[26] *Telika kephalaia,* also translated "headings of purpose," identified below as the legal, the just, the beneficial, the possible, and the appropriate.

to you by an example, let the topos be against a temple robber. In this case, the prooemia[27] will not concern the intent (of the doer) but will deal with a generalization, such as the following: "It is appropriate, men of the jury, to hate all wrong-doers, but especially those whose audacity is directed against the gods"; secondly, "If, then, you want to encourage other evil-doers, let this one go, but if not, he should be punished"; third, "In appearance, only the defendant is on trial, but in truth you who are judging him are on trial as well; for I suspect that being false to your oaths may be [13] worse than the crime." Then, before going on to the action itself, one should speak about its contrary, (saying, for example,) that "The laws have provided for worship of the gods, have set up altars, have adorned them with offerings, have honored them with sacrifices, festive assemblies, and processions." Then the judgment with explanation of the cause: "Rightly; for the gods' good will preserves cities, and if it were otherwise cities would necessarily be destroyed."

Go on now to the case at hand: "Since these things are so, what has this man dared?" And speak of what has been done, not as explaining it but as making it seem dreadful, and (say) that "He has defiled the whole city, its people both jointly and severally, and there is fear lest the crops fail, there is fear lest we be defeated by our enemies," and more like that. Next, go on to comparison, (saying) that "He is more dangerous than murderers, the difference can be seen by comparing the victims: murderers attack human beings, he has abused the gods in his drunkenness. He is like tyrants, and not all of them but like the most dangerous; for what seems the most dreadful thing about them is that they seize on offerings to the gods." And you will introduce comparisons to lesser things by way of reproach; for they are damaging: "Is it not a dreadful thing to punish a thief and not a temple robber?" Also, it is possible for you to attack the rest of his life on the basis of his present deed, as "From small beginnings he advanced to this final act, so that [14] you have in one and the same person a thief and a housebreaker and an adulterer." You will consider the maxim which describes how he came to this, (saying) that "Not wanting to work on the land, he wants to get rich from actions like this." If you were speaking against a murderer (you would also tell) the consequences: "A wid-

---

[27] Some rhetoricians of the empire used "prooemia" in the plural to mean a series of statements made in the prooemion of a speech; cf., e.g., Anonymous Seguerianus §37.

owed wife, orphaned children." Also use rejection of pity. You will reject pity by the so-called "final headings" of the legal, the just, the beneficial, the possible, the appropriate, and by vivid description of the crime: "Do not, I beg you, gaze at him as he now sheds tears, but on him as showing contempt for the gods, on him as he advances to the shrines, on him as he forces the doors, on him as he seizes the dedications." And end with an exhortation: "Why do you delay? Why are you still deliberating about what has long ago been judged?" So much for the present. You will learn the more complete method later.

7. ON ENCOMION

Encomion (*enkômion*) is an exposition of the good qualities of a person or thing, in general or individually; in general, for example, an encomion of man,[28] individually, for example, an encomion of Socrates. We also praise things; for example, justice, **[15]** and dumb animals, for example, a horse; and there have even been encomia of plants and mountains and rivers. The term *enkômion,* they say, comes from the fact that poets sang hymns praising the gods in *kômai* (villages) in ancient times; they used to call narrow places *kômai*.[29]

Encomion differs from *epainos* (praise) in that *epainos* can be short; for example, "Socrates is wise," while encomion is found in a longer passages.[30] Do not overlook the fact that they include *psogoi* (invectives) with encomia, either naming it euphemistically or because both use the same topics. How does encomion differ from common-place? In some cases both seem to coincide; for example, an encomion of a war hero and a topos in favor of a war hero. They say, however, that the difference is in the purpose or outcome; for in common-place the goal is (for the subject) to receive a gift,[31] while encomion is a bare testimony of virtue.[32]

---

[28] E.g., Sophocles, *Antigone* 332ff.: "There are many wondrous things and nothing more wondrous than man. . . ."

[29] This is apparently an etymological proposal, deriving *kômê*, "village," from an (unattested) usage meaning "crowded alleys"; cf. Aphthonius, ch. 8, below.

[30] Aristotle (*Eudemian Ethics* 2.1.12) says that *epainos* is praise of the subject's general character, *enkômion* of particular deeds.

[31] The author is thinking of a topos about a war hero who was imagined as entitled to a gift for his valor. This was a common subject in declamation; cf. D. A. Russell, *Greek Declamation* (Cambridge University Press, 1983), pp. 24–25. In the case of denunciations of temple robbers, murderers, or other malefactors, a commoner subject of topoi, punishment rather than reward was the ostensible objective.

[32] Public epideictic oratory in the time of the Roman Empire, flattering a wealthy or powerful person, might also produce a gift from the recipient.

Encomiastic topics are (the subject's) national origin, such as Greek, city, such as Athenian, family, such as Alcmaeonid. You will mention also any marvelous occurrences at birth, for example from dreams or signs or things like that. **[16]** After this, nurture; for example in the case of Achilles, that he was nurtured on lions' marrow and by Cheiron;[33] then upbringing, how he was trained or how educated. Of course, the nature of mind and body will be examined and each of these divided into several qualities. You will say about his body that it was beautiful, large, swift, strong; about his mind that it was just, temperate, wise, brave. After this you will draw on his pursuits; for example, what sort of life he led: Was he a philosopher or an orator or a general? Most important are deeds; for deeds are included among pursuits; for example, having chosen a soldier's life, what did he accomplish in it? As for externals, they include relatives, friends, possessions, servants, luck, and the like. Moreover, from the topic of time comes how long he lived, much or little. Each provides the starting point of encomia; for you will praise one who had a long life because of that fact and one who did not in that "he had no share of the diseases of old age."[34] Further, from the manner of his death, (for example,) how he died fighting for his country; and if there was anything unusual about it, as in the case of Callimachus, because his corpse remained standing.[35] And you will praise him because of who killed him; for example, that Achilles died at the hand of the god Apollo. You will examine also events after death: if they held games in his honor, as for **[17]** Patroclus (*Iliad* 23); if there was an oracle about his bones, as with Orestes;[36] if he had famous children, as did Neoptolemus.[37] The best source of argument in encomia is derived from comparisons, which you will utilize as the occasion may suggest.

Similarly in the case of dumb animals, where possible; for you will praise them from the place where they occur, and you will add to the place of their birth the name of the gods to whom they are dedicated, as is the owl to Athena, the horse to Poseidon. Similarly, you will say how they are nurtured, what kind of mind, what kind

[33] Cf. Apollodorus the Mythographer 3.172 and John of Sardis, ch. 10, below.
[34] Cf. Isocrates' *Encomium of Evagoras* 71.
[35] Callimachus was killed in the battle of Marathon, 490 B.C. On his upright corpse, see Plutarch, *Parallel Stories* 1 = *Moralia* 305C.
[36] An oracle told the Spartans they must bring the bones of Orestes to Sparta in order to defeat the Tegeans; cf. Herodotus 1.67.
[37] The kings of Molossus in Epirus, including Pyrrhus, who defeated the Romans at Heraclea in 280 B.C., claimed descent from Achilles' son Neoptolemus.

of body, what functions they have; how they are useful, how long they live. And you will draw comparisons and generally use the relevant topics.

You will praise activities from their inventors; for example, Artemis and Apollo invented hunting, or from those who practiced them, (saying) that heroes used them. But the best method in such encomia as are concerned with activities is to consider those participating in them, in terms of what are their states of mind and body; for example, hunters are manly, daring, quick-witted, vigorous in body. From this you will not fail to understand how one should praise gods, but remember that encomia of gods should be called "hymns."

Surely growing things (can be praised) in a similar way: from the place [18] where they grow; from the god to whom they are dedicated, as the olive is to Athena; from nurture, for example, how they are raised. If they should need much care, you will marvel at that; if little, at that too. You will speak of the plant's budding as a feature of its body, of its beauty, whether it is ever-blooming, as is the olive; then of its utility, on which you will most linger. You should add comparisons everywhere.

And surely you will undertake an encomion of a city without difficulty from these topics; for you will speak about its origin, (saying) that its people are autochthonous,[38] and about its growth, how it was nurtured by gods, and about education, how the people have been taught by the gods. And you will examine, as in the case of a man, what sort of manners the city has, what sort of institutions, what pursuits it follows, what it has accomplished.

8. ON SYNCRISIS

<Syncrisis (*synkrisis*) is a comparison of similar or dissimilar things, or of lesser things to greater or greater things to lesser.>[39] Syncrisis has been included in common-place, where we amplify the misdeeds by comparison, and in encomion, where we amplify the good features of the subject by comparison, and also in invective, as having the same function, but since some good authorities [19] have made it an exercise by itself, a little must be said about it.

Well then, it proceeds by use of encomiastic topics; for we com-

---

[38] Literally, "sprung from the earth" = "the original inhabitants," a claim of the Athenians; cf., e.g., Isocrates' *Panegyricus* 24.

[39] This is the definition as given in Priscian's Latin version of the text but lacking in the Greek original.

pare the cities from which the men came, and family with family and nurture with nurture and pursuits and deeds and external factors and manner of death and what follows death. Similarly, if you compare plants, you will evaluate against each other the gods who gave them, the places where they grow, their cultivation, the utility of their fruits, and so on. Similarly, if you compare activities, you will mention those who first took up the activities and you will set those engaged in them side by side with each other in terms of the quality of mind and body. You should apply the same principle in all cases.

Now sometimes we introduce comparisons on the basis of equality, showing the subjects we compare as equal, either in all respects or in most; sometimes we prefer one or the other, while also praising what we placed second. Sometimes we blame one thing completely and praise the other; for example, if you were to deliver a comparison of justice and wealth. There is also comparison with the better, where you bring in the lesser **[20]** to show it is equal to the greater; for example, if you were to compare Odysseus to Heracles. This requires a vehement orator and the forceful style (*deinotês*), and the working out requires rapidity[40] everywhere because of the need of making quick changes back and forth from one to the other.

<h2 style="text-align:center">9. ON ETHOPOEIA</h2>

Ethopoeia (*êthopoiia*) is an imitation of the character of a person supposed to be speaking; for example, what words Andromache might say to Hector.[41] It is called personification (*prosôpopoiia*) when we personify a thing, like Elenchus (Disproof) in Menander[42] and as in Aristeides' speech where "The Sea" addresses the Athenians.[43] The difference is clear: in ethopoeia we imagine words for a real person, in prosopopoeia we imagine a non-existing person. They say it is image-making (*eidolopoiia*) when we attribute words to the dead, as does Aristeides in *Against Plato on Behalf of the*

[40] *Gorgotês,* "rapidity," is one of the "ideas" of style discussed by Hermogenes, *On Types of Style* 2.1; cf. Wooten, pp. 65–70.
[41] As in *Iliad* 6.406–39. On this chapter, see Patillon *Théorie du Discours*, pp. 300–304.
[42] Frag. 545, ed. Koch.
[43] Aelius Aristeides, the most famous sophist of the mid–second century after Christ, is the only post-classical orator cited by late Greek rhetoricians; however, the address of The Sea to the Athenians does not occur in his numerous extant works.

Four; for there he has attributed words to Themistocles' companions.[44]

There are characterizations of both definite and indefinite persons; of indefinite, for example, what words someone would say to
his family when about to go away from home; of definite, for example, what words Achilles would say to Deidamia when about to
go to war. Those characterizations are single where someone [21] is
imagined as making a speech by himself; those are double when he
is speaking to someone else. By himself, for example, What would a
general say when returning from a victory? To another, for example, What would a general say to his army after a victory?[45]

Throughout the exercise you will preserve what is distinctive
and appropriate to the persons imagined as speaking and to the occasions; for the speech of a young man differs from that of an old
man, and that of one who rejoices from that of one who grieves.
Some personifications are ethical, some pathetical, some mixed.
Ethical are those in which the characterization of the speaker is
dominant throughout; for example, what a farmer would say when
first seeing a ship; pathetical are those in which there is emotion
throughout; for example, what Andromache would say over the
dead Hector; mixed are those which have a combination of ethos
and pathos; for example, what Achilles would say over the dead Patroclus; for there would be pathos because of the slaughter of Patroclus and ethos in Achilles' plans for the war.[46]

The elaboration proceeds by the three times. Begin with the
present, because it is difficult; then run back [22] to earlier times,
because they have a large share of happiness; then change to the future, because what is going to happen is much more dreadful.[47] Let
both figures and diction contribute to the portrayal.

---

[44] Cf. Aristeides 3.367ff., where Miltiades, Themistocles, Pericles, and Cimon
("the Four") are imagined as coming back to life and answering Plato's attack on
them in *Gorgias*. According to a scholiast on the passage, Sopatros claimed this was
ethopoeia rather than eidolopoeia since the speakers were represented as alive. The
best example of eidolopoeia in ancient oratory is probably Cicero's evocation of
the ghost of Appius Claudius Caecus in *Pro Caelio* 33–34; speeches by ghosts
occur in Greek and Latin tragedy.

[45] Presumably the contents and style of the second speech would be influenced by perception of the audience, but the author may have misunderstood his
source. "Double" ethopoeia would better describe two speeches on the same subject by different characters, such as is often found in historical writing.

[46] I.e., his plans for revenge will reveal character; cf. *Iliad* 18.324–42.

[47] The author continues to think of a speech for Andromache or Achilles.

10. ON ECPHRASIS

Ecphrasis (*ekphrasis*) is descriptive speech, as they say, vivid (*enargês*) and bringing what is being shown before the eyes.[48]

There are ecphrases of persons and actions and times and places and seasons and many other things: of persons, as in Homer (of Thersites in *Iliad* 2.217), "He was bandy-legged, lame in one foot"; of actions, for example, the description of a land battle and a naval battle; of occasions, for example, peace, war; of places, for example, harbors, beaches, cities; of times, for example, spring, summer, harvest. There may also be a mixed ecphrasis, as the night battle in Thucydides (3.22 and 7.44); for night is a portion of time and the battle is an action.

In describing actions we shall treat them by starting from what went before and continuing with what happened in them and what followed. **[23]** For example, if we were speaking an ecphrasis of a war, first we shall mention events before the war: recruiting the soldiers, the expenditures, the fears; then the attacks, the slaughter, the deaths; then the victory trophies; then the paeans of the victors and the others' tears and slavery. But if we are describing places or seasons or persons we shall take material from narration and from the beautiful or useful or unexpected.

Virtues (*aretai*) of an ecphrasis are, most of all, clarity (*saphêneia*) and vividness (*enargeia*); for the expression should almost create seeing through the hearing. Moreover, of course, the word choice ought to correspond to the subject. If the subject is flowery, let the style be so too; if the subject is dry, let the style be similar.

You should know that some of the more exact teachers do not make ecphrasis an exercise, on the ground that it has already been included in fable and narrative and common-place and encomion; for there too, they say, we describe places and rivers and actions and persons. Nevertheless, since some writers of no small authority number ecphrasis among the exercises, we have followed them to avoid any criticism of carelessness.

---

[48] *Enargeia*, meaning clarity of style, is a stylistic term often used by Dionysius of Halicarnassus and other critics of Hellenistic and Roman times. In Hermogenes' *On Ideas of Style*, however, as in Aristotle's *Rhetoric* (3.2), the word for clarity is *saphênia*.

11. ON THESIS

[24]   They have given a definition of thesis (*thesis*) to the effect that it is a consideration of some subject viewed apart from any specific circumstance; for thesis seems to take the place of a general piece of advice, not directed to any specified person but with quite general application to any person, basing its development solely on the attributes of things. Whenever we investigate whether one should marry we do not apply what we say to such and such a person, for example, to Pericles or Alcibiades, or to particular circumstances or at a particular age or in a certain fortune in life, but we look at the matter in itself, simply setting aside all these things and making an examination of the attributes of the subject; for example, whether someone ought to do this because the results are of a certain sort for those engaging in it. Thus, if we choose a specific person and some circumstance and **[25]** give an account of reasons in this way,[49] it will be an hypothesis, not a thesis.

Some theses are political,[50] some not. Political are those falling among common thoughts; for example, whether one should teach rhetoric and things like that. Those are not political which belong to some field of science and are appropriate for those versed in it; for example, whether the sky is spherical, whether there are many worlds, whether the sun is made of fire. These subjects belong to philosophers, while orators should practice the others. Some call these "practical" theses and the others "theoretical"; for the former concern things that can be done, whereas the purpose of the latter is speculation.

Thesis differs from common-place in that common-place is an amplification of a subject on which people agree, while thesis is a question about something in doubt.

Some theses are simple, some are posed in relation to something, some are regarded as double. If we discuss whether one should marry, the thesis is simple; if whether a king should marry it is relative; if we discuss whether one should engage in athletics rather than farm the land it is double, for it is necessary to dissuade from one pursuit and exhort to the other.

The logical divisions in discussion of theses are what are called "final **[26]** headings": justice, advantage, possibility, appropriateness; for example, that it is just to marry and to make the same con-

---

[49] E.g., a declamation in which Andromache debates whether to remarry after the death of Hector.

[50] I.e., they relate to life in society.

tribution to life that one has received; that it is advantageous, for
many consolations come from it; that it is possible, for it is possible
to marry from such considerations; that it is appropriate in not
seeming to live like savages. This is how you will argue in favor of
the proposition and you will rebut it from the opposite arguments.
You will also refute the arguments found on the other side of the
issue. At the end there will be exhortations and reference to the
common customs of all mankind.

12. ON INTRODUCTION OF A LAW

Some include the introduction of a law among exercises. Since in
pragmatic[51] debate also, proposals for laws and objections to them
create a question for discussion, they say the difference is as follows:
in pragmatic debate there are surrounding circumstances, in exercises there are not; for example, in a time of lack of money someone introduces a motion to sell public offices; here you have the lack
of money as an occasion. This is not true in an exercise, where the
theme would be simply "Someone introduces a motion to sell public offices," without an occasion or other circumstances specified.[52]
[27]   The subdivisions are clarity, justice, legality, advantage,
possibility, appropriateness. Clarity as in Demosthenes (cf. 20.93),
"To know and understand that these things are just is simple and
clear to all"; legality, whenever we say that something is contrary to
the ancient laws;[53] justice, whenever we say that something is contrary to nature and morals; advantage, whenever we say that it does
harm both now and for future time; possibility, whenever we say
that it cannot be done; appropriateness, whenever we say that it
hurts our reputation.

---

[51] *Pragmatikê;* here meaning deliberative oratory; cf. Hermogenes, *On Stases*
p. 38,4–5, ed. Rabe.
[52] As a progymnasma, introduction of a law is analogous to thesis, whereas in
declamation, with fuller identification of the circumstances, it becomes hypothesis.
[53] I.e., unconstitutional.

Chapter III

The *Preliminary Exercises* of Aphthonius the Sophist

Aphthonius studied rhetoric with Libanius in Antioch sometime in the second half of the fourth century after Christ. Some of his themes of exercises and some of the topoi he develops can also be found in writings by Libanius, but they are the common stock of the schools and Aphthonius need not have taken them directly from Libanius. According to the Byzantine encyclopedia Suda, *Aphthonius also wrote a commentary, now lost, on the rhetorical treatises of Hermogenes, and Photius in the ninth century mentions reading declamations by Aphthonius.[1] His* Progymnasmata *became the first text in the standard Hermogenic corpus, chosen for that honor, according to the commentators, because it included examples of all exercises as well as brief and clear descriptions of each. Despite its canonical status, it sometimes seems inferior to other surviving accounts, for the examples of exercises it provides are often weakly argued and even some of its divisions and definitions (e.g., in the account of encomion) are less satisfactory than what is found elsewhere.*

Aphthonius' work survives in the numerous manuscripts of the Hermogenic corpus. Some manuscripts have marginal notes, and in addition introductions and commentaries were written by teachers in the Byzantine period. The most important extant commentaries, largely compendia of earlier discussions, are those by John of Sardis, probably dating from the ninth century, and John Doxapatres from the eleventh.[2] Aphthonius' text was the source for an extant progymnasmatic handbook in classical Armenian, attributed to Moses Khorentsi,[3] and for Latin textbooks in the Renaissance. According to D. L. Clark,[4] between

[1] For evidence about Aphthonius' life, see Hugo Rabe in *Rheinisches Museum* 62 (1907) 263 and the Preface to his edition, pp.xxii–xxvii. There survives a short letter of thanks from Libanius to Aphthonius, no. 11 in the edition of Foerster.

[2] For John of Sardis, see below; Doxapatres' commentary can be found in *Rhetores Greaci*, ed. Walz, vol. 2, pp. 81–564.

[3] See the Preface to Rabe's edition, pp. xv–xvii. Rabe questioned the attribution to the Armenian historian Moses, who lived in the fifth century, and attributed the work to a later Moses.

[4] "The Rise and Fall of Progymnasmata in Sixteenth and Seventeenth Century Grammar Schools," *Speech Monographs* 19 (1952): 259–63; see also J.-C. Mar-

*1507 and 1680, ten different Latin translations of Aphthonius were
published in a total of 114 printings. The most popular, reprinted at
least 73 times from 1546 to 1699, combined some translations by the fif-
teenth-century Dutch humanist Rudolf Agricola and others by Joannes
Maria Catanaeus with notes by Reinhard Lorich and model Latin
themes composed by Petrus Mosellanus. This material then was
adapted into English by Richard Rainolde in* A Book Called the
Foundacion of Rhetorike, *published in London in 1563.⁵ Rainolde describes "fable, narracion, chria, sentence, confutation, confirmacion,
commonplace, praise, dispraise, comparison, ethopeia, discripcion, thesis, and legislatio," with examples of each theme, including the fable of
the ant and grasshopper and the thesis on marriage, derived from Aphthonius' handbook.*

An Anonymous Prolegomenon,
or Introduction, to the *Progymnasmata*
of Aphthonius the Sophist

*By the fifth century after Christ, teachers of rhetoric had created com-
prehensive textbooks by combining various works into a single corpus for
their own and others' use. The most important of these compilations
was the Hermogenic corpus, which included the* Progymnasmata *of
Aphthonius, Hermogenes'* On Stasis *and* On Ideas of Style, *and
works* On Invention *and* On the Method of Forcefulness *attributed
to Hermogenes, probably erroneously. Commentaries were added to
these works and prolegomena, or introductions, were composed to the
corpus as a whole and to individual works. These prolegomena were
modeled on introductions to philosophy composed by Neo-Platonist
philosophers and show the influence of the Neo-Platonic system of organization of learning.⁶ Some introductions to progymnasmata were
edited by Hugo Rabe in a volume entitled* Prolegomenon Sylloge
(Leipzig: Teubner, 1931); *among them is an extended introduction to
Aphthonius' work by John Doxapatres, who lived in the eleventh century, and a shorter, probably earlier one, by an unknown writer, which
is translated here for the first time. It cannot be dated except to say that
the references to Gregory of Nazianzus and John Chrysostom at the*

---

golin, "La rhétorique d'Aphthonius et son influence au XVIᵉ siècle," in *La rhétorique à Rome* (Paris: Les Belles Lettres, 1979), pp. 239–69.

⁵ Reprinted, New York: Scholars' Facsimiles and Reprints, 1945.

⁶ See Kennedy, *Greek Rhetoric Under Christian Emperors,* pp. 116–22, and
J. Mansfield, *Prolegomena: Questions to Be Settled before the Study of an Author or
a Text* (Leiden: Brill, 1994), p. 52.

end indicate it is by a Christian who lived no earlier than the fifth century after Christ and perhaps much later. It gives, however, a picture of how rhetorical instruction was conceived in late antiquity. The translation is based on Rabe's text, pp. 73–80.

[p. 73 Rabe]   One should (as in philosophy) also consider the eight headings as they apply to rhetoric, and they are these: the goal (*skopos*), the utility, the authenticity, the arrangement, the reason for the title, the division into parts, the manner of teaching, and—instead of asking to what part of the discipline the subject belongs, which is the usual question in writings on philosophy—why is Aphthonius honored above others who have discussed rhetorical progymnasmata?

(1. The Goal) We wonder how it is that although there are fourteen progymnasmata, teachers think one goal can be assigned to all, and we reply [74] that just as the exegetes have attributed one goal to Porphyry's *Eisagoge*,[7] in which he teaches about the five predicatives, and just as in the case of the thirteen divisions of stasis in the book *On Stases* by Hermogenes, the exegetes of that work describe one goal, and similarly there is one goal in *On Inventions* and one in *On Ideas*, so here there is nothing strange if one goal is assigned to a work describing several progymnasmata. Aphthonius' goal in the hypothesis of his *Progymnasmata* is to train and accustom us to the species and parts found in rhetoric, and in addition to the parts of political discourse. Now rhetoric is divided into three species, the deliberative, the judicial, and the panegyrical, since the hearers have come together either to judge or deliberate or celebrate. Alternatively, as rhetoric developed jointly with the human mind, it should be divided into parts corresponding to the parts of the mind. The parts of the mind are logical, passionate, and appetitive.[8] Deliberative rhetoric corresponds to the rational part; for just as *logos* exists in us to direct us to beneficial things, so deliberation turns us away from things not beneficial and incites us to the beneficial. Judicial rhetoric corresponds to the passionate; for they say that anger is a boiling of blood around the heart from the desire to distress others in return;[9] and similarly, it is judicial "to ward off a man when one is the first to be wroth."[10] [75] The panegyrical corre-

[7] The *Introduction* to Aristotle's *Categories* by the Neo-Platonic philosopher Porphyry (A.D. 232–305).
[8] Neo-Platonic teaching; cf. Plato, *Republic* 4.441a.
[9] Cf. Aristotle, *Rhetoric* 2.2.1.
[10] *Iliad* 19.183, with change of one word.

sponds to the appetitive; for longing has the good and beautiful as its objective.[11] Again, each of these species is divided into two parts; for the deliberative is divided into exhortation and dissuasion and the judicial into accusation and defense and the panegyrical into encomion and invective. There are four parts in a political discourse: prooemia, narrations, proofs (*agônes*), and epilogues. Now the progymnasmata train us for the species and parts of rhetoric, since some of the progymnasmata, such as myth and thesis and chreia and maxim, belong to the deliberative species, and refutation and confirmation and common-place belong to the judicial, and encomion and invective and comparison belong to the panegyrical. They also give us preliminary training for the parts of a political speech; for fable practices us in features of prooemia, and narrative and ecphrasis in narrations, and refutation and confirmation in proofs, and common-place in epilogues.

(2. The Utility) (Progymnasmata) are useful for us in the species and parts of rhetoric, and furthermore in the parts of the political speech.

(3. The Authenticity) That the work is genuine is quite clear from the unanimous voice of everyone.

(4. The Arrangement) We inquire about the order of the present work in relation to the other exercises in rhetoric, and we say that it is rightly placed before the others since it is, indeed, an introduction to all of rhetoric, introductions necessarily preceding what they introduce.[76]

(5. The Title) The fifth heading is the reason for the title.[12] Here we ought to inquire what kind of name is "Aphthonius," then what the name "sophist" means in the present title and why he called the work *Progymnasmata* and not *On Progymnasmata* and why he said *Progymnasmata* rather than *Gymnasmata* and what it is to "exercise" (*gymnazein*) and why *Progymnasmata* without adding the qualification "for Rhetoric."

The name Aphthonius is a proper noun and a derived one and most appropriate for an orator because it is his nature to give forth streams of speech "ungrudgingly" (*aphthonôs*), that is richly and without suffering—thus, without "grudging" (*phthonos*)—to pour the running water of his teaching on those who are learning. The verb *sophizô* is understood in two ways; sometimes it means "I

[11] According to Aristotle, *Rhetoric* 1.3.5, the characteristic topic of epideictic is *to kalon*, what is honorable, good, or beautiful.
[12] I.e., *The Progymnasmata of Aphthonius the Sophist*.

teach" and "I make someone wise (*sophos*)" by discoursing to him on the truest wisdom, but sometimes it means "I deceive" and "I reason falsely," since "to teach" (*sophisai*) someone is understood in terms of the result and "to be a sophist" is taken in two ways, depending on what is being signified. Sometimes *sophizôn* has a meaning like that brought out here; for Aphthonius was a "teacher" (*sophistês*) of students, unfolding the principles of the art of rhetoric to them, but sometimes it is someone who engages in deceit and is devious and a false-reasoner, as in the words "O sophist of evil, how you have undermined what belongs together?"[13]

He inscribed the book "Progymnasmata" and not "On Progymnasmata" because it is customary to prefix a composition with the name of the subject, as a speech about Themistocles is entitled "Themistocles" and one about a constitution is entitled "Politeia." In another sense, **[77]** by entitling it "Progymnasmata" he made clear that this is a book by which we are trained for rhetoric, but if he had entitled it "On Progymnasmata" he would have shown that it does not provide preliminary exercises but is a discussion of the subject. The nominative case is indicative of the subject itself; that is why definitions signifying the nature of things are expressed with this case. Deviations from the nominative indicate not the essence of the thing but something about it. *Gymnazesthai* is, literally, "to exercise oneself in the nude" and to learn military drill or to train for athletic contests, the diaulos perhaps or pancration or boxing or wrestling or another such event, as Xenophon in the *Cyropaideia* (3.1.20) described Cyrus doing with his companions when practicing military exercises. *Gymnazesthai* has been taken from this and applied by catachresis to all verbal and practical education, and when someone says "I am exercising" he is not really saying "I am making an attempt to acquire knowledge in the nude"—which would be the literal meaning—but simply "I am educating myself in something." We say, then, that a *pro-gymnasma* is what comes before the *gymnasia,* since the books of Hermogenes on stasis, invention, ideas, and the method of forcefulness are a *gymnasma* and

---

[13] John Doxapatres explains the meaning of "sophist" more clearly, *Prolegomenon Sylloge*, pp. 136–37, ed. Rabe: The term sophist can mean a teacher of rhetoric or even philosophy, and can also mean a deceitful speaker. In contrast with a *rhêtôr*, who speaks in actual trials, as did Demosthenes, a "sophist" like Libanius primarily composed declamations on imaginary subjects, and delivered epideictic orations. Doxapatres says Aphthonius is called a sophist either because he was a teacher or because he wrote declamations. The source of the quotation, "O sophist of evil . . ." is unknown. This translation was proposed to me by Dirk Schenkeveld.

training and true education in rhetoric, and the *Progymnasmata* of Aphthonius are an introduction to those works and, as it were, a brief unfolding of the subject and a sort of habituation, which oils young students and stimulates them to study of those more advanced works. He called them only "progymnasmata," not adding "to rhetoric," **[78]** not unreasonably. Just as Porphyry, when writing an introduction to philosophy, the Queen of the Arts, entitled it "Porphyry's *Introduction*," not adding "to Philosophy," since such is understood implicitly because philosophy embraces the other sciences, so Aphthonius entitled his book "Progymnasmata" without qualification, a work which is training in the greatest and most practical of the technical arts.

(6. The Division into Parts) The division into headings cuts the present book into exercises practicing us in the deliberative species and the judicial and the panegyrical, and again into things analogous to prooemia and those that preserve the likeness of a narration and those that fulfill the function of the proofs and epilogues.

(7. The Mode of Teaching) Although there are four modes of teaching—divisional, definitional, demonstrative, and analytic[14]—, in the present composition Aphthonius uses only two, the divisional when he divides each of the progymnasmata, saying that "some fable is rational, some ethical, some mixed," and that "some narrative is dramatic, some historical, some political," similarly of the others; and he uses the definitional when he defines the progymnasmata, saying that fable is a fictive statement imaging truth and that narrative is an exposition of a thing that has happened or as though it has happened, (and so on). But some say that he also used the analytical means in **[79]** speaking of the origin of fable; for they say he goes from the subordinate and posterior to the superior and prior, or from fable to the persons from whom it had its birth.[15] To go from the posterior to the prior is characteristic of the analytical means; for example, the four elements are first,[16] man is subsequent. Man is then analyzed into these elements.

Heading eight: Why the *Progymnasmata* of Aphthonius is preferred to the works by Hermogenes and others. We say it is because it is clearer than the others and more easily learned. Hermogenes and the others set out the bare methods without examples and have

---

[14] These categories appear in writings of some later Neo-Platonists and other prolegomena; cf. Rabe's note *ad loc.*

[15] At the beginning of ch. 1 Aphthonius first defines fable, then mentions its inventors.

[16] Earth, air, fire, and water.

made the study of progymnasmata difficult for students at the introductory level, while Aphthonius has not only described the
methods as clearly and distinctly as possible, but in desiring to illu-
minate what he says with examples he has made his work more
adapted and appropriate to the needs of the young.

Some people,[17] asking to what part of learning the present work
should be attributed, say that it does not belong to theoretical
knowledge, since it does not discuss physics or theology or mathe-
matics, but it does not belong to practical knowledge either; for it
does not teach how to cultivate morality. Rather it belongs to what
lies between these, methodical and instrumental[18] knowledge, and
this is the discipline of logic. For it teaches rules and methods.

Some also inquire about its stylistic character. There are three
characters of style: grand, plain, and middle. What has pompous
words but plain thought is grand, as are the works of Lycophron;[19]
what has elevated thought but plain words is plain, as are the writings of The Theologian;[20] what has neither elevated thought nor
pompous diction but both moderate is middle, as are the writings of
Chrysostom[21] for the most part. Aphthonius uses all three: the
grand in ethopoeia, the relaxed and plain in ecphrasis, and the middle in some of the others.

The *Preliminary Exercises*
of Aphthonius the Sophist

*This translation is based on the edition of Aphthonius by Hugo Rabe
(Leipzig: Teubner, 1926). There is an earlier translation by Ray
Nadeau in* Speech Monographs *19 (1952), pp. 264–85, revised by
Patricia B. Matsen in* Readings from Classical Rhetoric, *ed. by Patricia P. Matsen, Philip Rollinson, and Marion Sousa, pp. 266–88.
Numbers in brackets refer to pages in Spengel's edition of 1854, which
remain the standard form of reference to the text; pages in Rabe's edition are indicated with* R. *The anonymous prolegomenon translated
above seems to indicate (p. 74 Rabe) that the work once began with an*

---

[17] I.e., Neo-Platonic philosophers.

[18] *Organikon*; cf. Aristotle's *organon,* the "instrument" of knowledge. This
passage is an adaptation of Aristotle's map of learning as described in *Metaphysics*
6.1, but the author fails to consider the possibility that progymnasmata might be
regarded as "productive" knowledge.

[19] Hellenistic grammarian and poet, author of the obscure monologue,
Alexandra.

[20] I.e., Gregory of Nazianzus (A.D. c. 330–390).

[21] John Chrysostom (A.D. c. 349–407).

*"hypothesis" stating the author's purpose in writing and probably out-
lining the contents. This, however, has not survived. Portions of a commentary on Aphthonius attributed to John of Sardis are translated
later in this volume.*

[p. 21 Spengel, p. 1 Rabe]

1. ON FABLE

See Gangloff, "Mythes," pp. 34–36.

Fable (*mythos*) originated with poets but has come to be used
also by orators for the sake of the moral. Fable is a fictive statement,
imaging truth. It is called Sybaritic and Cilician and Cyprian, varying its names with its inventors, but calling it Aesopic has largely
prevailed because Aesop composed fables best of all. Some fables
are rational, some ethical, some mixed; rational when a human
being is imagined as doing something, ethical when representing
the character of irrational animals, mixed when made up of both,
irrational and rational. **[2R]** When the moral for which the fable has
been assigned is stated first, you will call it a *promythion,* when
added at the end an *epimythion.*

AN ETHICAL FABLE OF THE CICADAS AND ANTS,
EXHORTING THE YOUNG TO TOIL

It was the height of summer and the cicadas were offering up their
shrill song, but it occurred to the ants to toil and collect the harvest
from which they would be fed in the winter. When the winter came
on, the ants fed on what they had laboriously collected, but the
pleasure of the cicadas ended in want. Similarly, youth that does not
wish to toil fares badly in old age.

[22]   2. ON NARRATIVE

Narrative (*diêgêma*) is an exposition of an action that has happened
or as though it had happened. Narrative differs from narration
(*diêgêsis*) as a piece of poetry (*poiêma*) differs from a poem (*poiêsis*).[22] The *Iliad* as a whole is a *poiêsis,* the making of the arms of
Achilles a *poiêma.*

Some narrative is dramatic, some historical, some political.
Imagined narrative is dramatic; narrative giving an account of early
events is historical; what orators use in their contests is political.
[3R] There are six attributes of narrative: the person who acted, the

---

[22] Cf. Hermogenes, above, p. 75.

thing done, the time at which, the place in which, the manner how, and the cause for which it was done.

The virtues of a narrative are four: clarity, brevity, persuasiveness, and hellenism.[23]

A DRAMATIC NARRATIVE CONCERNING THE ROSE

Let anyone who admires the rose for its beauty consider Aphrodite's wound. The goddess was in love with Adonis and Ares in turn was in love with her,[24] and the goddess was to Adonis what Ares was to her: a god was in love with a goddess and a goddess was pursuing a mortal. The emotion was the same even if the species was different. Struck with jealousy, Ares wanted to do away with Adonis, thinking the death of Adonis would be the end of the love. Ares attacks Adonis. Learning what had been done, the goddess hurried to his rescue, and in her haste, falling on a rose, she stumbled among the thorns and pierces the bottom of her foot. The blood from the wound dripped on the rose and changed its color to the now familiar appearance; the rose, originally having been white, changed to the appearance it now has.

[23]   3. ON CHREIA

Chreia (*khreia*) is a brief recollection, referring to some person in a pointed way. **[4R]** It is called chreia because it is useful (*khreiôdês*). Some chreias are verbal, some active, some mixed. One that makes the utility clear by what is said is verbal; for example, Plato said the twigs of virtue grow by sweat and toil. An active chreia is one signifying something done; for example, when Pythagoras was asked how long is the life of men, he hid himself after appearing briefly, making his appearance a measure of life.[25] A mixed chreia consists of both a saying and an action; for example, when Diogenes saw an undisciplined youth he struck his pedagogue, saying, "Why do you teach him such things?"[26]

This is the division of the chreia, and you should elaborate it with the following headings: praise, paraphrase, cause, contrary, comparison, example, testimony of the ancients, brief epilogue.

---

[23] *Hellenismos,* or purity of Greek. Aphthonius adds this to the three traditional virtues of the narration as found, e.g., in Theon, ch. 5; cf. above p. 29, n. 107.

[24] See John of Sardis' note, translated below, and Ovid, *Metamorphoses* 10.298–559.

[25] Cf. the fuller version in Theon, above, p. 17.

[26] There is an elaboration of this chreia by Libanius, vol. 8, pp. 74–82, ed. Foerster.

A VERBAL CHREIA:
ISOCRATES SAID THE ROOT OF EDUCATION
IS BITTER BUT THE FRUITS ARE SWEET[27]

(Praise) It is right to admire Isocrates for his art; he made its name[28] most illustrious, and in his practice he showed how great the art was and proclaims its greatness, rather than having been himself proclaimed by it. **[5R]** Now it would take a long time to go through all the benefits he has brought to human life, whether in proposing laws to kings[29] or in advising private individuals, but (we can note) his wise teaching about education.

(Paraphrase) One who longs for education, he is saying, begins with toils, but yet the toils end in an advantage.[30] The wisdom of these words we shall admire in what follows.

[24] (Cause) Those who long for education attach themselves to educational leaders, whom it is frightening to approach and very stupid to abandon. Fear comes on boys both when they are there and when they are about to go to school. Next after the teachers come the pedagogues,[31] fearful to see and more dreadful when they beat the boys. Fright anticipates discovery, and punishment follows fright; they go looking for the boys' mistakes but regard the boys' successes as their own doing. Fathers are more strict than pedagogues, dictating the routes to be followed, demanding boys go straight to school, and showing suspicion of the market place. And if there is need to punish, fathers ignore their natural feelings.[32] But the boy who has experienced these things, when he comes to manhood wears a crown of virtue.

(Contrary) If, on the other hand, out of fear of these things someone were to flee from teachers, run away from parents, and shun pedagogues, he is completely deprived of training in speech and has lost ability in speech with his loss of fear. All these considerations **[6R]** influenced Isocrates' thought in calling the root of education bitter.

[27] There is an elaboration of this chreia by Libanius, vol. 8, pp. 82–97, ed. Foerster.

[28] Aphthonius seems not to realize that the word *rhêtorikê* does not occur in Isocrates' writings.

[29] I.e., Nicocles and Demonicus.

[30] Cf. Isocrates 1.47.

[31] I.e., the slaves who accompanied boys to and from school and supervised their activities generally.

[32] I.e., they make no allowance for human nature, or for the possible bad effects of severe punishments.

(Comparison) Just as those who work the earth cast the seeds in the ground with toil but reap the fruits with greater pleasure, in the same way those exchanging toil for education have by toil acquired future renown.

(Example) Look, I ask you, at the life of Demosthenes, which was the most filled with labor of any orator but became the most glorious of all. He showed such an abundance of zeal that he took the ornament from his head, because he thought the ornament that comes from virtue was the best;[33] and he expended in toils what others lavished on pleasures.[34]

(Testimony) Thus, one should admire Hesiod's saying (cf. *Works and Days* 289–92) that **[25]** the road of virtue is rough, but the height is easy, the same philosophy as found in the maxim of Isocrates; for what Hesiod indicated by a "road" is what Isocrates called a "root," both expressing one thought, but with different words.

(Epilogue) Looking at all this, one should admire Isocrates for his wise and beautiful speculation about education.

[7R]   4. ON MAXIM

Maxim (*gnômê*) is a summary statement, in declarative sentences, urging or dissuading something. Some maxims are protreptic, some apotreptic, some declarative; and some are simple, some compound, some credible, some true, some hyperbolic: protreptic, as (*Odyssey* 15.74), "One should be kind to a visiting stranger, but send him on his way when he wants to go"; apotreptic, as (*Iliad* 2.24), "A man who is a counselor should not sleep all the night";[35] declarative, as (Demosthenes 1.20), "There is need of money, and without it nothing needful can be done"; and simple, as (*Iliad* 12.243), "One omen is best, to fight for one's country"; and compound, as (*Iliad* 2.204), "Many rulers are not good; let there be one ruler"; and credible, as,

---

[33] Hair was commonly regarded as an adornment of the head. According to the *Lives of the Ten Orators* (848C), preserved with the works of Plutarch, there was a story that Demosthenes, when still young, withdrew into a cave to study and shaved half of his head to keep himself from going out until his hair had grown back. Cf. John Doxapatres, p. 281,6–12 Walz: "For either he cut the hairs from half his head, as (Aphthonius) says, so that he would not go out of the house, or because he disliked adorning his head and regarded it as nothing."

[34] John of Sardis, translated below, says he spent money on books or on oil for his lamp.

[35] There are two elaborations of this maxim by Libanius, vol. 8, pp. 102–117, ed. Foerster.

"Each man is as those he likes to be with";[36] and true, as "It is not possible for anyone to lead a life without suffering";[37] **[8R]** and hyperbolic, as (*Odyssey* 18.30), "Earth nourishes nothing feebler than man."

This is how the maxim is classified, and you should elaborate it with the headings for the chreia: praise, periphrase, **[26]** cause, opposite, comparison, example, testimony of the ancients, short epilogue.

A chreia differs from a maxim in that a chreia sometimes reports an action, whereas a maxim is always a saying, and in that a chreia needs to indicate a person (as speaker or doer), whereas a maxim is uttered impersonally.

PROTREPTIC MAXIM:
"ONE FLEEING POVERTY, CYRNUS, MUST THROW HIMSELF INTO THE YAWNING SEA AND DOWN STEEP CRAGS" (THEOGNIS 175)

(Praise) By fashioning advice (*parainesis*) in place of myths, Theognis prevented his poetry from being attacked. Although seeing that (other) poets thought highly of telling myths, he collected in verse recommendations for the right way to live, avoiding myths himself but at the same time preserving the charm of verse while introducing the profit of advice. And one might praise Theognis for many things, but especially for his wise remarks about poverty.

(Periphrase) And what does he say? Let one living with poverty be content to fall (off a cliff), since it is better to cut life short than to make the sun a witness of shame. **[9R]** This is his wise statement, and it is easy to see how beautifully it is said.

(Cause) For one who lives in poverty, first, when among boys, does not practice virtue, and when coming among adults he will do all the most objectional things: going on an embassy he will betray his country for money, in the assembly he will speak for silver, and when called to sit as a juror he will give his votes for a bribe.

(Contrary) Not such are those freed from poverty: when boys, they practice the noblest things, and when coming among adults they do everything splendidly, **[27]** sponsoring choruses at festivals and paying assessments in war time.

(Comparison) Just as those held by a dreadful bond are hindered by it from acting, in the same way those living in poverty are constrained from freedom of speech.

---

[36] Euripides, frag. 812, ed. Nauck.
[37] Menander, frag. 411, ed. Kock.

(Example) Consider Irus, who had been born as one of the Itha-
cans but did not share the same security with the other citizens;
rather, his lack of means was so great that his name was changed by
poverty; for having originally been called Arnaius, his name was
changed to *Iros,* deriving his surname from acting as a servant.[38] But
what need to mention Irus? When Odysseus, ruler of Ithaca,
feigned poverty on his return to his own land, he shared the evils of
poverty, had things thrown at him in his own house, and was mal-
treated by the servant girls. Such is poverty, and hard to bear even
when it is only apparent. **[10R]**

(Testimony) Therefore, I have to admire Euripides who said[39]
that it is a bad thing to be in want, and that it is impossible for nobility to counteract poverty.

(Epilogue) So how is it possible to admire Theognis enough
when he said such wise things about poverty?

5. ON REFUTATION

Refutation (*anaskeuê*) is an overturning of some matter at hand.
One should refute what is neither very clear nor what is altogether
impossible, but what holds a middle ground. Those engaged in
refutation should first state the false claim of those who advance it,
then add an exposition of the subject and use these headings: first,
that it is unclear and incredible, **[28]** in addition that it is impossible and illogical and inappropriate, and finally adding that it is inexpedient. This progymnasma includes in itself all the power of the
art (of rhetoric).[40]

REFUTATION:
WHAT IS SAID ABOUT DAPHNE IS NOT PROBABLE[41]

(The False Claim) It is irrational to attack poets, but they themselves stimulate us to oppose them because they first made up sto-

---

[38] In *Odyssey* 18.5–7 the suitors give Arnaeus the name *Iros,* cognate with Iris,
messenger of the gods, because he carried messages when ordered; John of Sardis,
ad loc., derives the name from *eirô,* "I speak."

[39] Cf. *Phoenician Women* 404–5 and *Electra* 37–38.

[40] Said also of confirmation, below; understanding of refutation and confirmation is basic to rhetoric.

[41] There are rather few versions of the story of Daphne; the most important
are those in Ovid, *Metamorphoses* 1.452–567, Hyginus, *Fables* 203, and Pausanias
10.7.8; Aphthonius' source is unknown. The Grove of Daphne was a famous sub-
urb of Antioch, doubtless familiar to Aphthonius. There is a brief narrative about
Daphne by Libanius, vol. 8, pp. 44–45, ed. Foerster: "Ladon begot the beauty of
Daphne, and Apollo marveled at her. Experiencing erotic feeling for her, he pur-

ries like this about the gods.[42] **[11R]** How is it not irrational for poets to have belittled the gods and for us to take poets seriously? I myself have been distressed for all the gods who been trampled in the mud, and Apollo especially, the god whom the poets themselves have made the leader of their own art. What follows, the story they have made up about Apollo's Daphne, is an example.

(Exposition) Daphne, they say, came forth from Earth and Ladon,[43] and since she excelled many in looks she acquired the Pythian as a lover. Since he loved her, he pursued her, but in pursuing he did not catch her. Instead, Earth received her child and gave birth to a flower with the same name as the maiden (*daphnê* = laurel). Apollo crowned himself with her in her changed form, and the plant becomes a crown, put on the Pythian tripod because of his desire for the mortal maiden, and he makes the bloom a token of his art. This is the story they have made up. It remains to test it from the following arguments.[44]

"Daphne came forth from Earth and Ladon." What proof did she have of her birth? For she was human, whereas they had another nature different from hers. How does Ladon join himself with Earth? By flooding her with his waters? Then all rivers may be called husbands of Earth; for all flood her. And if a human has come forth from a river, it is time for a river also to come forth from human beings; **[29]** for descendants reveal their begetters. **[12R]** What name do they give to the marriage of a river and earth? A hymeneal is for conscious beings, but earth does not have the nature of conscious beings. Thus, either Daphne must be classified among streams or Ladon be defined as human.

But let it be so, let it be granted to the poets that Daphne was

---

sued her when he could not persuade her. She prayed to Earth not to be taken and, on fulfillment of her prayer, she disappeared. Her body became a tree, and the tree was the laurel. The god did not cease in his longing, but changed his feelings for the girl to the branches of the tree and is a lover of her leaves."

[42] Aphthonius is apparently thinking of the attacks in elegiac verse on conventional views of the gods by Xenophanes of Colophon in the late sixth century B.C. Note echoes of Xenophanes' philosophy in the confirmation of the myth in the next chapter.

[43] Ladon was the name of a small river in the northwestern Peloponnesus. Ovid and some others identify the Peneius river in Aetolia as Daphne's father.

[44] Spengel's text indicates a progression of arguments from unclear to impossible, inappropriate, illogical, and inexpedient; Rabe omitted the labels as not original. There is no specific claim that the myth is unclear; most of the arguments involve impossibility, improbability, or lack of logic, though the myth is criticized as inappropriate.

born from Earth and Ladon. By whom was a daughter so born brought up? For even if I concede her birth, her upbringing becomes impossible. For where did the child have a place to live? "With her father, of course." And what human endures living in a river? Her father would fail to realize he was drowning her in his streams rather than feeding her with his waters. "But the child lived under the earth with her mother." Then she was unnoticed (in the darkness), and being unnoticed had no one who saw her. Desire could not come into being for one whose beauty was hidden.

If you want, let this also be granted to the poets. How did a god feel love and how did he betray his nature with longing? Sexual passion is the most troublesome thing that exists, and to bear witness of such dreadful things among gods is impious; for if the gods have all diseases, how are they superior to mortals? If they endure love, the most dreadful thing, how are they exempted from many other woes, since they endure the most severe? But their nature knows not longing, and the Pythian did not appear as a lover.

[13R] And how, when pursuing the maiden, did the Pythian come off second to a mortal woman? Men are stronger than women, and do women have more strength than gods? Did something inferior to mortal men even overcome gods? Why did the mother receive the fleeing maiden? Did she think the marriage a bad one? How had she herself become a mother? Was that from a good marriage? And why did she deprive her child of something fine? Thus, either she had not been a mother or she is to be thought a bad one. [30]

Why did Earth act inconsistently with her usual deeds? She was distressing the Pythian by saving her daughter, and was she trying to win him over again by bringing her back? There was no need to try to win him over if she wanted to annoy him. Why did the god crown himself with the tree beside the tripods? The bloom became a symbol of pleasure, but prophecy is a sign of virtue. How then did the Pythian reconcile things unnaturally combined? What? Was the pretext mortal but the experience immortal?

Let this be enough about the poets, lest I seem to be speaking poets' language.

6. ON CONFIRMATION

Confirmation (*kataskeuê*) is the corroboration of some matter at hand. One should confirm things that are neither very clear nor wholly impossible but that hold a middle ground. One who is confirming should use arguments opposed to those of refutation and first mention the good repute of the claimant, **[14R]** then, in turn, provide an exposition, and use the opposite headings: clear instead of unclear, credible instead of incredible, and possible instead of impossible and logical instead of illogical and appropriate instead of inappropriate and expedient instead of inexpedient.

This exercise includes all the power of the art (of rhetoric).[45]

CONFIRMATION:
WHAT IS SAID ABOUT DAPHNE IS PROBABLE

One who speaks against poets seems to me to be speaking against the muses themselves; for if poets utter what is transmitted to them by the intent of the muses, how would one seeking to rebuke the saying of poets not be speaking **[31]** against the muses? For my part, I respect the judgment of all the poets, and most of all that of the wise man who said that Daphne was beloved of the Pythian, the kind of statement that some disbelieve.

"Daphne," he says, "came forth from Earth and Ladon." Why, by the gods, is this incredible? Were not water and earth the source of all things?[46] Do not the elements precede the seed of life? But if all that exists comes forth from earth and water, Daphne corroborates the common origin of all **[15R]** by coming forth from Earth and Ladon. Born whence all things are born, in appearance she excelled the others, and reasonably so; for the first things given up from earth come forth with natural beauty; for many changes of bodies in which beauty is seen have come to pass, but what appeared first of all is the most blooming. Probably then Daphne did excel in appearance, since she was the first of those born from earth.[47]

Since Daphne excelled in beauty, the Pythian conceived a love for the girl, and very logically; for everything beautiful that lives in the cities of men came forth from gods; and if beauty is one of the more blessed of the good things on earth, because beauty is a gift of the gods, beauty had a god as a lover; for what gods give, all gladly accept.

---

[45] Cf. above, n. 40.

[46] Xenophanes, frag. 29 and 33, ed. Diels-Kranz. Despite the use of Xenophanes' philosophical teachings in this passage it is unlikely that the myth of Daphne and Apollo figured in his poetry.

[47] Aphthonius seems to assume that Daphne was the first woman, and that the first would necessarily be the most beautiful. The composition as a whole is filled with invalid assumptions and logical non-sequiturs. Refutation was a much easier exercise than confirmation.

The god in love chose to heal his suffering. Such virtues lead their possessors[48] to violence, and without labors it is not possible to get virtue; thus he was laboring in love and though laboring he failed. For it is not possible to perceive how far virtue can go; thus, they say the Pythian loved, not thereby raising questions about the nature of the gods but making clear that the nature of virtue is the cause; and what is pursued leaves a mark on what is pursuing.

When the girl flees, **[32]** her mother receives her. All mortal things are born with such a nature: from what they came forth, **[16R]** to that they hasten.[49] Thus Daphne goes back to Earth, having come forth from Earth. And after receiving the maiden, Earth yielded up a plant. Both deeds are proper for Earth: humans fall to her and trees grow from her. And the plant that appeared became a source of honor to Apollo; for gods do not leave even growing things outside their concern but crown themselves with what comes into existence; for first-fruits of earth are dedicated to gods. And it has become a symbol of prophetic power, something I think also fitting; for they (i.e., the poets) name the maiden Sophrone, and prophecy comes from *sôphosynê*.[50] Well then, because the girl did not experience physical pleasure, she is dedicated to virtues; for it is not possible for anyone to see the future who has suffered the sickness of lack of self control.

These are my reasons for admiring the poets, and because of this I honor measure.[51]

7. ON COMMON-PLACE

Common-place (*koinos topos*) is language amplifying evils that are attached to something.[52] It is so called from fitting all in common who take part in the same deed; **[17R]** for speech against a traitor applies in common to all who share in the deed. It is like a second speech (for the prosecution) and an epilogue (in a trial); thus common-place does not have a prooemion, but we make up a form of prooemia for the sake of practice for the young. After that, you will put first a heading from the opposite, then you will introduce the statement, not as teaching it, for it is understood, but as stimulating

[48] Reading *ktômenous* as suggested to me by D. A. Russell.
[49] Xenophanes, frag. 28, ed. Diels-Kranz.
[50] *Sophrosynê* = moderation, self-control; here perhaps chastity.
[51] I.e., poetic meter and ethical moderation.
[52] Retaining *tini* with editors before Rabe. John of Sardis, *ad loc.*, gives the lemma as "inherent goods and evils," leaving open the possibility of common-places on virtue as found in the other handbooks.

the hearer. After that, you will introduce the comparison, attributing greater fault to the accused by means of the contrast; then
comes the heading called "intent," [33] attacking the state of mind
of the doer; then a digression, conjecturally criticizing his past life;
then rejection of pity, and at the end of the exercise the "final headings":[53] legality, justice, advantage, possibility, honor, result.

A COMMON-PLACE AGAINST A TYRANT [54]

(Prooemium 1) Since laws have been established and courts of justice are part of our government, let one seeking to annul the laws be
subject to the laws for punishment. If he were going to become
more democratically inclined by acquittal of the present charge,
perhaps one would let him off from trial; but since he will be more
violent if he is acquitted now, how is it just at present to provide
forgiveness for his initiation of tyranny? [18R]

(Prooemium 2)[55] Now all men who have been chosen by lot to
serve on juries receive no harm from their acquittal of the accused,
but acquittal on a charge of tyranny will cause harm to those making the judgment; for making judgment does not survive once a
tyrant has gained power.

(Contrary) It seems to me that you will rather more accurately
consider the state of mind of the man before you if you consider the
intentions of our ancestors. As a benefit to us they invented a constitution free of domination, and quite rightly so. Since different
accidents befall mankind at different times and cause the judgments
of men to alter, they sought out laws to balance the vagaries of fate
by the equal application of the laws, working out for themselves
therefrom a single standard of judgment for all. This becomes the
law for the cities, a rectification of the evils that accidents create.

(Exposition) Taking no thought of these things, [34] this man
has plotted some most evil purpose: to change the basis of the constitution. He debated with himself in some such way as this: "Why
is my situation what it is, O gods? Since I am clearly superior to the
common people, shall I put up with being constantly treated as the
equal of others and allow Fortune to bestow wealth upon me in
vain? If I am subject to the same conditions as the many and the
poor join together in judgment of me, whatever seems best to the

[53] On final headings, see above, p. 79, n. 26.
[54] There is an elaboration of this common-place by Libanius, vol. 8, pp. 195–
203, ed. Foerster.
[55] On the concept of multiple prooemia, cf. above, p. 80, n. 27.

many becomes a law for me. What escape will there be from these conditions? I shall seize the acropolis and put aside the laws, **[19R]** curse them, and thus I shall be a law to the many, not the many to me." These are the ideas he considered, though not bringing them to fulfillment; for the gods' good will prevented it. May the things for which we owe thanks to the gods not also protect this man today.

(Comparison) A murderer is a dreadful thing but a tyrant is a greater evil. The former does wrong against some ordinary person, but the other alters the whole fortune of the city. Thus, to the extent that causing grief on a small scale falls short of shedding the blood of all, to that extent murder is a lesser thing than tyranny.

(Intention) It is characteristic of all other men, even if they do very dreadful things, at least to distinguish their intention from their action, but the tyrant alone cannot say his daring is unintentional. If he had unwillingly attempted tyranny, perhaps one would excuse him from trial; but since he acted after much planning, how is it just to dismiss something fully intended before the actions?

(Digression) All other persons brought before you for judgment **[20R]** are held responsible only for their present activity, and often they are let go because of their past life, but the one before us is being judged on the basis of both parts of his life: he did not live his past life with moderation and his present life is worse than his past. **[35]** So let him be judged for both, both the harm he did earlier and what he did thereafter.

(Rejection of pity) Will anyone then try to win his release by emotional appeal? Probably his children will. But when they come into court weeping, think that the laws stand before you; surely it is much more righteous to cast a vote for them than for the children of this man; for (if you pity him) this man's tyranny will have been secured by means of his children, but it is through the laws that you have acquired the right to make judgment. Thus, you will more justly vote in favor of that by which you have been made judges.

(Legality) And if it is the law to honor those who free their fatherland, it follows that it is just to punish those who enslave it.

(Justice) It is just for him to submit in your court to a penalty equal to what he has done.

(Advantage) The fall of a tyrant will be a benefit; for it will make the laws stand up.

(Possibility) It will be easy to exact punishment from the one before us; for it is not the case that just as he needed armed guards for the establishment of his tyranny, so we shall need **[21R]** allies to put down the tyrant; rather, the vote of the judges will suffice to abolish the whole power of a tyranny.

(*Honor and result are omitted; John of Sardis*, ad loc., *says they are not needed*.)

8. ON ENCOMION

Encomion is language expressive of inherent excellences. It is so called from singing in villages (*kômai*) in ancient times. They used to call narrow passages *kômai*.[56] It differs from hymn and *epainos* in that a hymn is a celebration of gods, an encomion of mortals, and an epainos is brief but an encomion is artistically developed.[57]

One should celebrate persons and things, both occasions and [36] places, dumb animals and plants as well: persons, like Thucydides or Demosthenes; things, like justice or self-control; occasions, like spring or summer; and places, like harbors and gardens; dumb animals, like a horse or ox; plants, like olive or vine. Collective as well as individual encomia may be given; collectively, like an encomion of all Athenians, individually, like an encomion of one Athenian. [22R]

This then is the division of the encomion. You should elaborate it with the following headings. You will construct a prooemion appropriate to the subject; then you will state the person's origin, which you will divide into nation, homeland, ancestors, and parents; then upbringing, which you will divide into habits and acquired skill (*tekhnê*) and principles of conduct;[58] then you will compose the greatest heading of the encomion, deeds, which you will divide into those of mind and body and fortune:[59] mind, as courage or prudence; body, as beauty or swiftness or strength; and fortune, as power and wealth and friends; after these a comparison, attributing superiority to what is being celebrated by contrast; then an epilogue rather fitting a prayer.

AN ENCOMION OF THUCYDIDES

It is right to honor the inventors of useful things, by which they made the finest contributions, and to attribute the visible results of

---

[56] Cf. the note on Hermogenes, above p. 81, n. 29.

[57] Cf. Hermogenes, *ibid*.

[58] *Nomos*; John of Sardis, *ad loc.*, understands this to mean becoming accustomed to observing the laws and not being corrupted by bribery. This division is not found elsewhere.

[59] Cf. above, p. 50, n. 156.

these contributions justly to those who showed the way. Therefore I shall praise Thucydides by choosing to honor him with his own eloquent language (*logoi*). It is a fine thing for all benefactors to be honored, but Thucydides more than others in that he discovered the fairest thing; for it is not possible to find anything greater than eloquent language among things that exist, nor to find anyone wiser than Thucydides about eloquence.[60]

Now Thucydides came from a land which provided him both life and artistry; for he came not from some other place **[37. 23R]** but from the home of speeches (*logoi*). And by having Athens as the mother of his life, he enjoyed kings for ancestors and the stronger part of his good fortune came to him from his earlier ancestry. With the double benefit of a strong ancestry and a democratic constitution, he enjoyed the advantage that each counterbalanced the other: he was prevented from being rich unjustly by the equality of law, and his political weakness was disguised by the greatness of his descent.

Born from such circumstances, he is nurtured under a constitution and laws that are by their nature better than others, and having learned to deal both with arms and words, he projected a career as both philosopher and general, neither depriving his words of arms nor describing battles without[61] practical understanding. He makes a single study of things which did not have a single art, thus bringing together things that differed in nature.

As he came to manhood he began to seek an opportunity for the demonstration of the skills in which he was well practiced. Fate soon produced the war, and he made the doings of all the Greeks his unique study and became a guardian of what the war brought; for he did not allow time to erase memory of what each state was doing. The capture of Plataea has become known from his work (2.2ff.), and the laying waste of Attica (2.19ff.), and the Athenians' circumnavigation of the Peloponnesus was described (2.23ff.). **[24R]** Naupactus witnessed sea battles (2.90ff.); Thucydides in his history has prevented these things from being forgotten. Lesbos was taken (3.29ff.) and the fact is still proclaimed; a battle was fought with the Ambracians (3.107ff.) and time has not obliterated the event. The illegal trial (of the Plataeans) by Lacedaimonians (3.68) is not un-

[60] What Aphthonius means by *logoi* here is not entirely clear. John of Sardis, *ad loc.*, paraphrases it as *syngrammata,* prose writings. Matsen, Rollinson, and Sousa, p. 276, translate *logoi* here as "history." Aphthonius is perhaps honoring Thucydides as an inventor of artistic Attic prose writing.

[61] Reading *amoirous* instead of *en merei* as suggested to me by D. A. Russell.

known; Sphacteria and Pylos, the great action of the Athenians
(4.8ff.), has not escaped memory. The Corcyreans speak in the assembly at Athens, the Corinthians make their reply (1.32ff.),
Aeginetans **[38]** bring accusations to Lacedaimon (1.67), and
Archidamus shows restraint at the assembly (1.79ff.), but Sthene-
laidas incites to battle (1.86). In addition to all this, Pericles scorns
the Laconian embassy (1.139ff.) and does not let the Athenians become angry when suffering the plague (2.59ff.). All these things,
once and for all, are preserved for all time in Thucydides' *History*
(*syngraphê*).

Then does anyone compare Herodotus to him? No, for
Herodotus tells a story for its pleasure, while Thucydides utters
everything for its truth. To the extent that pleasure is something
less than truth, to that extent Herodotus falls short of the beauties
of Thucydides.

Many other things could be said about Thucydides, if the mass
of his praises did not fall short of telling everything. **[25R]**

AN ENCOMION OF WISDOM

Wisdom is a fortunate thing to acquire, but impossible to praise ad-
equately; so much happiness is associated with it that it is regarded
as a common possession of gods. Different gods care for different
things: Hera presides over marriage, Ares over war, together with
Athene; Hephaestus works bronze with fire; Poseidon is the leader
for sailors; each of the gods has a different art, but all share in wisdom, and Zeus in particular beyond all others; for he is wiser than
all to the extent that he is more powerful than the other gods, and
wisdom confirms the rule of Zeus. Gods acquired wisdom together
with their nature, the possession went forth to earth, and children
of gods brought it into human life. Therefore it also occurs to me
to marvel at the poets, because they made Palamedes and Nestor
children of gods, as well as any other of the first men who are celebrated in song as most wise, even though they were not gods by nature. Otherwise, they would have been made gods themselves and
would demonstrate their participation in virtue by community of
birth. **[39]** But because they acquired the virtue of gods they were
thought children of gods and seem to be a reminder of gods, whose
(own) wisdom came forth as a property of their birth. **[26R]**

To continue, wisdom controls the critical occasions of peace
and war; for some things are well thought of only in time of peace
and others are admired only during war time, but wisdom alone

knows how to prevail in both, as if they were one; for she governs in war as though quite ignorant of peace, and she controls peace as though never knowing battles. And wherever she rules is thought to be hers alone; for she gives laws in time of peace and uses all sorts of forms of tranquility, but in wars she leads the way to victory. Wisdom prevails in arms, and she does not allow another to succeed in assemblies but knows how to control both equally, those who fight and those who speak. Wisdom alone implements the plans of gods; for she alone, like a god, knows the future. She opened the land to farmers and she allots the sea to sailors; fruits cannot be gathered without wisdom nor, again, can one board a ship without a skilled pilot. Thus, everything of which the sea boasts and whatever the land provides to humans, all these things are discoveries of wisdom. She does not allow to lie hid the secrets which heaven holds to itself; for wisdom alone has discovered for mankind the size of the sun's circuit and the course of each of the stars. Now the wiseman is not ignorant of things beneath the earth, **[27R]** and wisdom alone has furnished knowledge of how we shall be when life is ended. She captured Troy; a wise plan[62] accomplished what much time was not able to do. And she destroyed the whole power of the Persians, accomplishing it by a single plan.[63] The Cyclops' eye was destroyed when Odysseus conceived a wiser plan. Thus, if anything succeeds, it comes from wisdom. **[40]** Will anyone, then, compare bravery to her? But whatever power can do is derived from wisdom, and if you deprive bravery of prudence, it is left open to attack.

Many other things could be listed about wisdom, but it is impracticable to go into them all.

9. ON INVECTIVE

Invective (*psogos*) is language expressive of inherent evils. It differs from common-place in that the latter aims at punishment, while invective contains only bald attack. It is divided into the same headings as encomion. One should blame the same number of things as one should celebrate: persons and things, both occasions and places, dumb animals and also growing things. One applies invective both in general and to a particular. **[28R]**

When composing prooemia you will describe the origin, which you will divide in the same way as in encomion, and you will set out

---

[62] The stratagem of the Trojan horse.
[63] The Athenians' strategy of leaving Athens and embarking on their fleet.

the upbringing and the deeds and the comparison and the epilogue
in the same way as in encomia.

AN INVECTIVE AGAINST PHILIP[64]

It is appropriate neither to leave virtue unpraised nor vice uncen-
sured, because there is profit in both cases, when good deeds are
praised and when evil deeds are blamed. It is right that all who are
wickedly disposed should be rebuked, and Philip most of all to the
degree that he exceeded all evil doers.

He came forth from people who are the worst of the barbarians
and were seeking to move from place to place because of their cowardice. The Argives threw them out first; then, wandering about,
they took refuge in the country they now hold,[65] **[41]** experiencing
two misfortunes in the settlement: yielding on the one hand to the
stronger and on the other expelling the weaker, from their cowardice and greed unable to agree on a settled abode. **[29R]** This is
what his people were like, and he came from an even less distinguished city. Macedonians are the worst of the barbarians, and Pella
is the most undistinguished city in the land of Macedonians, from
which the people do not do well even when sold as slaves.[66] And
coming from such a place, he had the worst ancestors in the land.
He was descended from a Philip who was not allowed to rule the
place because of his birth; then came his father, Amyntas, who
needed the help of others to become king; for the Athenians restored him after he had been driven out. And seen to be from such
ancestors, he was held as a hostage among the Thebans,[67] and although living in the middle of Greece, he did not change his manners because of this association but added barbaric intemperance to
Greek ways of life. Despite all the differences between Greeks and
barbarians, he was the same in both cultures, wreaking equal
wickedness among unlike races.

And his first act as king was to enslave his relatives, showing his
distrust of those from whom he came. Then he attacked and destroyed his neighbors, and after carrying off the Paeonians he set

[64] I.e., Philip II, king of Macedon, 359–336 B.C. There is an elaboration of
this psogos by Libanius, vol. 8, pp. 296–301, ed. Foerster.

[65] Cf. Herodotus 8.137; Thucydides 2.99.

[66] Cf. Demosthenes 9.31, of Philip: ". . . not even a barbarian from a country
that one could acknowledge with credit; he is a pestilent Macedonian, from whose
country it used not to be possible to buy even a slave of any value."

[67] Cf. Diodorus Siculus 16.2.2. The translation is based on reading *progonôn*
for *menôn* as suggested to me by D. A. Russell.

upon the Illyrians and attacked and seized the land of the Triballi, taking all that belonged to tribes that had the misfortune of being nearby. He captured the bodies of the barbarians in battle, but their minds he did not get with their bodies; **[30R]** although enslaved by arms, they dreamed of revolt, and regions that were enslaved in fact remained independent in their reckonings. After bringing the neighbors of these barbarians to terms, he continued his advance against the Greeks. First, he subdued the Greek cities in Thrace, capturing Amphipolis and worsting Pydna and taking Potidaea as well, neither separating Phera from Pagasae **[42]** nor Magnesia from Pherae, but all the cities of Thessaly were captured and bore slavery as a symbol of their common race.[68]

It is worth giving an account of the death of this man; for whereas, in advancing, he reduced many places and treacherously enslaved those who made sworn treaties with him, the gods, angered at his broken treaties, brought a fitting death upon him. They did not remove him in battle nor make a war hero the witness of his death, but they destroyed him in the midst of pleasure, making pleasure a fair shroud for Philip's sins, so that both in life and when killed he got witnesses of his incontinence.[69]

Who then will compare Echetus to him?[70] Although Echetus cut off bits of his victims' extremities, he left the rest of the body, **[31R]** but Philip destroyed whole bodies with whole parts. To the extent that the destruction of the whole is worse than destruction of a part, Philip was more terrible than Echetus.

When Philip was alive he knew not when to stop, but the one who is describing him must stop somewhere.

10. ON SYNCRISIS

Syncrisis (*synkrisis*) is a comparison, made by setting things side-by-side, bringing the greater together with what is compared to it. When comparing we should either set fine things beside good things or poor things beside poor things or good beside bad or small beside

[68] Cf. Demosthenes 1.12–13. Spengel proposed a lacuna here, balancing the "first" at the beginning of the sentence with mention of Philip's subsequent move on Phocis. This, however, probably demands too much careful composition on the part of Aphthonius.

[69] Philip was assassinated at a wedding banquet by a Macedonian noble with a private grudge against him; cf. Plutarch, *Alexander* 9.5–10. On Philip's death, cf. John of Sardis, *ad loc.*

[70] Echetus is only known as a king, proverbial for cruelty, mentioned in *Odyssey* 18.83–87, 116, and 21.308.

larger. As a whole, syncrisis is a double encomion or <a double> invective or a speech made up out of encomion <and invective>. Every
topic of syncrisis is quite forceful, but especially that comparing
small things to greater ones. It is appropriate for us to compare as
many things as we blame and celebrate: both persons and things, occasions and places, dumb animals, and, in addition, plants. **[43]** It is
not necessary in making comparisons to contrast a whole with a
whole, for that is flat and not argumentative, but compare a heading
to a heading; this at least is argumentative.[71] Since dividing is a feature of encomion, **[32R]** <you should elaborate comparison with the
same headings as encomion, except for comparison>.[72] There is no
comparison in it, since the whole exercise is a comparison.

A COMPARISON OF ACHILLES AND HECTOR

In seeking to compare virtue to virtue, I shall measure the son of
Peleus against Hector; for virtues are to be honored for themselves,
but when measured against each other they become more worthy of
imitation.

Well then, they were not born in the same land, but nevertheless each in a land to be praised. The one came from Phthia, where
the eponymous hero of Hellas came from, and the other from Troy,
whose original founders were descendants of gods.[73] To the extent
that having been born in similar places is no derogation of praise,
Hector is not excelled by Achilles. And while both were born in a
praiseworthy land, both had equal ancestry; for each descended
from Zeus. Achilles was son of Peleus, Peleus of Aeacus, and Aeacus of Zeus; similarly, Hector was son of Priam and (grandson) of
Laomedon, and Laomedon was son of Dardanus, and Dardanus
had been a son of Zeus. And having been born descendants of Zeus,
they enjoyed similar forefathers: of Achilles, Aeacus and Peleus, of
whom the former brought Greeks the end of droughts,[74] and the
other was granted marriage with a goddess as a prize of valor for
slaying the Lapiths; **[33R]** Hector's ancestor was Dardanus who
earlier dined with the gods, and his father was Priam, the ruler of a
city whose walls were built by gods.[75] Indeed, to the extent that

---

[71] I.e., proceeding point by point.
[72] The supplement is adapted from Rabe's conjectural emendation.
[73] The Hellenes were originally a small tribe in Thessaly; the name may have
spread southward during the Dorian invasion. The founders of Troy were descendants of Dardanus, son of Zeus.
[74] Cf. Isocrates 9.14–17.
[75] I.e., Apollo and Poseidon.

marrying gods and dining with them is similar, to that extent Hector is comparable to Achilles. And having descended from such ancestors, both were brought up for bravery. **[44]** The one was reared by Cheiron,[76] while Priam was tutor to the other, giving demonstrations of his own courage. Since training for courage was equal in both, it brings equal glory to them.

When both came to manhood, they acquired equal prestige from one war. First, Hector was leader of the Trojans and, while alive, the protector of Troy; during that time he continued to have gods aiding him in the fight and when he fell he made Troy fall with him. Achilles was the leader of Greece in arms; terrifying all, he subdued the Trojans and had the help of Athene in the fight, and his death took away the superiority of the Achaeans. The one (Hector) was defeated and killed through the agency of Athene, the other (Achilles) fell, struck by Apollo. Both were descended from gods and were destroyed by gods. They received the end of their life from the same source as their birth. To the extent that their life and death were nearly equal, Hector is nearly equal to Achilles.

There are many other things that could be said about the virtue of both, if it were not that both had nearly equal fame from their deeds.**[34R]**

11. ON ETHOPOEIA

Ethopoeia (*êthopoiia*) is imitation of the character of a proposed speaker.[77] There are three different forms of it: apparition-making (*eidôlopoiia*), personification (*prosôpooiia*), and characterization (*êthopoiia*). Ethopoeia has a known person as speaker and only invents the characterization, which is why it is called "character-making"; for example, what words would Heracles say when Eurystheus gave his commands. Here Heracles is known, but we invent the character in which he speaks. In the case of eidolopoeia, the speaker is a known person, but dead and no longer able to speak, like the character Eupolis invented in his *Demoi* and Aristeides in *On the Four;*[78] **[45]** which is why it is called "apparition-making."[79] In the case of prosopopoeia, everything is invented, both character and

---

[76] Cf. John of Sardis' note, *ad loc.*

[77] On this chapter, see Patillon, *Théorie du discours*, pp. 300–304.

[78] For Eupolis, cf. Kock, I, p. 229; for Aristeides, see above, p. 84, n. 43.

[79] The status of the speaker at the time the speech is imagined as being given is what determines whether it is ethopoeia or eidolopoeia. A speech Heracles might have given while alive is an example of ethopoeia, a speech he might have given after death is an eidolopoeia.

speaker, as Menander invented Elenchos (Disproof);[80] for *elenchos* is
a thing, not a person at all; which is why this is called "person-mak-
ing"; for the person is invented with the character.**[35R]** So much
for the distinctions.

Some characterizations are pathetical, some ethical, some
mixed. Pathetical are those showing emotion in everything; for example, what words Hecuba might say when Troy was destroyed.
Ethical are those that only introduce character; for example, what
words a man from inland might say on first seeing the sea. Mixed
are those having both character and pathos; for example, what
words Achilles might say over the body of Patroclus when planing
to continue war; for the plan shows character, the fallen friend
pathos.

You will elaborate the characterization in a style that is clear,
concise, fresh, pure, free from any inversion and figure.[81] Instead of
headings, there is a division into the three periods of time: present,
past, and future.

AN EXERCISE IN CHARACTERIZATION:
"WHAT WORDS NIOBE MIGHT SAY
WHEN HER CHILDREN LIE DEAD"[82]

How great is the change in my fortune! —childless now, once seeming blessed with children. Abundance has turned into want and I
who earlier seemed the mother of many children am now not the
mother of one! As a result, I ought not to have given birth to start
with, rather than giving birth **[36R]** to tears. Those deprived are
more unfortunate than those not having given birth; for what has
once been experienced gives pain when taken away. Alas, I have a
fate much like that of my parent. I was begotten by Tantalus, who
was banished from the gods after he had feasted with them, and descended as I am from Tantalus, I confirm the relationship by my
misfortunes. I had an acquaintance with Leto **[46]** and because of
it I fare badly and the connection led to the loss of my children.
Connection with a goddess brings me in the end to misfortune. Before entering rivalry with Leto I was a mother to be envied, but
having become famous I am at a loss for offspring, which I had in

---

[80] Menander, frag. 545, ed. Kock.

[81] See the explanation of these terms by John of Sardis, *ad loc.*

[82] According to myth, Niobe, mother of twelve or more children, boasted she
was at least equal to Leto, who had but two, Apollo and Artemis. Those two killed
Niobe's many. There are two elaborations of this ethopoeia by Libanius, vol. 8, pp.
391–96, ed. Foerster.

abundance before the rivalry. Now my lot is one of weeping for each child and grieving at the loss of what was a source of pride.

Where can I turn? What can I hold to? What kind of tomb will suffice for the destruction of so many dead children? My honors have ended in misfortunes. But why do I laments these things, when it is possible to ask the gods to change my nature for another? I see but one escape from my misfortunes, to change into a substance that feels nothing.[83] Yet I am more fearful lest even in that form I may continue weeping.

12. ON ECPHRASIS

Ecphrasis (*ekphrasis*) is descriptive language, bringing what is shown clearly before the eyes. [37R] One should describe both persons and things, occasions and places, dumb animals and, in addition, growing things: persons, as Homer does, "He was round shouldered, dark skinned, woolly haired";[84] things, as description of a naval battle and an infantry battle,[85] as does the historian (i.e., Thucydides); occasions, like spring and summer, saying what flowers they produce; places, as the same Thucydides (1.46) speaks of Chimerium, the harbor of the Thesprotians, telling what shape it has. In making an ecphrasis of persons one should go from first things to last, that is, from head to feet; and in describing things, say what preceded them, what is in them, and what is wont to result, and describe occasions and places from what surrounds them and what is in them.

Some ecphrases are single, some compound: single, like [47] descriptions of an infantry or naval battle, compound, like those combining things and occasions together, as Thucydides (7.43–44) describes the night battle in Sicily; for he specified how the battle was conducted and what the night was like.

In composing an ecphrasis, one should make use of a relaxed style[86] [38R] and adorn it with varied figures and, throughout, create an imitation of the things being described.

---

[83] Zeus changed her into a weeping stone on Mount Sipylon, pointed out to later travelers.

[84] Of Eurybates in *Odyssey* 19.246.

[85] Cf. Libanius, vol. 8, pp. 460–64 and 489–90, ed. Foerster.

[86] I.e., without periods and enthymemes; cf. John of Sardis, *ad loc.*

ECPHRASIS OF THE SHRINE OF ALEXANDRIA,
WITH ITS ACROPOLIS

Citadels, then,[87] have been built in cities for the common security; for
they are the highest points in the cities, and they are not themselves
more fortified with buildings than they fortify their cities. The middle of Athens has embraced the acropolis of the Athenians, and
Alexander had a height prepared in his own city, constructed to suit
the name he gave it;[88] for he set it on the highest point of the city, and
it is more sensible to call it an acropolis than that on which the Athenians took counsel.[89] Its appearance is as this account will describe.

*What Aphthonius calls the acropolis of Alexandria and describes
in the following passage is better known as the Serapeum (or Sara-
peum), an extensive shrine on a low hill in the southwestern quarter of
the city. The Serapeum was dedicated to Serapis (Sarapis), a composite Egyptian and Greek god deliberately created to be patron of the new
city. Although Alexander may have intended that something be built on
this hill, construction of the shrine probably did not begin until the third
century B.C. at the instigation of Ptolemy III, and the site was much
enlarged and adorned by his successors. In A.D. 389 the shrine was destroyed at the instigation of the Christian Patriarch Theophilus under
authority from the emperor Theodosius (see Eunapius 457, Sozomen
7.15). Aphthonius' description was perhaps written before that date,
but probably relies on another description (dating from after construction of Diocletian's pillar in A.D. 297; cf. below) of a place Aphthonius himself may never have seen and had difficulty describing clearly.
But no such description is known.*

An *akra* projects up from the land, going up to a considerable
height, and is called an "acropolis" for two reasons: because it is
raised to a height and because it has been set on the high point of a
city. Roads leading to this acropolis are not alike; for here there is an
incline (*anodos*) and there an entrance way (*eisodos*). The roads
change their names, being called by their function: here it is possible to go on foot and the way is public and a road for those going by
carriage; on another side, flights of steps have been constructed

[87] Unlike the other examples of composition, this begins with connective par-
ticles (*de ara*), contributing to the relaxed style; see John of Sardis' commentary on
this ecphrasis, translated below.
[88] I.e., the name "acropolis," but the sentence is clumsy and possibly the text
is corrupt. Alexander's city is of course Alexandria.
[89] The Areopagus?

[39R] where it is not possible for carriages to go. Flight of steps follows flight of step, always increasing from the lesser and leading upward, not ceasing until there have been a hundred steps; for the limit of a number is the end **[48]** that reaches perfect measure.[90]

At the top of the stairs is a Propylaeon, enclosed by latticed gates of moderate height, and four very large columns rise up, providing several openings into one entrance passage. Above the columns stands the Oecus, fronted by many smaller columns which are not all of the same color, and when compared they add ornament to the design. The roof of the building rises in a dome, and around the dome is fixed a great memorial of things that are.[91]

On going into the acropolis itself, one enters a single open space, bounded by four equal sides, and its figure is rather like that of a war machine (i.e., a hollow rectangle). In the middle is a courtyard, surrounded by a colonnade. Stoas continue the courtyard and the stoas are divided by equal columns, and as for their measure, it is the largest possible. Each stoa ends **[40R]** in another crosswise colonnade and a double column divides it from another stoa, one ending and the other beginning again. Small covered structures are built inside the stoas; some are reading rooms for books, offering an opportunity for the studious to pursue knowledge and arousing the whole city to the possibility of wisdom; others were built as shrines to the ancient gods. Gold adorns the roof of the stoas and the capitals of the columns are made of bronze, overlaid with gold. The decoration of the courtyard is not all the same; different parts were done differently. One part has a representation of the contests of Perseus. A column higher than the others stands in the middle, making the place conspicuous.[92] A visitor, up to this point, does not

[90] "In its completed form the plateau on which the Temple stood was approached from the north and south sides by a carriage road and from the east side by a flight of 200 steps," John Marlowe, *The Golden Age of Alexandria* (London: Victor Gollancz, 1971), p. 60. For more information about the Serapeum, see I. A. Rowe, "Discoveries of the Famous Temple and Enclosure of Sarapis at Alexandria," *Annales du Service de l'Antiquité del'Egypte*, Cahier supplémentaire 2 (1946).

[91] "At the top of the steps was a Propylaeum supported by four large columns and approached between two obelisks. Immediately inside the Propylaeum was an Oecus, or circular hall, covered by a gilded dome resting on a double ring of columns," Marlow ibid. The "great memorial of things that are" was probably a religious and historical fresco.

[92] This monument, some 80 feet high, was known as "Pompey's Pillar," but was actually erected to commemorate a visit to Alexandria by Diocletian in A.D. 297, when he suppressed a revolt.

known where he is going unless he uses this column as a sign of the
ways. It makes the acropolis visible by both land and sea. The beginning of things are carved around the top of the column.[93]

Before one comes to the middle of the courtyard there is a
structure divided into two parts that serve for gates, which are
named for the ancient gods. **[49]** Two stone obelisks rise up and
there is a fountain considered better than that of the Pisistratids.[94]
[41R] This marvel came into being as the work of an unbelievable
number of designers; for as though one was not sufficient for the
work, a total of twelve architects were seen.

Coming down from the acropolis on one side one comes to a
level place resembling a stadium, which has become the name of
the place. On another side there is a place similarly divided but not
of equal length. The beauty (of the acropolis) is greater than I can
say, and if anything has been left out, this has been incidental to
our wonder. It has been omitted because it was impossible to describe.[95]

13. ON THESIS

Thesis (*thesis*) is a logical examination of any matter under inspec-
tion. Some theses are political, some theoretical; political are those
involving an action affecting a city; for example, whether one
should marry, whether one should sail, whether one should build a
fortification; for all these actions affect a city; theoretical are those
only examined in the mind; for example, whether the heaven is
spherical, whether there are other worlds. These matters cannot be
tested by humans and are only examined in the mind.

Thesis differs from hypothesis in that an hypothesis has atten-

[93] I.e., allegorical representations of the four elements of fire, water, air, and
earth, according to John of Sardis, *ad loc.*

[94] For the Pisistratids' fountain, cf. Thucydides 2.15. Marlowe, op. cit., pp.
60–61, describes the shrine thus: "The Temple itself was in the middle of the
quadrangle formed by the flattened plateau. Round the perimeter of the quadrangle were lecture-halls, libraries, storerooms, etc., opening on to a cloister supported
by columns. This cloister was joined to an inner colonnade surrounding the Temple by four double rows of columns running at right angles from the center of each
side of the cloister, forming the shape of a cross, with the Temple at the intersec-
tion. The Temple was rectangular in shape and surrounded by a colonnade, of
which the capitals were gilded. The floor and walls of the Temple were of marble
and the walls were covered with metal sheets of gold, silver, and bronze. At the east
end was a huge statue of Serapis. . . . An east window behind the statue was so
arranged that the first rays of the rising sun lit up the features of the god."

[95] This is perhaps to be taken as an excuse for failing to describe the temple
and cult statue of the god Serapis.

dant circumstances, whereas a thesis is without particulars.[96] Attendant circumstance includes person, action, cause, etc.; for example, whether one should build a fortification is a thesis, an inquiry **[42R]** not including a person, but "When the Persians are advancing, the Lacedaimonians debate whether to fortify Sparta" is an hypothesis; for it includes as personal agent the Lacedaimonians in debate, and as action the fortifying of Sparta, and as cause the advance of the Persians. Thesis is the first progymnasma to include antithesis **[50]** and solution (*lysis*) of the question.[97] Now then, thesis is divided, first, into what is called the approach (*ephodos*),[98] which you will speak in place of prooemia; then you will use the final headings: legal, just, advantageous, possible.

A THESIS: WHETHER ONE SHOULD MARRY[99]

Let one who seeks to honor everything in brief praise marriage; for it came forth from heaven, or rather it filled heaven with gods and created a father of them, from whom the name "father" is given. By having given birth to gods, marriage removed them from the need to guard against mortal nature.[100] Then, coming on the earth, it brings reproduction to all the rest, and having produced creatures that do not know how to survive death, it contrived continuance of their race by successive generations.

And first of all, marriage raises men to bravery; for since it knows how to get children and wives, for whom war is fought, it gives men strength by means of its gifts. Then, it makes them just as well as brave; for marriage makes men both just and brave because it endows them with children, for whose sake men feel fear and do just things. **[43R]** And surely it makes them wise as well, in that it stirs them to take thought for their dearest ones. Paradoxi-

---

[96] As a "dialectical" exercise it also usually relies on argument and avoids ethos and pathos.

[97] I.e., objection to the thesis by an imaginary opponent and rebuttal of the objection.

[98] Latin *insinuatio*, "the subtle approach"; cf. *Rhetoric for Herennius* 1.6 and John of Sardis, *ad loc.*, "He said it is called *ephodos* rather than prooemion either as being a path (*hodos*) to the narration—for an *ephodos* provides a praiseworthy reason for a narration —or as providing an entrance into the subject without being obvious."

[99] There is an elaboration of this thesis by Libanius, vol. 8, pp. 550–61, ed. Foerster.

[100] I.e., to guard against death and destruction; cf. John of Sardis, *ad loc.* D. A. Russell, however, suggests to me that Aphthonius may mean "relieved Nature from the need to watch over them."

cally, marriage knows how to bring about self-control, and self-control has been co-mingled with desire for the pleasures (of sexual intercourse); by putting a legal limit on the pleasures, self-control provides pleasure to lawful action, and what in itself is a subject of accusation is admired when joined with marriage. If, then, marriage produces gods, and after them each of the generations in turn, and creates brave and just men and makes them wise and temperate, how should one not admire marriage as much as possible?

(Antithesis) "Yes," he says, "but marriage is a cause of misfortunes."

(Solution) You seem to me to be attacking fortune, not marriage. **[51]** Fortune, not marriage, occasions the things that men suffer when they fare badly, and what marriage gives men is not a gift of fortune. As a result, marriage is more to be admired for its fine features than to be attacked for the evils fortune provides. But even if we should attribute to marriage the worst experiences of human beings, why should one refrain the more from marriage? Difficulties that belong to actions do not bring about avoidance of action. Let me examine skills one by one to see what it is you really object to. Thunderbolts trouble farmers **[44R]** and hailstorms cause them loss; but farmers whose land has been struck by a thunderbolt do not abandon the land; they continue farming even if some damage comes from heaven. Again, men meet with misfortunes when sailing the seas, and storms befall them and wreck their ships; but they do not stop sailing because of what they have suffered in turn; they attribute misfortune to chance and await the profit that comes from the sea. Moreover, battles and wars destroy the bodies of antagonists, and yet men do not avoid battles because they may fall while fighting; because fighters are admired, they are content to risk death and disguise the present danger for the sake of the attendant good. One should not avoid what has much good in it because of some negative features but bear up under evils for the sake of the good things. Thus, it is not logical to conclude that, while farmers and sailors, and soldiers as well, bear troubles that come upon them for the sake of benefits that come with these difficulties, marriage, in contrast, should be dishonored because marriage brings some annoyance.

(Antithesis) "Yes," he says, "but marriage has made women widows and children orphans."

(Solution) These are the evils of death, and nature knows the experience, **[52]** but you seem to me to be blaming marriage because it does not make humans into gods, and to accuse marriage because it did not include mortal suffering for the gods. Why, please tell me, **[45R]** do you attack marriage for what is death's business? Why do you attribute to weddings things that nature knows? Grant that he will die who was born to die. But if human beings die because they have been born, and when they die bereave the spouse and make an orphan of a son, why do you say that marriage brought about what was only the result of nature? On the contrary, I think that marriage corrects orphanhood and widowhood. Someone's father dies and thus a child is an orphan; but (the mother's next) marriage brings another father for the orphans, and the suffering does not come from marriage but is disguised by marriage, and marriage is the obliteration of bereavement, not its cause. Then, nature brought widowhood from death, but marriage changed it with wedding songs; one whom death made a widow marriage has given a husband to live with, as though standing guard over its gift. The things it brought at first, it gave back again when they were taken away; thus marriage knows how to abolish bereavement, not how to bring it. And surely, though a father is deprived of children by their death, by marriage he secures others, and he becomes a father for a second time who was not allowed to be one the first time. Why then do you change the fine features of marriage into a charge against marriage? You seem to me not to be trying to attack but to be bringing praise to the wedding song; for by forcing us to enumerate the pleasures of wedding songs, you have become an admirer, not an accuser of marriage; **[46R]** and you force us to marvel at critics of marriage, and you make the accusations against marriage a catalogue of its benefits.

(Antithesis) "Yes," he says, "but marriage is wearisome."

(Solution) What knows how to end weariness better than marriage does? **[53]** Whatever wearies is removed by wedding songs and there is relief to everyone in coming into intercourse with a wife. How great it is for a man to go to bed with a woman! With what joy is a child expected, and when expected then appears, and having appeared he addresses his father and advances to the practice of a skill and works together with his father, haranguing the people in the assembly and caring for his father in old age and becoming everything he should be!

(Epilogue) It is not possible to describe in a word what marriage knows how to bring about. Marriage is a mighty thing, both producing gods and allowing mortals to seem to be gods by cleverly teaching how to survive. It teaches justice to those who practice it, and spurs them on to consider self-control and bestows those pleasures that are not obviously to be blamed. Thus, it has been established among all that marriage should be most highly valued.

14. ON INTRODUCTION OF A LAW

Some have also allowed that the introduction of a law is an exercise. It is almost a complete hypothesis **[47R]** without preserving all the features of an hypothesis; a person is introduced but not one known in all respects.[101] As a result, it is more than a thesis but less than an hypothesis; for in so far as its overall form admits a person, it goes beyond a thesis, but because it does not keep the attendant circumstance clear, it falls short of an hypothesis.

Now introduction of a law is a double exercise, a speech in support of and speech of attack against a proposed law. Law is "an invention and gift of the gods, an opinion of wise men, a correction of willing and unwilling errors, and a city's common covenant" (cf. Demosthenes 25.16). This (i.e., argument for or against) is the division of the introduction of a law, and you will elaborate it with the headings by which you elaborate deliberation about future action, i.e., legal, just, advantageous, possible. You will provide prooemia **[54]** and after the prooemia what is called the "contrary"; then you will use the aforementioned headings, by which it also differs from thesis.

A SPEECH IN OPPOSITION TO A LAW REQUIRING THE KILLING OF AN ADULTERER WHEN TAKEN IN THE ACT[102]

I shall not entirely praise the law nor criticize what has been introduced in every respect. In that it adversely affects adulterers, I praise what is put before us, but because it does not require a vote by judges[103] I criticize the plan. If the mover of the law is avoiding appeal to the courts because of having observed bribery of judges, **[48R]** he is proved to have a poor opinion of judges; but if he thinks they judge justly, as you here judge justice, how is it just to praise judges but to take operation of the law away from those who judge

---

[101] The reference is to the person who is imagined as having introduced the law. In a declamation (i.e., an hypothesis) in contrast to a progymnasma, introduction of the law might be attributed to a specific historical person, who could then become a topic in the speech.

[102] As in many cultures, Greek law allowed a husband to kill his wife's seducer, but only if taken in the act and without premeditation; there was no legal require-

crimes? In the case of all other laws that contradict existing laws, some differ from laws in certain cities and agree with laws in others. Only this present law has been advanced in opposition to all laws. You (members of the assembly) seem to me to scrutinize the law in a much better way if you judge it as you do all other public matters—appointment of generals, the priesthoods, the decrees. Almost everything that is done best in time of peace or war undergoes the scrutiny of judges, and he is a general whom the judge has approved and a priest whom a judge has confirmed, and a decree is valid that has been examined in the presence of others, and victors in war are not awarded prizes until after having been judged. How then is it not illogical for everything to be subject to scrutiny and for the law before us alone to remove the vote of judges?

(Antithesis) "Yes," he says, "but the wrongs done by adulterers are great."

(Solution) What? Are not those of murderers greater? **[55]** And do we think traitors are less wicked than others, and are temple robbers of less account than **[49R]** traitors? Yet whoever is caught doing these things faces judges and neither does a traitor suffer punishment without the judge giving vote, nor does death come to a murderer unless the prosecutor proves the crime, nor do those who rob the higher powers[104] suffer until there is an opportunity for the judges to learn about these matters. Is it not strange then for greater crimes to face a decision among the judges and not any of these, as it were, to seem to exist unless a judge has given vote, while only an adulterer is to die unexamined, although he should all the more be judged in that he is a less serious criminal than others.

(Antithesis) "What is the difference between killing an adulterer and handing him over to judges, if he will sustain death equally from both?"

(Solution) There is as much difference as between tyranny and law and between democracy and monarchy. It is characteristic of a tyrant to kill whomever he wants but of law to put to death justly one who has been convicted. The demos presents for public scrutiny whatever it is considering in the assembly, but the rule of one man punishes and does not allow debate, two things which the

---

ment in Athens that an adulterer be killed, and the offended husband could accept monetary compensation for the wrong; cf. Lysias 1.27–36.

[103] Or members of a jury. The situation envisioned is that of the lawcourts in classical Athens, where there was no distinction between judges and jurymen.

[104] I.e., the gods, as in stealing from a temple.

people and law have done in entire contrast to the one who has chosen to rule and tyrannize alone. **[50R]** How then will killing the adulterer not differ from handing him over to the judges? And in addition, one who by himself kills the adulterer makes himself master of the doer, while one who turns him over to trial makes the court master of the doer, and it is surely better for the judge than for the accuser to be his master. Furthermore, one who on his own killed an adulterer is suspected of killing him for some other reason, while one who has handed him over to be judged seems motivated by justice alone.

(Antithesis) "Yes," he says, "but falling immediately on the spot will be a harsher punishment; **[56]** lapse of time before judgment will be an advantage to the adulterer."

(Solution) If brought to trial, he will have the opposite experience; for his life hereafter will be more unpleasant; for he will find the expectation more terrifying than the experience. To expect to suffer is worse than having suffered, and delay of punishment seems additional punishment. One who thinks he will die dies many times and will have a more awful expectation of his end. As a result, the adulterer who falls immediately does not perceive it. Quickness of punishment deceives the sense. A death occurring before it is expected is painless, while one often expected, once taking place, measures the punishments by the expectations. Put the two side by side and consider them. The man who killed an adulterer on his own has no witness of the punishment, but the man who handed him over to judges provides a large audience, and it is more painful to be punished in front of many spectators. In another way too it will be an advantage to adulterers to die secretly; **[51R]** for they will leave in the minds of many a suspicion that they fell because of personal enmity, but if what has happened is examined among judges, the one put to death will meet with an unambiguous decision. So it is in the adulterer's interest to be killed in secret rather than to be handed over to judges.

(Epilogue) An adulterer is a terrible thing, and he has exceeded the utmost degree of wrong. As a result, let him first be tried, then let him be executed, and let him be judged rather than suffer punishment before judgment. Thus the executed adulterer will make more clear the origin of children. No one will be in doubt about the father of a child if adulterers are eliminated in the future. The wrong is part of our common nature, and so let a common vote do away with it when it occurs; since I am afraid that, if the circumstances of an adulterer' death are concealed, he will leave behind many others like himself. Others will emulate those of whose death they know not the cause, and the punishment will become not the end but the beginning of suffering.

Chapter IV

The *Preliminary Exercises* of Nicolaus the Sophist

What is known about Nicolaus is derived from two entries under that name in the Byzantine encyclopedia Suda, *both probably referring to the same person, and a short passage in Marinus'* Life of Proclus *(10). These sources indicate that he came from Myra in Lycia, studied in Athens with the Platonist Plutarch and the sophist Lachares, and taught rhetoric in Constantinople during the reigns of Leo, Zeno, and Anastasius (i.e., from before A.D. 474 until after 491). He was probably one of the professors at the educational institution called by modern scholars "The University of Constantinople," founded by Theodosius II in 425.[1] The first article in the* Suda *attributes to him progymnasmata and* meletai *(declamations, or perhaps progymnasmatic exercises), the second an* Art of Rhetoric *(which may have included or been identical with the* Progymnasmata)[2] *and* meletai. *His brother, Dioscorius, is said to have been the teacher of the sons of the emperor Leo and was consul in A.D. 442. To hold these positions, Dioscorius must have been a Christian. Nicolaus' known connections are otherwise with pagans, and his treatise gives no hint of Christian sentiments. On the basis of Marinus' description of Nicolaus' meeting with his fellow-countryman Proclus, on the latter's arrival as a student in Athens, Felten proposed that Nicolaus was born about 410, but a later date has been also been suggested.[3] As noted above, he probably died some time after 491.*

The manuscript evidence for Nicolaus' Progymnasmata *is slender. The full text, from the beginning to the end of the chapter on encomion, is known from only one late manuscript (British Museum 11889 of the fifteenth century), where it is interspersed with the text of Aphthonius'*

---

[1] On the University, see Kennedy, *Greek Rhetoric*, pp. 165–67. Nicolaus' text often sounds as though it had been transcribed from lectures.

[2] Cf. the use of "Art," below, p. 144. On a few occasions (e.g., below, pp. 144 and 154) Nicolaus indicates he will elsewhere discuss some aspect of rhetorical theory more advanced than that needed for beginners. Perhaps his *Progymnasmata* was the first part of a larger rhetorical corpus, like that attributed to Hermogenes.

[3] By Kurt Orinsky, as reported by E. Richsteig in *Philologische Wochenschrift* 41 (1921): 691–701.

*account of the exercises; there are also some fragments of the chapters
on fable and narrative in a manuscript in Munich. Nicolaus' accounts
of the last five exercises do not survive in their original form, but evidence for them has been collected by editors from citations in Byzantine
commentaries on Aphthonius. The version of the whole text in Spengel's* Rhetores Graeci *(vol. 3, pp.* 449–498), *published in 1856, ante-
dates Johannes Graeven's discovery of the British Museum manuscript
by forty years and was entirely based on quotations in the commentaries
on Aphthonius. Evidence from the British Museum manuscript, as well
as from all other known sources, was utilized by Joseph Felten in his
Teubner text of 1913, which is the basis for the translation here. Numbers in brackets refer to pages in Felten's edition. For a French translation and commentary, see Henry Fruteau de Laclos,* Les Progymnasmata de Nicolaus de Mura dans la tradition versicolore des
exercises préparatoires de rhétorique, *thèse Montpellier, 1999.*

*At the beginning of chapter 1 Nicolaus indicates that his discussion
of progymnasmata is primarily based on earlier accounts, and he often
cites the views of unnamed predecessors. Verbal echoes suggest that he
may have known the works attributed to Theon and to Hermogenes,
but, perhaps surprisingly, he seems not to have used Aphthonius's work,
at least not directly. Although there are some similarities to statements
found in the* Art of Rhetoric *attributed to Anonymous Seguerianus,
Felten's belief (pp. xxxii–xxxiii) that these are derived from the
rhetorical handbook of Cornutus was based on his acceptance of the
mistaken views of Graeven that Anonymous Seguerianus is an epitome
of Cornutus' work. Anonymous Seguerianus is now thought to be an
abstract of doctrines of Alexander, son of Numenius, Neocles, and other
rhetoricians of the second century after Christ.[4] Nicolaus may have
drawn on these sources, on Anonymous Seguerianus' abstract, or on
later works that incorporated earlier teaching. Regrettably, it must be
admitted that when Nicolaus tries to explain something in his own
words, the result is often cumbersome and confusing.*

*In the portion of his work preserved in its original form Nicolaus'
method is to comment on why the exercise should be taken up in the
order indicated, how it is to be defined, how it differs from other exercises, what are the different kinds and headings into which the exercise
is divided, for what species and parts of an oration the exercise provides
training, and whether the exercise is to be regarded only as a part of
some larger rhetorical composition or whether it can in itself constitute*

[4] Cf. Dilts and Kennedy, pp. x–xv.

a whole. These last two topics, largely ignored in other handbooks, are of special interest to him.

A collection of examples of progymnasmata attributed to Nicolaus can be found in Walz, Rhetores Graeci, vol. 1, pp. 266–420; some progymnasmata preserved as works by Libanius have also been attributed to Nicolaus; cf. Hock and O'Neil, The Chreia, vol. 2, pp. 125–26 and 198–233.

1. PREFACE

[p. 1 Felten] I have not undertaken this book, my dear boys, with the intention of writing an art of rhetoric for you—so many have compiled "Arts" that there is, so to speak, nothing left to say—; but wishing to prepare you to meet the larger treatises as well, drawing on various sources I have collected everything into this one book that I perceived as necessary for those needing an introduction. Thus, you should not be surprised if you find each exercise discussed elsewhere, even as is likely in the same language, nor should you look down on what is here if some things are found in other books also; for those of you who can learn what is here will be able to understand more difficult things as well.

Now the first thing to be considered is why we begin with progymnasmata. We shall say in reply that rhetoric was by nature always present among men but was hard to grasp and did not provide its own easy use; thus it was not evident to all. [2] Each individual, taking up some part of this art, handed it on to those who came after him and thus little by little it developed certain divisions and methods. Once these had been understood, the benefits from rhetoric already became clearer, but nevertheless young men found the subject difficult to manage; for it did not seem to be easy for those taking it up to see, straight off from the beginning, all that was contained in it. As a result, the use of progymnasmata came about; for in them we do not practice ourselves in the whole of rhetoric but in each part individually.

Now let us first learn what rhetoric is; for different teachers have defined rhetoric differently. Diodorus[5] defines it thus:

---

[5] The reading of the manuscript and scholia. Felten conjectured Theodorus on the basis of Quintilian 2.15.16, where however the correct name is Eudorus. Theodorus of Gadara's definition as quoted by Quintilian in 2.15.21 differs in important respects from what Nicolaus cites here. The Diodorus cited here cannot be identified; he may have been one of Nicolaus' teachers. His definition is close to that of Aristotle, *Rhetoric* 1.2.1: "the *dynamis* of discovering in each case the available means of persuasion."

"Rhetoric is a *dynamis*[6] of invention and expression, with orna-ment, of the available means of persuasion in every discourse." What is a *dynamis*? A neutral thing which can be used well or badly, like wealth, strength, and a cutting blade; for one might use these things both for good ends and for the opposite. Well then, he called rhetoric a *dynamis* since one might use it both for good purposes and for those not good. He called it inventive and expressive [3] since it is the function (*ergon*) of the rhetor in every proposed prob-lem to think of what must be said and to arrange these things and to express them in the best way. The phrase "the available means of persuasion in every discourse" is added because of the end (*telos*) of rhetoric, since its end is to speak persuasively in accord which what is available. Thus the definition "a *dynamis* of invention and ex-pression, with ornament, of the available means of persuasion in every discourse." Its function is in every proposed problem to think of what must be said and to arrange these things and express them in the best way. Its end is not to persuade in every case, but to speak persuasively in accord with what is available. This is why Gorgias defined it as "the worker of persuasion."[7] It is called "rhetoric" ei-ther from speech being "flowing" (*rhydên*) or from the rhetor's speaking in support of the law; for law in the Doric dialect is *rhêtra*.[8]

Rhetoric, at the most general level, is divided into three species: judicial (*dikanikon*), deliberative (*symbouleutikon*), panegyrical (*panêgyrikon*). Each of these is characterized by the persons pre-sumed to be present; for the hearers have been collected either to render judgment or to deliberate or to celebrate a festival. [4] Everything in accusation and defense is specific to judicial rhetoric, and its end is the just; exhortation and dissuasion belongs to delib-erative, and its end is the advantageous; of panegyric, also (called) epideictic, the forms are the encomiastic and invective, and its ob-jective is the honorable.

There are five parts of a speech: prooemion, narration, antithe-sis, solution, and epilogue. Prooemion is language preparing the hearer and making him well disposed toward the proposed speech; the function (*ergon*) and end (*telos*) of the prooemion—for some have wanted it to be the same thing[9]—is to create attention and re-

---

[6] I.e., a faculty or power.

[7] Cf. Plato, *Gorgias* 453a.

[8] The root *rhê/rha* refers to speech and is found also in Greek *erô* and Latin *orator*. A *rhêtra* is a decree.

[9] This is, e.g., the *telos* in the definition of Anonymous Seguerianus (§9), the *ergon* in a definition attributed to Cassius Longinus; cf. Spengel-Hammer, p. 208,8.

ceptivity and good will. Narration (*diêgêsis*) is an exposition of the facts in the hypothesis favorable to the speaker's side of the case or in the best interest of the speaker; and this is said because there is a narration only of matters in doubt in the law courts;[10] or it is defined as an exposition of things that have happened or as though they had happened. Its function and end is to provide the hearer with an account and clarification of the action. Antithesis (*antithesis*) **[5]** is an objection from the opposing person, rebutting credibility in us and misdirecting the hearer to a more specious thought.[11] Solution (*lysis*) is the removal of harm done by the objection and the returning of the hearer to the original proposition, persuading him to come to agreement about the question at hand. Epilogue (*epilogos*) is language introduced after the demonstrations have been given, providing a summary of subjects and characters and emotions. Its function, Plato says (*Phaedrus* 267d), is, at the end (of a speech), to remind the listeners of what has been said.

We have made this division of the subject to clarify the advantage coming from progymnasmata. Some of them practice us for judicial speech, some for deliberative, and some for the third, the panegyrical. Looked at in another way, some of the progymnasmata teach the use of prooemia, some of narrations, others of arguments in antitheses and solutions, and there are also some that practice use of epilogues.

We must speak about each in turn, and first about the fable. Just as by avoiding what is difficult in complete hypotheses[12] **[6]** those who arranged these things invented the use of progymnasmata, so they put the fable first among them as being naturally plain and simpler than the others and as having some relationship to poems. In their transition from poems to rhetoric, students should not all at once encounter things that are strange and unusual to them. Let us speak first, therefore, about fable.

2. ON FABLE

See Gangloff, "Mythes," pp. 36–38.

Fable (*mythos*), then, is false speech, imaging truth by being persuasively composed. The speech is false since it is admittedly made up of falsehoods, but it images the truth since it would not accomplish its purpose if it did not have some similarity to the truth.

---

[10] Elsewhere there is *diêgêma*; cf. below, ch. 3.
[11] Cf. the use of antithesis and solution in Aphthonius' exercises on thesis and law.
[12] I.e., in declamation on judicial and deliberative themes.

It becomes like truth from the credibility of the invention. It is called *mythos* from *mytheisthai,* that is, "to speak," not because we do not speak in the other exercises but because in it we first learn how to speak in public. Some have called it *ainos* from the advice (*parainesis*) it gives.[13]

Let some fables be called Aesopic, some Sybaritic, some Lydian, some Phrygian, [7] getting these epithets from certain places or persons. In Sybaritic fables the characters are limited to rational animals, in Aesopic there is a combination of irrational and rational, and Lydian and Phrygian fables use only the irrational.[14] There are also some fables making use of gods—an example is "Hera's Home-life with Zeus"—but I think these are more appropriate for philosophical study, where it is possible to understand the allegorical meanings in them.[15] You should know that some people call fables about the gods "mythical narratives" rather than *mythoi,* including them with discourses about metamorphoses and similar works. Whichever they are called, philosophers are the ones to explicate the allegories in them. For our part, we shall concern ourselves with what is credible or incredible in public speaking.

Since it has been said that a fable should be composed so as to be credible, we should consider how it may become credible. Many things can contribute to this: mention of places where the creatures imagined in the fable are accustomed to pass their time; from the occasions on which they are wont to show themselves; from words that harmonize with the nature of each; from actions which do not surpass the kind of thing each does—so we do not say that a mouse gave advice about the kingdom of the animals [8] or that a lion was captured by the savor of cheese—and if there is need to attribute some words to them, if we make the fox speak subtle things and the sheep naive and simple-minded things; for such is the nature of each; and so that the eagle is introduced as rapacious for fawns and lambs, and the jackdaw does not so much as think of anything like that. If there should ever be need to invent something contrary to nature, one should set the scene for this first and should connect the moral of the fable with it; for example, if the sheep were being described as having a friendly talk with the wolves, first you should set the scene for this friendship and anything else of that sort.

[13] Cf. Theon, above, p. 24.

[14] A view rejected by Theon, above, p. 24, and ignored by other writers.

[15] Possibly the fable had some connection with the sacred marriage ritual performed at the Daedala; cf. Plutarch, *Roman Questions* 29.

We have said that some progymnasmata are deliberative, some judicial, and some panegyrical. Now fable clearly belongs to the deliberative kind; for we are exhorting to good deeds or dissuading from errors. But to some[16] fable has already seemed useful in practice of all three species of rhetoric. "In so far as we are exhorting or dissuading," they say, "the special feature of deliberation is preserved, but when we make an onslaught on crimes, the judicial part is being kept, and when we use the plain style and develop our theme with simplicity **[9]** while at the same time including an element of praise, we are not far from the panegyrical genre. Furthermore," they say, "it is customary to include *mythoi* among panegyrical hypotheses."[17] Those thinking in this way have assigned fable first place among the exercises, "since it practices us," they say, "in the three parts of rhetoric." But that it clearly belongs to the deliberative part, no one should doubt; for in addition to its power of enchantment,[18] it benefits those who are persuaded, dissuading them from bad things, advising them to desire good things, and together with its sweetness accustoming them to take advantage of its benefit.

Practice in fable would also contribute—there being five parts of a speech—to instruction in composing the narration; for in forming the fable we learn how one should narrate what is happening.

An *epimythion* is language added to the fable **[10]**, making clear its moral. This is done in three ways: either paradigmatically or enthymematically or prosphonetically.[19] Paradigmatically, for example: "This fable teaches us to do or not to do some particular thing"; enthymematically, when we say, "One not doing this particular thing deserves criticism." And prosphonetically, for example: "And you, my boy, keep away from this or that." Some put the moral at the beginning and call it a *promythion;* others, prescribing a more sensible and consequential organization, have thought it necessary always to attach the moral to the end of the fable, saying, "If, because the young do not enjoy accepting advice that is explicitly stated, we invented the fable in order that by being persuaded and beguiled by the pleasantry of it they may promptly accept advice offered in this way, how is it not necessary to put at the end of the

---

[16] Their identity is unknown.

[17] Isocrates' *Busiris* might be taken as an early example. *Mythos*, of course, includes myths generally, as well as fables.

[18] *Psychagôgia,* "leading the soul"; cf. Plato, *Phaedrus* 261a.

[19] I.e., offering the fable as an example, or drawing a conclusion from it, or addressing advice to someone.

fable the moral drawn from it? **[11]** Since, if they would accept the advice otherwise, the use of a fable is unnecessary."

The language should be rather simple and not contrived and should be devoid of all forcefulness and periodic expression, so that the advice is clear and what is said (by the speakers in the fable) does not seem more elevated than their supposed character, especially when the fable consists of actions and speeches by irrational animals. As a general rule, one should employ language that is rather simple and deviates little from that used in ordinary conversation.

3. ON NARRATIVE

After fable should come narrative (*diêgêma*), as being more argumentative than fable but simpler than all the other exercises. Narrative, as stated a little earlier,[20] is an exposition of things that have happened or as though they had happened. Some have said that narrative (*diêgêma*) differs from narration (*diêgêsis*) in that, they say, "narration is the exposition of the matters under debate in the lawcourts in a way advantageous to the speaker, while narrative is the report of historical and past happenings." Others have called **[12]** narration the exposition of true events and narrative that of things as though they happened. The majority, however, say that narrative concerns a single event, narration a combination of many actions; the difference is the same as that between *poiêsis* and *poiêma:* Homer's subject as a whole is *poiêsis,* but the part about the wrath of Achilles or some similar part is a *poiêma.*[21]

There are three kinds of narrative, differing from each other. Some is descriptive, some dramatic, some mixed. Descriptive is everything that is said by one person alone narrating everything, as found in Pindar's poems; dramatic is everything that is said by the supposed characters rather than by the author, as in comic and tragic drama; mixed is made up of both forms, as are the works of Homer and Herodotus and any others like them, in some passages being stated by the author, in others by different characters.[22] Furthermore, some narratives are mythical, some historical, some pragmatic, which they also call judicial, and some fictive. Mythical are those not worthy of unquestioned belief and having a suspicion of falsehood, like stories about the Cyclopses and Centaurs; historical narratives are concerned with ancient events that are admitted

[20] Cf. above, p. 133, where the term used is *diêgêsis.*
[21] Cf. above, pp. 75 (Hermogenes) and 96 (Aphthonius).
[22] Cf. Plato, *Republic* 3.393a–394b.

to have happened; **[13]** for example, the events concerning Epidamnus (as described by Thucydides); pragmatic or judicial are things said in public debates; and fictive are narratives in comedies and all those in other dramas.[23] Mythical narratives share with fables the need to be persuasive, but they differ because fables are agreed to be false and fictional, while mythical narratives differ from others in being told as though they had happened and being capable of having happened or not having happened. Further, fictive narratives share with fables the fact that both have been made up, but they differ from each other in that fictive narratives, even if they did not happen, could happen in nature, while fables neither happened nor could happen naturally.

The elements of a narration (*diêgêsis*) are six; person, action, place, time, cause, manner. Person is, for example, the one doing something, the person of Demosthenes or of Meidias; action is what is being accomplished, for example, an insult; place is where it took place; for example, in the theater; time is when, for example during a festival; cause is the reason, for example, hatred; manner is how it is done, for example, by words or by fists. There are some who add a seventh element, the material, separating **[14]** it from the manner and attributing acting illegally and violently to manner and to material the use of a sword, perhaps, or a stone or a spear or something else like that.

The virtues of a narration, according to some, are five: brevity, clarity, persuasiveness, charm, grandeur,[24] but according to others only persuasiveness; for they thought that the other four were common to all speech. However, in the opinion of the more exact writers[25] there are only three virtues: clarity, brevity, persuasiveness. It must be recognized that it is very difficult for those giving attention to brevity also to give due care to clarity; for often we either make the language unclear for the sake of brevity or for clarity's sake we have to speak at length. It is necessary, then, to be on the lookout whether the brevity is proportional, neither leaving out anything necessary nor including more than is needed; for then it will be a virtue of speech, but if something useful seems omitted, brevity

---

[23] Events narrated in tragedies can be historical, as in Aeschylus' *Persians,* or regarded as historical, as in plays about the Trojan war.

[24] The text continues "and the use of correct Greek words (*hellenismos*)," which Felten bracketed, but cf. Aphthonius, above, p. 97. The commentary by Maximus Planudes (Walz, p. 14,22ff.) says "some have added pleasantry and grandeur instead of the use of *hellenismos.*"

[25] Cf. Theon, above, p. 29, and n. 107 thereon.

will be classed among the faults. How brevity might be created and how persuasiveness is added to speech is a bigger task for a would-be instructor than [15] can be taught in an introduction. However, when one is forced to consider clarity and brevity together, whoever is going to make the best judgment will use both if they can go together, but if not, he will use the more pressing, and this is apt to be clarity; for a speech will not be harmed so much from length as from obscurity. Among many other things, use of the nominative case will contribute to clarity in narratives; for it makes the language easy to understand by continual pauses, which is not easily done in the oblique cases.[26]

Narrative practices us equally in all parts of rhetoric: I mean in deliberative, judicial, and panegyrical speech; for we need narrative in all of these. Furthermore, in as much as a political speech is divided into five parts, narrative is, on the one hand, one of the five, but often we also use it in the arguments and especially in proofs based on example, and even in epilogues, [16] whenever we are reminding the audience of what has been said. Thus we practice it in different ways; for example, in direct discourse, in indirect discourse, in the form of a question, in comparison, and asyndetically.[27] In direct discourse, for example, "Phaethon was child of the Sun," and so forth; this is called "direct" because of use of the nominative case. In indirect discourse, which is so called from use of oblique cases: for example, "There is story that Phaethon,[28] child of the Sun. . . ." In the form of a question, when we speak as though asking something: "What then? Was not this and that the case about Phaethon?" In a comparison, whenever we say that "instead of being self-controlled, he loved strange things, and instead of controlling his love, he mounted the chariot," and so on. And asyndetically, whenever we proceed to say, "Phaethon longed to mount the chariot; he persuaded his father; he took the reins." Since the exposition takes different forms in this way, we shall use direct discourse for the sake of clarity in historical accounts or where we need clarity, and indirect discourse and questions in the arguments and the refutations,[29] and asyndeton in epilogues, and the comparative form where occasion allows; [17] for there are

---

[26] I.e., a succession of simple sentences, or simple clauses joined by connectives, will be easier to follow than sentences with relative clauses or genitives absolute.

[27] Cf. Theon, above, pp. 35–38; Hermogenes, above, p. 76.

[28] Accusative case in Greek, with an infinitive to follow.

[29] Cf. Hermogenes, above, p. 76.

many places in all species of rhetoric and parts of a speech where we need this treatment.

Some progymnasmata are parts, some are wholes and parts; those are parts that are always found as parts of other hypotheses; those are parts and wholes that are sometimes worked in as parts of something else, sometimes themselves make up a whole theme. Now narrative is only found as parts of something; for it always fills the use of a part and never is sufficient for a whole theme in political speaking, unless one would say, and say quite wrongly, in the case of ecphrases, which are, so to speak, parts of narratives, as will be said in the chapter on ecphrasis.

4. ON CHREIA[30]

After narrative should come the chreia; for this would be the best sequence. There are some who assign it before both fable and narrative and say that it should be put first since it shows the way to good and avoidance of evil. "The young," they say, "should be taught about these things first."[31] To which the following response should be given. It is not unreasonable to assign it a place after the fable and the narrative, because it requires the use of more logical divisions. **[18]** Those others who made it the first exercise have not accorded it the same divisions as is done now, but thought recitation (of a chreia) in all cases and numbers was alone enough for young men who were just proceeding from the study of the poets and coming to the study of rhetoric to practice declamation of political speech, and they used it in this way; for example, Pittacus of Mitylene, having been asked if anyone escapes notice of the gods when doing wrong, said "Not even when thinking of it." First, the students recited it in the nominative case and then in the other cases; for example, in the genitive: The statement of Pittacus of Mitylene is remembered, having been asked if anyone escapes notice of the gods when doing wrong: "Not even when thinking of it." In the dative: To Pittacus of Mitylene, having been asked if anyone escapes notice of the gods when doing wrong, it occurred to say, "Not even when thinking of it." In the accusative: They say Pittacus the Mitylenean, having been asked if any one escapes notice of the gods

---

[30] For a translation and discussion of this chapter, see Hock and O'Neil, vol. 1, pp. 237–69.

[31] Theon alone of writers of extant progymnasmatic works put the chreia first; the reason he gives (above, p. 8) is that it is short and easily remembered. His account includes grammatical inflection along the lines mentioned here. The source of Nicolaus' quotation is unknown.

when doing wrong, to have said: "Not even when thinking of it."
The vocative case is clear from its name; for we address the statement to the one who said it: You, O Pittacus the Mitylenean, having been asked if any one escapes notice of the gods when doing
wrong, said: "Not even when thinking of it." And similarly in the
dual and plural number, if it is possible for the sake of practice perhaps to attribute the statement to two or more Pittacuses. [19] But
now one should not assign the chreia first, for the following reason:
so long as it was not divided into headings, students were able to be
exercised well in the use of language by declension through the
cases, but now since it is divided in headings, it would be well to assign it a place after narrative.[32]

A chreia is a pointed and concise saying or action, attributed to
some specific person, reported for the correction of some things in
life. It is a "saying or action" since it is found both in words and in
deeds. It is "pointed" since the strength of the chreia lies in its
being well aimed. It is "concise" as distinguished from reminiscences. It is attributed to some person to distinguish it from a
maxim, for a maxim is not always attributed to a person. It is reported for the correction of some things in life, since for the most
part some good advice is involved. The differences (between the
chreia and the maxim) will be discussed in the chapter on maxim.

[20] It is called chreia ("something useful"), not that the other
progymnasmata do not fulfill some use, but either because it has
been especially honored with this common name as characteristic,
in the way that Homer is called "the poet" and Demosthenes "the
orator," or because originally someone made use of it primarily
from some circumstance and need.

At the most general level, there are three kinds of chreias: some
of them are verbal, some actional, some mixed. "The most general
level" is added because chreias have many differences from each
other, as must be learned from fuller study of the art or its material.
Verbal are those describing only sayings; for example, "Isocrates
said that the root of education is bitter but the fruits are sweet." Actional are those describing only actions; for example, "When Diogenes saw a disorderly youth in the marketplace, he beat his pedagogue with his staff." Mixed describe both sayings and actions; for

[32] Nicolaus' statement could apply to Theon's account of the chreia in that the
latter did not identify headings for its elaboration. The change of the chreia from
a grammatical to a logical exercise may relate to increased teaching of the simpler
progymnasmata by rhetoricians rather than by grammarians.

example, "When a Laconian was asked where the walls of Sparta were, holding up his spear, he said, 'There.'"

[21]   They say, also, that some chreias are transmitted because of some utility and some only because of their charm. An example of a useful one is, "Isocrates said that the root of education is bitter but the fruit is sweet." It refers to the need to endure difficulties for the pleasure that follows them. An example of a charming one is, "When Olympias, the mother of Alexander, heard that her child was claiming to be the son of Zeus, she said, 'When will the boy stop slandering me to Hera?'" It seems to be a pleasantry. And again, "Damon the trainer, they say, had twisted feet and when he lost his shoes at the baths he expressed the hope that they would fit the feet of the thief." This seems to be only a pleasantry. Yet to me, together with the pleasantry they seem to contain good advice: one dissuades a child from calling himself the son of Zeus, and the other teaches us to avoid theft as a most unacceptable thing. As a result, one should not trust those who refute chreias; for there are some who refute them and fables as well. To these people one should say that they ought not [22] to refute acknowledged good things because no one will believe them, nor acknowledged falsehoods because their falsehood is evident. Thus one should not refute either fables or chreia. No sensible person is unaware that the fables are fictional, nor will anyone be persuaded by somebody deflecting the good advice in the chreia, and surely the good in the fables themselves, which we look to when forming fables, does not allow those speaking against them to seem to be credible.[33]

Some chreias make clear how things are, some how things should be. The following says how they are: "Aesop the fablist, having been asked what is the strongest thing in human society, said 'Speech,'" for this is the strongest thing. The following says how things should be: "Aristeides,[34] having been asked what is justice, said, 'Not to covet what belongs to others,'" for that ought to be the case. To know this helps us with our division; for if the chreia makes clear how things are, after the prooemion and paraphrase we praise it as being true; but if how things should be, we praise it as being right. Furthermore, some chreias are simple, some responsive. [23] Simple, for example, "Isocrates said that the root of edu-

---

[33] In the second paragraph below Nicolaus seems to recommend refutation of chreias on the part of more advanced students as practice for judicial declamation. Inconsistencies in his text often result from his following a variety of sources.

[34] Aristeides "the Just," fifth-century B.C. Athenian statesman.

cation is bitter but the fruits are sweet"; responsive are those in answer to a question; for example, "When Plato was asked where the Muses dwell, he said, 'In the souls of the educated.'"

Since some progymnasmata are parts and some are both parts and wholes, the chreia would belong to those that are parts; for alone by itself it will not make up a complete hypothesis. Further, since some progymnasmata contribute to practice on judicial themes, some to that of panegyric, and some to that of deliberative speaking, the chreia clearly would be of the deliberative sort; for it always either exhorts to some good or hinders from some evil. But it would also contribute to the others; for in those where we are praising something, we are taking thought about composing encomia, and in those where we are refuting the probability and the applicability of the examples, we are concerned with judicial rhetoric. Further, there being five parts to a political speech—that is, prooemion, narration, antithesis, solution, and epilogue—, chreia provides practice in all; for we begin with a prooemion, then we praise the speaker or doer, and we narrate in turn; then we give a paraphrase of the chreia, and we argue, even if we do not [24] include an antithesis; then we show that it has been well spoken or done, and we end with an epilogue in which we advise emulating what is said.

A chreia is divided into the following headings, beginning with brief praise of the speaker, not extended in length nor using all the encomiastic headings, lest the prooemion become longer than the body of the composition. The first heading, then, is this praise of the speaker or doer; then, after it, paraphrase of the chreia, to which we add a statement of its probability and truth, then supporting examples, and finally the judgment of others, after which, if there be need, we proceed to a brief exhortation. You should know, however, that after probability some put comparison, which is part of probability, occurring in it in the form of an enthymeme. For some demonstrations are enthymematic, some paradeigmatic, and in argument from probability we use the enthymematic, in argument from example the paradeigmatic. So much for a short progymnasma; as to how one should use demonstrations, that we shall learn in discussing more complete hypotheses. These, however, are things a teacher needs to show in the course of his division.

[25]   5. ON MAXIM

Maxim (*gnômê*) is a general statement, giving some counsel and advice for something useful in life. Although it shares the same divisions as the chreia, it differs in that the chreia consists of both words and deeds, the maxim of words alone; also in that a maxim is a general statement and not usually attributed to some person, while a chreia is always attributed to a person. In addition, a chreia includes reference to some circumstance, while a maxim consists in a number of words, for while furnishing an enthymematic demonstration of the subject, at the same time it provides general advice. Finally, they differ because a maxim always teaches either the choice of a good or avoidance of an evil, while a chreia is also cited for the sake of its charm alone. One might discover several other differences as well.

Since [26] a reminiscence (*apomnêmoneuma*) shares advice-giving with the chreia and the maxim, it is necessary to explain its differences from them. It differs from the maxim in almost all the ways the chreia does, and from the chreia in the length of its statement; for a chreia is expressed in few words, while a reminiscence uses more. Xenophon is a witness of this in his work called *Memorabilia*.

Maxims also differ from each other. Some maxims are true, some credible; true when we say, (for example,) (*Iliad* 2.24–25): "A councilor should not sleep all through the night, / A man to whom the people are entrusted and who cares for many things." For it is not appropriate for the leader of many to sleep all through the night. The following, for example, is credible: "Whatever man enjoys being with the wicked," is himself like them; "I never asked, since I know that he is such as those with whom he likes to be."[35] This is credible because it happens that even a good man may be misled by associating with the wicked. Further, some maxims are simple, some double. This, for example, is simple: "It is not possible for anyone to find a life without suffering."[36] [27] And this, for example, is double (Theognis, 35–36): "You will be taught good things from good men; but if you mingle / With the bad, you will lose the wit you have." Again, some maxims are stated without a reason, some have a reason added: without a reason, for example, "The master of the house is the one real slave";[37] with a reason, for example, (*Odyssey* 1.302) "Be brave, that one who comes hereafter may speak well of you"; for the reason to turn to bravery is added.

---

[35] Euripides, *Phoenician Women*, frag. 812, ed. Nauck. Quoted better in Hermogenes, above p. 78.

[36] Menander, frag. 411, ed. Kock.

[37] From some now lost comedy.

Again, some maxims make clear how things are, as do chreias, and others how things should be: how things are, for example, "Most men are bad"; how things should be, for example, "Nothing too much." They add some other divisions among maxims, some calling these "species," some "differences" from each other, saying, for example, that some maxims are commands, as that "Be brave," some wishes, as the one that says (Euripides, *Medea* 598), "May a prosperous life not become a source of woe to me." Some are prohibitory, for example, (*Iliad* 7.111) "Do not wish to fight in rivalry with a better man than you"; some determinative, for example, (*Odyssey* 17.218) **[28]** "Since god always leads the like to the like." In addition, they say that some maxims are ignoble, as for example, "Let me be called bad for making a profit";[38] some are noble, as (*Iliad* 12.243), "One omen is best, to fight for one's country."

The school of Siricius[39] adds these distinctions and others add many more, but these should be evaluated on another occasion; now it is enough to say about them only that of the five parts of a speech—prooemion, narration, antithesis, solution, epilogue—and of the three parts of rhetoric—panegryical, judicial, deliberative—maxim gives practice in the same things as does chreia. Since these were separately explained above, there is no need here to repeat the same words. And of course the division of headings is the same.

And since some progymnasmata are parts, some parts and wholes, maxim would be one of the parts; for by itself, without other material, it does not constitute a complete hypothesis, unless someone thought it enough, by denial alone, to reply to a whole speech: "Do not wish to fight in rivalry with a better man than you" (*Iliad* 7.111).[40] **[29]** More rightly it should be thought one of the parts, as is the chreia as well. It has often been said, and by all writers of "Arts," that the maxim is divided into the same headings as is the chreia. We mentioned this also in remarks about the chreia.

6. ON REFUTATION AND CONFIRMATION

After maxim there should come refutation (*anaskeuê*) and confirmation (*kataskeuê*); for once we have been practiced by the chreia

[38] From some now lost tragedy.

[39] Siricius was a sophist of the early 4th cent. C.E., according to the *Suda* author of progymnasmata and declamations.

[40] This is only one line in a longer speech. A better example might be the maxim, "A bad crow from a bad egg," attributed to the judges in the legendary trial of Corax and Tisias; cf., e.g., *Prolegomenon Sylloge*, ed. Rabe, p. 27; it is also told of Protagoras and Euathlus; cf. Diogenes Laertius 9.8.25.

and the maxim in paradeigmatic and enthymematic demonstrations, these teach us in greater detail how to engage in debate in reply to antitheses, so that in complete hypotheses we shall be able to offer a solution to the objections of the opponents and easily confirm what seems to us to be best.

Now refutation is a statement in rebuttal of something that has been credibly stated and confirmation is the opposite, a statement offering confirmation of something that has been credibly stated. The term "credibly" is added in both cases in order that we may know not to refute acknowledged truths or acknowledged falsehoods but statements open to credible argument on either side of a question; for by (attempted) refutation of acknowledged truths [30] we shall not seem truthful—for no one will pay attention—nor by refuting falsehoods either—for no one needs to be persuaded—, and conversely in the case of confirmation, we do not confirm acknowledged truths; for everybody is already persuaded of them—nor acknowledged falsehoods—; for no one will tolerate it. Thus, practice in such composition should be directed to what is credible.

You should know that the order of these exercises is indifferent; for after refutation we do not always then confirm nor shall we definitely do the opposite, but, without fear, we can use whichever of them we want first.

They say that these exercises are divided into the following headings: incredible, impossible, inappropriate, inexpedient, inconsistent, and further headings derived from circumstantial factors: place, time, person, or anything else like that. You should know that some have tried to require a definite order in the treatment of these headings, saying that incredibility should be put first, then one should go on to the impossible, then the inexpedient, then [31] the inconsistent. Others, again, used what they regarded as the right order for a different set of divisions. We say, however, that all the headings do not apply to all refutations and confirmations, nor is there one definite order, but these are the headings from which we refute and confirm, and a student doing the exercises carefully and considering how many and what sort of headings to use should be himself in control of the order, or rather follow the order of the discourse to be refuted. For example, we are assigned to refute the story of Daphne,[41] thus to refute a narrative. Here we shall look at the first part[42] of the narrative to see whether it is impossible or in-

[41] Cf. the treatment by Aphthonius, above, pp. 101–3.
[42] Nicolaus has in mind a statement by statement analysis and refutation.

credible, and thus we shall use the elaboration of that heading. Then we shall do the same with the second and third part of the narrative, and continue through all of it similarly. In this way, the speech will not be thrown into confusion, since if we are forced to cut up the narrative in terms of the order of the headings, rather than taking up the headings in accord with the order of the narrative, confusion will necessarily result; for we are then probably talking about the first incidents last and the last first. Thus, as I said, we should follow the order of the subject before us, as we find Demosthenes did [32] in his speech *Against Timocrates* and elsewhere. For attacking the law of Timocrates as inexpedient and taking this up first, after scrutiny of the law, starting over again from the beginning, he sets out in turn other seeming inexpediencies and carries on the debate.

In addition to this, you should know that nothing will prevent you from considering one part of the narrative under several headings; for example, perhaps under the inexpedient and the incredible and some other one. And we shall use the same heading in all parts and contrive variety by difference in the elaboration. The most contentious heading, and the one most useful to us, is what is called "inconsistency" (*makhomenon*), where we show that the opponent is speaking in contradiction of himself and in opposition to his own proposition. Demosthenes is a witness for this in the same speech; after scrutiny of other laws to which that of Timocrates was opposed, he reads a law previously introduced by this same Timocrates and shows that the present law is opposed to it. [33] The inconsistency of the circumstances will often assist in making the discourse refutable; for example, in what places was Daphne? or at what times?, or if something else like this occurs.

Furthermore, you should realize that some argue by setting out part by part and others fight against the (opponent's) speech as a whole. To me, part by part conflict seems rather better; for in that way the discourse becomes more contentious. But nothing prevents us, having narrated the whole case after the prooemion, from taking this up again then part by part; for the result of this will be that the scrutiny becomes clearer.

We shall use the same headings also in confirmation, drawing them from the opposite arguments.

Since there are, as many believe, three parts of rhetoric, practice in these progymnasmata is mostly concerned with the judicial; for the topic of the advantageous (*sympheron*), which is characteristic of deliberative rhetoric, is not scrutinized here in the first instance but is brought in as connected with other demonstrations. And you will find that there is practice here of all five parts of a speech, except for epilogues; for there will be exercise of the concepts of prooemia and of narrations [34] and antitheses and solutions. Common-place, about which we shall speak next, fits in with the teaching of epilogues.

We have repeatedly said that some progymnasmata are parts, some both parts and wholes. Refutation and confirmation are among those occurring only as parts, although I realize that some people think it is possible for these progymnasmata also, by themselves, to make up an hypothesis. As an indication of this they mention Aristeides' speech *On the Four*,[43] which they regard as a refutation. Those who claim this are clearly ignorant of the distinct species of rhetoric called a "reply-speech" (*antirrhêsis*)[44] and think a reply-speech is a refutation. Refutation and confirmation should be regarded as among those exercises only occurring as parts and never able, by themselves, to make up an hypothesis, even if they seem to constitute almost all the parts of a speech. Those who confuse a refutation with a reply-speech are being illogical, on the one hand discussing everything, but on the other not identifying the differences and failing to see what their analysis leaves out in terms of the whole speech and what is characteristic of a reply-speech.

In these progymnasmata one should [35] use prooemia that are more contentious than those for chreias and maxims; for as we move ahead to greater things from lesser things[45] we need to take proportionally more care about each of the exercises discussed.

7. ON COMMON-PLACE

Some put common-place after ecphrasis, others before refutation and confirmation, still others elsewhere, but those assigning it the best place in the sequence place it after refutation and confirmation. And rightly so, because if the progymnasmata were invented in the first place in order that by being practiced in them first we may then undertake complete speeches, and if, all in all, each of the exercises

---

[43] Cf. above, p. 84, n. 43. For the debate, see the scholia on Aristeides vol. 3, p. 437 ed. Dindorf, and Sopatros' prolegomena.

[44] An unusual concept; the closest parallels are perhaps in Philodemus; cf. *Rhetorica* 1. p. 284, ed. Sudhaus, and *De Signis* 7 and 11, ed. Gomperz.

[45] I.e., from the simpler, relatively non-argumentative exercises, to more difficult ones involving argument.

seems to provide practice in a suitable way for one of the parts of a speech, if we are imitating the succession and order in speeches it is necessary to put common-place right after refutation and confirmation. For since there are five parts of a speech—prooemia, narrations, antitheses, solutions, epilogues—, among which epilogues are the final part, after [36] being exercised in the other forms through what has been said already, and especially after being taught how one should use arguments and how to fight against what seem to be strong objections, which was what we were doing in refutation and confirmation, we quite rightly should take up the progymnasma exercising us for epilogues, which is the common-place. Chreia and maxim taught how one should work up prooemia; how we should make use of narrations we learned in the progymnasma called narrative, and, of course, also in refutation and confirmation we narrated the whole account against which we were contending before arguing our case point by point. Refutation and confirmation provided exercise in antitheses and solutions. Thus there is now left the epilogue, for which common-place fills the need.

Common-place (*koinos topos*) is an amplification and attack on an acknowledged evil; or as others define it, an amplification of an acknowledged evil or human goodness. First, we must explain why it is called "common-place." Now it is "common" because it is not directed against a specified person, for example, against Timarchus for prostitution or Lycophron for adultery, but simply against any prostitute or adulterer.[46] It is called *topos* because rhetorical arguments (*epikheirêmata*) are called *topos*, so it is a common epicheireme, [37] or because, as though setting out from some common spot, we easily compose attacks on specified kinds of persons.

We said that some have defined common-place as an amplification of an acknowledged evil or human goodness. Those saying this seemed to sensible writers of handbooks to be mistaken: "Amplification of acknowledged good things," they say, "should not be done in common-place, since (if we do that) we shall, without realizing it, in common-place be using encomion, which is the main thing in the panegyrical part of rhetoric. For what is an encomion other than an amplification of acknowledged good things?" To those saying this,[47] we must reply that what is said in common-place has to be

---

[46] Timarchus is known from the prosecution of him by Aeschines, Lycophron from the defense of him by Hypereides.

[47] I.e., those including amplification of good things in the progymnasma called common-place.

said on behalf of someone.[48] Shall we speak on behalf of those against whom we have just spoken, or on behalf of others? If on behalf of those against whom this is a prosecution—for example, against a murderer and (then) on behalf of a murderer—the subject is no longer something acknowledged; but if on behalf of others who have performed acknowledged good deeds, such a speech seems more to fit the definition of encomion. As a result, to have to speak on behalf of someone should not be identified as part of a common-place, which should entirely be a running attack on **[38]** an acknowledged and ascertained human evil, so that we shall be speaking as in a second speech."[49]

Others give the following definition: common-place is an amplification and running attack on some acknowledged evil action. These writers include under common-place everything deserving a prejudicial attack, failing to recognize that there are some things that should more rightly be classified as invective (*psogos*) rather than as common-place. These are things for which there is no one punishment defined by the laws; for example, against a drunkard or against one doing some completely bad thing and deserving blame but not in violation of any law that sets a penalty for the doer by way of prohibition. Against such a person one would not use common-place rather than invective, but, as the occasion might arise, against an adulterer and against a temple robber[50] and against others for whom penalties have been set by the laws. The main difference between common-place and invective is that in the case of common-place the judges are being urged to punish the wrongdoer, while in invective hearers are being incited to hatred of the individual against whom the attack is being made. They differ further in that in common-place the person attacked is not specified, but in invective he is named, since we are making an attack on a person rather than on a deed.

They say the following about the divisions of common-place: **[39]** "Some common-places we say are simple, some double; simple, for example, against a temple robber or against a traitor; dou-

[48] E.g., on behalf of someone prosecuting another for a crime.

[49] Originally, as seen in Theon's account (above, pp. 42–43), common-place was regarded as the amplification of a good or bad action or good or bad character type, but increasingly teachers focused on denunciation of an evil, as of practical utility to an orator, leaving praise to be taught in exercises in encomion. By a second speech Nicolaus is thinking of the second speech in a prosecution, largely devoted to denouncing the crime; cf. below, pp. 150 and 153.

[50] A traditional example, but desecration of pagan temples was probably no longer a crime after prohibition of pagan worship in A.D. 391.

ble against a temple-robbing priest or against a traitorous general."[51] But these writers are mistaken in thinking to make commonplaces double by the addition of the general or the priest; for example, if one were to speak against a murderous adulterer—which is possible—or a murderous thief or any other such thing in which there are two crimes, either one of which is subject to a separate judgment. A topos against a traitorous general or a temple-robbing priest should not be called double; for the addition of priest and general would, of course, furnish a larger supply of things to say in the denunciation—we shall have a different supply of things to say against one who is simply a traitor and against a traitorous general—but we would not end up with double topoi, since what would one say against a general if the word "treason" was dropped, or against one described only as a priest?

Since it has been said that common-place fulfills the need of an epilogue and that it should be elaborated as in a second speech, we should inquire whether in common-place we shall include a prooemion or go straight to the division of the subject. We say that one should use prooemial concepts (*prooimiakai ennoiai*), even though some orators went directly into the main subject; **[40]** for we find that others, including Demosthenes himself, after working out the whole hypothesis, often at the very point of starting the epilogues, have made use of something like prooemia to secure continued attention. All in all, the use of prooemia and of epilogue in Demosthenes' works is indistinguishable; for he uses prooemial concepts both in the beginning and the middle of speeches and even at the end, and he uses epilogues both in the middle and in the ending. If it is a second speech, and they dispense with prooemia for that reason, they have a good artistic reason; for the previous speech contained everything that had to be done in the way of prooemia, but nevertheless some prooemial concepts are necessary so that the speech may not seem to be acephalous.[52] It has been generally agreed that prooemia take the place of a "head," and Demosthenes seems to have used them in his second speeches; for example, in *Against Androtion* and in *Against Timocrates*. Even in his *Reply to Leptines* **[41]** he arranged a kind of prooemion, though brief.

If this is accepted, we must ask whether we shall use a single

[51] Cf. Theon, above, p. 43. The use of *topos* for common-place in this passage also recalls Theon.

[52] I.e., seemed to begin too abruptly, without a "head." Cf. Plato, *Phaedrus* 264c4.

prooemion in common-place or more than one.[53] We say that both
one and more than one are possible; for if common-place is taken
up for the sake of practice, there is nothing to prevent our exercising ourselves in one and in more. The extent of prooemia is not determined, but the speaker's needs will define it as more or less.
Some have gone as far as having five prooemia and the speech was
not harmed. Thus, as I was saying, we shall use numerous prooemial concepts in common-place. But if the virtue of a prooemion is
to fit the specific need of the hypothesis and for the same one not to
fit all hypotheses, in a common-place, where the person against
whom we are speaking is not specified, how could prooemia specific
to the subject be found? We say, in consequence, that in common-
place we should fit the prooemia to the nature of the subject instead
of to a specified person; for example, that it should fit a denunciation of every adulterer, if that is the subject, but not be the same as
is used against a traitor, or one for use against a traitor should not
be the same as one against a temple robber, and so on, so that each
seems suitable only for the subjects at hand. Thus they will have
their own qualities. Every prooemion, to speak of them compre-
hensively, is derived from the following four things: from the action
or from the opponent **[42]** or from the judges or from the speaker;
and this must be observed in every speech.

Different authorities make different divisions in common-place.
Some put first the action which is under judgment, others scrutinize the defendant's previous life, which they call "before the fact,"
and still others go directly to the comparisons. Yet those who make
good divisions do not approve any of these arrangements; for they
deny the need to put things preceding the action first—it would be
strange to look back at a way of life in the past before considering
life in the present—nor to put the action itself first—for the need
now is not one of teaching[54] but of sharpening disapproval; we are
not going to narrate what the audience has learned in the previous
speech, but we shall not turn to comparisons either without first
amplifying the present circumstance.

As a result, (the best authorities) put first, after the prooemia,
consideration of the opposite, which some call "praise of the thing
wronged." This heading is of the following sort: if we are speaking,
for example, against an adulterer, we shall praise self-control; if
against a tyrant, democracy and all the good things in it; if against

---

[53] On the concept of multiple prooemia, cf. above, p. 80, n. 27.
[54] I.e., not one of proving that an acknowledged evil deed has been committed.

a traitor, loyalty to the city; and in sum, we shall praise opposites in all cases. After having worked this up as needed, we shall go on to the deed, not narrating it but making it seem dreadful and showing that it is one of the worst possible things, [43] and right away we shall connect to it what is called "the network" (*periokhê*), in which we show how many other wrongs are implicated with the one under discussion; for example, that laws are being harmed, as are law-courts, councils, all the good institutions of the city together, and, in a word, we shall use *reductio ad absurdum*,[55] saying that from this one crime all the worst things result. At this point comparisons have their place, in which, above all, we take care to use homogeneous things.[56] Things are said to be homogeneous that have the same causes; for example, if we are speaking against a grave-robber, we shall work up a comparison with thieves, with temple-robbers, with all those daring to do such things for profit. The comparisons will be from the greater, from the lesser, or from the equal; we shall demonstrate that the action is equal to some greater thing and greater than some equal thing, and we shall cite the penalty assigned to a lesser crime, saying it would be absurd for someone to be held to account for a drachma and for this defendant to remain unpunished for robbing a temple. We should understand that comparisons will not always fall under these three topics nor in a definite order, but the person making the divisions will know which kind needs to be put first or second or third and which kind is relevant or which to omit.

After having worked out the comparisons we shall immediately use the headings called "before the fact." We shall take care here that [44] these are homogeneous. While conjecturing about what has been done earlier and saying that after these things the defendant did what he is now accused of, we ought to provide credibility to our words from examination of things like to those now being judged; for example, if, as it happens, against someone being tried for grave-robbing, we say that it is probable, after committing many earlier thefts, that he finally turned to this source of profit. This heading of "before the fact" is similar to what is named "a second-ary accusation" (*parakatêgorêma*)[57] in complete hypotheses, which we bring in here not primarily to judge the allegations but by men-

---

[55] *Eis atopon apagogê;* but that is a device of refutation. What Nicolaus has in mind is amplification of the implications of an illegal or immoral action by claiming that it undermines society as a whole.

[56] *Homoiogenê;* cf. Apsines 1.3ff. for another use of the concept.

[57] A term in Stoic philosophy, not found elsewhere in rhetorical texts.

tioning them to provide credibility to the present indictment. For example, Demosthenes, wishing to show that Meidias deliberately engaged in a wanton act against him when he was a choregus, reminded the jury of his former evil deeds and outrages against others, in order to strengthen the present charge from his past conduct. Thus, after attacking the defendant in the common-place on the basis of what he has done both now and in the past, we shall come to what are called the "final" headings; why they are called that we shall explain in due time,[58] but they are the advantageous, the just, the legal, the possible, the honorable, the necessary, and the easy, from among which we shall use those that apply. There is no need [45] to go through all of them and the advantageous will be the dominant topic.

After working out the headings we shall deny him the only remaining basis for safety. This is named "the rejection of pity," an appeal to pity being what defendants are accustomed to use after there is no hope they can be acquitted. Having stated and enlarged upon it as much as possible, we shall refute the defendant's appeal by means of whichever of the final headings we can use and through what is called hypotyposis. Hypotyposis is a heading bringing what has been done before the eyes and by description (*ekphrasis*) making us spectators of monstrous actions. In the case of this heading we must watch out that we do not, unwittingly, describe shameful deeds, which can result when we are making speeches against an adulterer or child abuser (*paidophthoros*). On such matters it is necessary to avoid detailed description, which will do more harm to us than to the defendant. If it is really necessary to go into such matters in detail, we shall avoid indiscretion by describing someone as a violent man who holds the laws in contempt and thus did not hesitate to do these monstrous acts. These are the headings into which common-place is divided.

In as much as some progymnasmata are parts and some [46] are both parts and wholes, common-place is sometimes among those exercises undertaken as parts and sometimes as wholes. It is possible for it to fill up the whole of an hypothesis, as we find in second speeches where, after previous speakers have completed a detailed prosecution together with proofs of the charges, second speakers use common-places, making an attack on those who have done wrong and exhorting the judges to vote condemnation. (Demosthenes') speech *Against Aristogeiton* is an indication of

---

[58] This promise is not fulfilled in the extant text.

this,[59] clearly being an epilogue; for nowhere are strong objections cited nor are there any contentious proofs, but everywhere a spirited attack.

It is characteristic of epilogues to adopt a forceful style and passionate complaints and generally to make the expression pathetic and to employ a rather pathetical delivery, all of which should be kept in common-place. For, as I said, it is an epilogue, even if it does not have all the features of an epilogue and differs in some ways. We shall learn on another occasion what the characteristics of an epilogue are and in what way it differs from common-place.[60]

Of the three parts of rhetoric, common-place provides practice in the judicial kind, as is clear to all who do not include in common-place speeches on behalf of heroes or tyrannicides or [47] those who have done something altogether good.[61] According to those who do include these things common-place also provides practice for panegyric.

8. ON ENCOMION AND INVECTIVE

The account of encomion is complicated, no longer limited to a single form (like descriptions of earlier exercises), and divided among many kinds. For speeches of arrival (*epibatêrioi*) and addresses to officials (*prosphônêtikoi*) and wedding speeches (*epithalamioi*) and funeral orations (*epitaphioi*), and, of course, also hymns to gods and every kind of speech of praise are listed under this species.[62] Here it is necessary only to say as much as is appropriate for beginners.

Since, generically speaking, there are three parts or species, or whatever one wants to call them, of rhetoric—deliberative and judicial and panegyrical—, the first thing that has been considered (by teachers) is why the third—I mean this panegyrical part, to which encomion belongs—has been put among the progymnasmata. For if each of the other progymnasmata was invented in order to exercise

[59] Although the reference seems to be to *Against Aristogeiton II* (Or. 26), Edwin Carawan suggests that *Against Aristogeiton I* (Or. 25) may be intended. It is probably a rhetorical exercise. Neither speech is now regarded as a genuine work by Demosthenes. On second speeches see John of Sardis, pp. 203–4 below.

[60] An epilogue would ordinarily summarize the proofs made earlier in the speech; this is not a feature of common-place.

[61] Nicolaus has explained why praise should not be included; cf. above, pp. 148–49.

[62] For these and other panegyrical genres, cf. *Menander Rhetor*, ed. D. A. Russell and N. G. Wilson, Oxford: Clarendon Press, 1981. Examples of them can be found among the speeches of Himerius, Libanius, and other sophists of late antiquity.

us for one of the complete hypotheses, why bring in this part, which is complete?[63] We say in reply what we have said earlier, that some progymnasmata **[48]** are parts, some parts and wholes. All those are parts which are practiced for the use of something else; those are parts and wholes which sometimes, by themselves, elaborate an hypothesis and sometimes constitute parts of other hypotheses. Encomion belongs with those that are parts and wholes. We are treating it as a whole whenever we use it to speak well of someone, and as a part whenever in the course of deliberative speaking we praise something or other that we are urging be done, or when prosecuting we both recommend the merit of our case and attack that of the opponent. An example of the former is Isocrates' *Panegyricus,* belonging to the deliberative species but constructed of encomiastic material; of the second, Demosthenes' *On the Crown* is an example; although belonging to the judicial species, it is all constructed by the orator as praise of himself and attack on Aeschines. Since, then, encomion is sometimes practiced as a part and sometimes as a whole, it has been included among progymnasmata.

Encomion (*enkômion*) is speaking well of some specified person or thing in a discursive way on the basis of acknowledged merits. **[49]** We say that speeches are "discursive" (*diexodoikos*) when they are extended in length and have explored all excellences. Encomion differs from praise (*epainos*) in that praise is constructed from few words—for example, mention of one good thing—whereas encomion is developed through an account of all the virtues and all the excellences of what is being praised.

The end of encomion is the honorable,[64] as justice is the end of judicial and the advantageous of deliberative speech. It is called encomion from the fact that people long ago used to make hymns to gods and speeches of praise of each other at a sort of village festival (*kômos*).

Each of its genres are distinct: I mean, for example, a wedding speech or an address to an official or a praise of Apollo (*sminthiakos*)

---

[63] The other exercises, at least for the most part, are regarded as preliminary training or parts for composing complete speeches in one of the three species; encomion, at first glance, seems to differ in being identical to a full panegyric. If so, should it not be taught in a more advanced stage of rhetorical studies? Nicolaus answers that encomion is also a part of other speeches and thus appropriately included among progymnasmata. Rhetorical schools tended to concentrate on judicial and deliberative declamation, leaving the progymnasma of encomion as important training for epideictic.

[64] *To kalon:* the good, fine, noble, honorable, beautiful, etc., depending on the nature of what is praised.

or any other speech at festivals, or a hymn to a god, and each of these genres has its own divisions, which is not part of elementary study. But in brief, it is necessary in the case of each of the hypotheses for its own heading to prevail; for example, in wedding speeches, praise of marriage, which is also called "arguing a thesis" (*thetikos*);[65] in a panathenaicus or any other speech of that sort, whatever relates to feasting, and in general, in each genre I mentioned, what provides the occasion for the hypothesis. Encomion, as we are using this term now **[50]**, we work out in the form of praise of a man who lived a life in accord with virtue. The godlike Plato in *Phaedrus* (270b) and others of ancient times divided subjects of praise into goods of the mind (*psychê*), goods of the body, and external goods.[66] Those of the mind are divided into prudence, justice, temperance, and courage; those of body into beauty, strength, size, and speed; external goods are divided into origin, friends, wealth, and such. We, however, shall not follow this division but the prevailing one.[67]

After the prooemia—in encomion we shall use whatever prooemia the need occasions rather than any particular one, in the same way as has already been repeatedly said—the first heading into which encomion is divided is what is called "from origin" (*apo tou genous*), which is derived from consideration of nationality,[68] native city, and ancestors. Either all of these are applicable or we shall use those that are; for example, if the city is illustrious and of high repute, then we shall spend more of the speech on that than on nationality, but if we have nothing notable to say about the city, then we shall take refuge in the nation. If we are unable to say anything worthwhile about either, then we shall begin straight off with the ancestors, and then add whatever can be said about the other things mentioned earlier, I mean nationality or native city. **[51]** For example, we wish to praise a certain Siphnion. Since there is nothing worth saying about Siphnos,[69] it will suffice for praise of it to say,

[65] I.e., whether one should marry; cf. Aphthonius above, pp. 120–24, and Nicolaus' on thesis, below, pp. 168–69.

[66] Plato mentions only goods of mind and body; external goods were a Peripatetic addition; cf. above, p. 50, n. 156.

[67] Theon, Hermogenes, and Aphthonius, more or less and in varying detail, follow the division of goods Nicolaus claims to reject. His account has most to say about external goods, only a little about virtues of the mind, and nothing about bodily advantages.

[68] I.e., Greek, Roman, Egyptian, Persian, etc.

[69] Cf. Demosthenes 13.34, on the insignificance of Siphnians and Cythnians compared with Athenians.

perhaps, that it lies near Attica and in the middle of the Cycladic islands. After that, keeping to the order prescribed by the art, we
shall come to what is more related to the subject, and while praising his more honorable relatives we shall hide the others in turn.
One should always hasten and press on to what especially belongs
to the subject alone; for example, I am saying that there probably
are many descendants from his most remote ancestors and, as it
were, many lines of descent and the same good words will fit many,
but only those descended from a father ought to boast in the father's
merits.⁷⁰ Thus we shall prefer to come to those. Yet we shall not
quickly nor casually run over memory of earlier ancestors, in order
not to seem to avoid mention of them because we know something
bad about them; but if we want to examine these things, we shall
approach them in a measured way, saying that it is out of place in
such a recollection not also to look at the virtues of his ancestors,
and if we wish to jump over them, we shall try to mention some
good reason in order not to seem to hide them intentionally.

After these remarks about origin we shall come to the circumstances of his birth; for example, if there is something we can say
about him at the time of his mother's birth pains, as it is said of the
mother of Pericles, **[52]** Agariste, that a god told her in a dream that
she would give birth to a lion,⁷¹ or the tradition about the mother of
Cyrus about the vine and the flood of water in a dream.⁷² Many
such stories have been passed down to us; for example, about Evagoras, the king of Cyprus,⁷³ and others.

After this, we shall take up the circumstances of his upbringing,
if we have something special to say about it that did not happen to
others, as in the case of Achilles, (saying) that he was fed on the
marrow of deer and taught by Cheiron⁷⁴ and all the things told of
him in turn. After this, his activities in youth; for example, did he
practice rhetoric or poetry or anything of that sort? Then, next,
things done by him. Here, or rather in all parts, so the language may
not become flat (*hyptios*), even though a level tone seems somehow
to fit panegyric, nevertheless, in order that it not be entirely dull be-

⁷⁰ I.e., collateral relatives need not be mentioned.

⁷¹ Cf. Plutarch, *Pericles* 3.2.

⁷² According to Herodotus (1.107–8), Mandane, mother of Cyrus, dreamed
she gave birth to a stream of water that flooded all Asia, and Astyages, her father,
dreamed of a vine that grew from her womb and overshadowed all Asia.

⁷³ Cf. Isocrates 9.21.

⁷⁴ Fed on the marrow of *lions*, according to Hermogenes, above, p. 82. On
Cheiron, cf. *Iliad* 11.832.

cause we are making only a bald and unelaborated list, we shall try
to refer his action to virtues and to introduce, in turn, comparisons.
For thus the flatness is dissolved and the discourse is made to seem
active (*enagonios*). If the subject has some weak side, we shall try to
cloak it with rather specious words, calling cowardice "prudence"
[53] and "foresight," and rashness "courage" and "high-spirited-
ness," reworking everything in a nobler direction.[75] As I said, one
should introduce comparisons everywhere, avoiding excessive flatness (*hyptiotês*) and aiming at an account of his virtues (*aretai*), in
order that the discourse may be alive (*empsykhos*).

The question should be asked whether encomion admits antithesis.[76] If there is need to make a test of what is acknowledged as
good, goods provoking an antithesis will not be acknowledged
goods; but if antithesis results from some particular material which
we are not able to conceal because the hearer seeks to know about it,
we shall demolish these things in the treatment and add stronger
rebuttals, in order to remove any harm done by the antithesis.[77]
There are examples of this in speeches of Aristeides and in Isocrates' *Panegyricus* and *Busiris*.[78] The antithesis in the *Panegyricus* especially deserves emulation, since it is well refuted. The refutation
introduced in the *Busiris* seems refuted more weakly. Antitheses occurring because of the special nature of the material will not establish a general rule in this species of rhetoric.

Invective[79] (*psogos*) is divided into the same headings, since we
complete the elaboration and division from opposite epicheiremes
and enthymemes; **[54]** for one kind of encomion is praise, the other
invective.[80] As a result, Isocrates' speech *Against the Sophists*, although all constructed from abuses about those offending against
the arts, has been classified among encomia. I am not unaware that
some criticize the title of that speech because he did not call it an
"invective of the sophists," but gave it the name "against" the

[75] Cf. Aristotle, *Rhetoric* 1.9.28–29.

[76] I.e., raise an objection to what is being said.

[77] Nicolaus' point seems to be that encomion does not admit consideration of
objections to what constitutes virtue but does allow possible objections to be raised
about the virtue or vice of some action, with rebuttal of those objections.

[78] Cf. the objections that might be raised to Athenian hegemony, *Panegyricus*
100, refuted in the following sections, and the objections that might be raised to
praise of the king, *Busiris* 30, dealt with in a less convincing fashion.

[79] The British Museum manuscript indicates a new chapter at this point, but
Nicolaus will resume discussion of praise below.

[80] The word "encomion," derived by the grammarians from the word for village, did not in itself connote praise.

sophists so that it would appear to be a common-place.[81] One should understand, however, that it is the underlying subject, not the title, that determines the genre of a work.

Now the difference between an invective and a common-place has been stated in the discussion of common-place, but nothing prevents our making a reminder of it now; for thus we shall know what sort of things should be listed under invective and what under common-place. When the subject under scrutiny is one for which some penalty has been defined in the laws, then we shall use the procedure in accord with the headings of common-place; but when the subject only brings reproach to one using it, then we elaborate it as an invective. As a result, in accordance with this statement, *Against the Sophists* would be classified under the panegyrical genre.

There are many other kinds (*eidê*) of speeches, as we indicated a little earlier, that are brought under panegyric, each needing its own description, as there also are subdivisions of the judicial and deliberative kind, and there is a need to say a little more about them; [55] for thus we shall be more attentive when we encounter technical works about those kinds of speeches. Some of the technical writers characterized speeches on the basis of the persons understood as present and set them among three kinds of rhetoric, saying that, since our hearers are either convened in an assembly or trying a case at law or participating in a festival, the speech being spoken must always belong to one of these kinds,[82] but others did not think we should name only three kinds and they extended the number to many more. It seems to me they were moved to think in this way by Aristotle; for that venerable man called history a fourth genre after the three mentioned, saying it was a mixture of the three.[83] But if one grants a fourth, as, therefore, one should,[84] nothing prevents us following others who, I think, went as far as thirty kinds, and probably even more could be found;[85] for there are as many kinds of

---

[81] "Common-place" in the sense of the progymnasma of that name.

[82] Cf. Aristotle, *Rhetoric* 1.3.

[83] The addition of history as a fourth genre is found in Rufus, *Art of Rhetoric* 2 (p. 399, ed. Spengel-Hammer) and Syrianus (vol. 2, p. 11, ed. Rabe), but not in extant writings of Aristotle. Nevertheless, it probably goes back to Hellenistic sources and is implicit in Cicero's discussions of historiography, e.g., *On the Orator* 2.62–64.

[84] This statement seems inconsistent with what follows; perhaps Nicolaus is admitting the logic of the position in the abstract, while feeling that in practice it leads to confusion.

[85] Cf. Quintilian 3.4.1–8. Menander Rhetor discusses some seventeen genres of epideictic.

speeches as there are human affairs. But anyone who does this will inadvertently create confusion. Thus it is necessary to try to bring all the subjects under the categories named by Cornutus[86] and Porphyry,[87] defining them on the basis of the subject proposed for discussion. One could [56] also call the division among those categories a "difference" and divide speeches up among the three species, if one took note of the persons who are the subjects and the end of each species of rhetoric. I mean, for example, the just as the end of judicial, which is shown from the vote of the jury judging in accordance with the laws. Would antirrhetic speeches,[88] then, be judicial, because they include arguments in reply to someone? But nobody would say that; for the hearers are not supposed to be going to impose any punishment fixed by the laws. Thus, these speeches of reply should rather be put under the panegyrical species. Speeches of admonition, speeches of thanks, and replies to defenses against charges when no legal punishment would follow and when constructed only for personal attack, —all speeches concerning such things can be classed under the three species of rhetoric, if one wants to force them (into these categories) and not accept cutting them up into a larger number of sub-genres but accepts interweaving of the materials from which they are constructed. In the cases of Isocrates' *Panegyricus* and Demosthenes' *On the Crown,* the latter acknowledged to be judicial and the former deliberative in species, if the materials have been taken from panegyric, what prevents the same mixtures and interweavings from occurring in the other [57] species, with the result that the speech has some other goal, found by considering the supposed audience, and is constructed from different material? Thus, Aristeides' speech *On the Four* would be called a speech of reply, and many other speeches of the same Aristeides, as well as those of sophists of his and later times, can be found that show that those who chose to remain within the concept of only three species are also making a fine judgment. But so much for these things.[89]

---

[86] Rhetorician, probably 3rd cent., A.D., mentioned by Syrianus (Walz IV, pp. 298 and 843) and other commentators on the Hermogenic corpus.

[87] Neo-Platonist of the third century; his *Eisagôgê* became the standard introduction to the study of logic.

[88] Speeches of reply, such as Aristeides' *On the Four;* cf. above, p. 147.

[89] The preceding discussion might have been clearer if Nicolaus had utilized a sequence of divisions from genus to species, with subdivisions of the genres of epideictic or taken some other approach. It seems to be his conclusion that the fundamental classification into three species is sound, even though some speeches do

We said above that encomion also busies itself with praise of things. Things are either lifeless but corporeal, like a shield or spear or stone or something of that sort, or incorporeal, like rhetoric and features of human activity generally. It is reasonable, therefore, to ask how we shall make an encomion of these things and if it is possible to use the same headings as when we praise a man. One should, then, understand that we shall use for them the topics available in encomion; for example, to take the case of activities, taking up those who invented or first used the activity instead of their origin, and instead of rearing, the training involved in them, and instead of their deeds, their uses in the life of humans and their benefits, and in each of the others **[58]** similarly. Since some praises of living things are general— for example, that of man or horse—and some are particular, like that of Socrates or some other persons, in the case of subjects of a general sort it is necessary to aim at what is possible.[90] In general, the speaker himself, as Isocrates said, needs to understand the divisions of the subject and to be a judge of utility and to compose speeches that accord with occasions and persons and things.[91]

They say,[92] "In encomion it is necessary regularly to use expression that is polished (*glaphyros*) and rather graceful (*habroteros*) and theatrical (*theatrikos*), with some solemnity (*semnotês*)." Just as we need expansiveness (*onkos*) and dignity (*axiôma*) in deliberative speeches, and in judicial speeches we need vehemence (*sphodrotês*), making the debate seem alive, so in panegyric we need what creates pleasure, as I said, with solemnity for people enjoying themselves at leisure.[93]

Everything that it was necessary for you to learn about encomion, my dearest boys, has been sufficiently said.

The original text of Nicolaus' handbook, as preserved in the British

---

not fit very well under any one species, and many kinds of panegyric need to be recognized.

[90] Possibly some reference to praise of particular persons or things is lost here, but Nicolaus may have thought what to say about them would be easily seen from their particularity, and in any event praise of individuals was discussed earlier in the chapter.

[91] Perhaps derived from the lost *Art of Rhetoric* sometimes attributed to Isocrates in antiquity. The advice is not unlike statements found in several of his speeches.

[92] The writers on progymnasmata consulted by Nicolaus.

[93] I.e., at a panegyris, or festival. Nicolaus seems to forget that he has associated encomion with funeral orations and other genres not given at a festival.

Museum manuscript, ends at this point. What follows is material attrib-
uted to Nicolaus in composite commentaries on Aphthonius from Byzan-
tine times, primarily found in eleventh century manuscripts in Paris
(Parisinus Graecus 1983 and 2977). These became the basis of Felten's
text from here on. The accounts of exercises do not follow quite the same
order of topics used by Nicolaus in earlier chapters and at times seem to
be summaries or restatements of his account in different language.

9. ON SYNCRISIS

[59]   Some have not included what is called *synkrisis* (comparison) among progymnasmata at all, on the ground that there has
been enough practice of it in common-places when we were making
a scrutiny of something that was then being judged in relation to
other wrongs, and in encomia, where we were trying to show the
greatness of what was being praised by setting it next to something
else; others have wanted it to be one of the progymnasmata but yet
put it before encomion. Neither of these groups deserves praise; for
it is not the case, when syncrisis has been taken up as a part (of a
larger discourse such as common-place or encomion), that it was
necessary for that reason for it to be no longer considered as consti-
tuting a whole, or if it was so considered for it not to be put after
encomion. When it is treated as a part, and especially in common-
place, its elaboration takes a different form, since we are comparing
something to an equal or a lesser or a greater, which will not be the
case in syncrisis by itself;[94] but neither in the exercise called encomion will there be an evaluation of a whole in comparison to a
whole, but of a part to a part. For example, in evaluating the noble
birth of a person we are praising, we wish to show that he did not
fall below the noble birth of, say, Achilles; here we take a short bit
of what is related about Achilles that **[60]** is enough for our purpose
and leave out everything else about the hero, since the incidental bit
happens to be more useful than that from which it is taken, and our
whole speaking effort is expended for this purpose. Syncrisis
should not be put before encomion, since then encomium becomes
double; for syncrisis is speech setting the better or worse side by
side. Or it can also be defined thus: syncrisis is parallel scrutiny of
goods or evils or persons or things, by which we try to show that the
subjects under discussion are both equal to each other or that one is
greater than the other. Thus, in what is called syncrisis, I mean in

---

[94] When comparison is used in common-place, its function is amplification
rather than evaluation.

this progymnasma, we shall now avoid comparison to the lesser, which we included in common-place for the purpose of censure. Well then, if syncrisis is a double encomion, how was it logical to put the double before the single? Therefore, syncrisis will not be assigned a place before encomion. It is one of the exercises that belongs both to parts and wholes; for it will be brought in as a part in encomia and common-places, and as a whole when, say, a prize for a virtuous life is offered and two men, distinguished in that way, contend with each other for the prize. **[61]**

We shall use here the same divisions as in encomion, only noting that the headings employed in syncrisis are double, and just as there, we shall seek out those that are possible, choosing them to fit the subjects or persons or actions. We shall compare as many things, whether fine or not, to each other as we praise in encomion or blame in invective. Thus, here there is no need to say more about these things. It is only necessary to add one thing, that whether we are making a scrutiny of good things or bad, we should not amplify our subjects by elimination of things that provide the basis of comparison, but our subjects will be great when they seem greater than the great, as in the Homeric line (*Iliad* 20.158, of Hector and Achilles, respectively), "The man who fled in front was good, but by far a better man pursued." For example, we want to show that Themistocles was better than Pausanias. Themistocles will not say to him that he did nothing good for the Greeks, but that "although you did many great things, my deeds are much greater than yours."[95] And similarly in comparison of the bad,[96] as Demosthenes showed us right in the prooemion of *Against Androtion* **[62]**; for Diodorus did not say that Euctimon had not been wronged at all by him, but that "He suffered many great wrongs, but I suffered much greater ones." Thus, by amplifying what happened to Euctimon his amplification of his own wrongs was not obvious.

The expression here ought to be stately (*pompikos*) and theatrical, though not departing from the solemn (*semnos*).[97] There being three parts of rhetoric, syncrisis would seem to belong to one, I mean encomion,[98] but it will exercise us also for the others; for when

[95] The situation envisioned is the contest for a prize described in Herodotus 8.123 and cast in the form of ethopoeia.

[96] In the previous paragraph we were told that comparison to the lesser is not appropriate in syncrisis, though it may be done in common-place.

[97] Solemnity was required of encomion in the previous chapter and is now carried over into comparison.

[98] I.e., panegyric.

engaged in deliberation we want to show that our proposals are finer than those spoken by others, and we shall do the same when giving an account of wrongs done and we shall try to show that the present ones are greater than all. All in all, the use of syncrisis takes many forms, as does that of encomion, both when employed by itself as a whole discourse[99] and when part of something else.

In terms of the five parts of the speech, while composing syncrises we are practicing for invention of prooemia and composition of narrations in which we mention the merits as though giving a narrative, and for the forcefulness of debates in which [63] we try to show that things are like or greater, and for the emotion of epilogues in which we bring the hypotheses to a close.

If we should be composing a comparison of flowers or plants or such things, we may use relaxed language (*aneimenê phrasis*), so as not to have to go though all the headings and not to seek ways of excusing ourselves (for omitting them), since the relaxed style is not expected to accord in every respect with the technical division of encomia of a more serious character.

10. ON ETHOPOEIA

Some who put ecphrasis right after comparison and ethopoeia after thesis have written as follows: "Ethopoeia has been rightly put after thesis; for in a certain sense there is a path leading from thesis, through ethopoeia, to complete hypotheses. For example, there is a thesis whether one should philosophize. The argument is constructed by the elaboration we mentioned in the discussion of thesis. 'A farmer urges his son to study philosophy' is an ethopoeia. The addition of the character of the father did not make a complete hypothesis, since it still omits the circumstance, although it indicated something more complete than was the case in thesis." This is what they have written. But we, following the prevailing custom [64] of putting ethopoeia right after comparison, reply that ethopoeia is speech suiting the proposed situations, showing ethos or pathos or both: "suiting the proposed situations" since it is necessary to take account of the speaker and the one to whom he is speaking; "ethos or pathos or both" since one looks either to the universal or to what came from the circumstance; for this is how ethos differs from pathos. For example, if we speak on the theme, "What words a coward would say when going out to battle," we

[99] Comparative essays are common in later Greek literature; those by Plutarch following sets of parallel lives are probably the best known.

shall give attention to the character generally belonging to cowards; but if we speak on, perhaps, "What words Agamemnon would say after taking Ilium," or Andromache when Hector fell, the emotions of the situation will give a supply of things to say.

Some ethopoeias are ethical, some pathetical, some mixed; ethical and pathetical are those which we have already cited, mixed those with both; for example, if I speak on the theme, "What words Achilles would say when going to war after the death of Patroclus"; for I shall add elements of emotion to the character and create a mixed ethopoeia.

Different writers regard what is called "prosopopoeia," being almost the same as ethopoeia, as differing from it in different ways. **[65]** Some call prosopopoeia that which specifies both the persons and the supposed circumstances, and ethopoeia what is in all respects freely made up,[100] which they also called a *rhêsis,* giving this name to the same thing. Those who have the best opinion think that in ethopoeia real persons are specified, while proposopoeia is that in which we invent persons and attribute words to them. This they attribute especially to the poets, who have the privilege of changing lifeless things into persons and giving them things to say.

Since there has been much difference of opinion about the division of ethopoeia by those discussing it, it is necessary to state the prevailing view, which is that it is divided into discussion of three times, present, past, and future; for what some call headings are enthymemes constructed about one of these times. We shall, therefore, begin from the present and run back to past time, then from there again return to the present; for we shall not immediately come to the future, but shall make brief mention of present constraints and in this way we shall consider what is going to follow. For example, the ethopoeia, "What words **[66]** Peleus would say when hearing of the death of Achilles." He will not right off recall his former happiness, but he will lament his present misfortune before contrasting it with the good things that came upon him in the past—marriage with a goddess, honor from the gods, many valiant deeds—; then he will weep for what has now befallen him, adding what circumstances, and from what sources, surround him, and thus, as it were, he will prophesy how many evils will likely befall him through the loss of one to aid him.

The expression (*apangelia*) should be in rather short phrases

---

[100] Cf. Hermogenes, above, p. 84.

and, as it were, <natural>,[101] not in full periods; for to be fussy about style is alien to emotion, and it is characteristic of those in joy and grief to say one thing after another, concisely, and in few words. A person careful of beauty in diction will not seem to have suffered on such an occasion.

This progymnasma is useful for the three kinds of rhetoric; for we often need ethopoeia when speaking an encomion and [67] in prosecuting and giving counsel. To me, it seems also to exercise us in the style of letter writing, since in that there is need of foreseeing the character of those sending letters and those to whom they are sent. Whether letter writing belongs to one of these three kinds or to another is not something to consider at this time, especially since, for introductory purposes, enough has been said about rhetorical genres in the discussion of encomia.[102]

We shall have no need of prooemia in periodic construction here where there is no use of any other linguistic device of the kind, nor of narrations keeping to a succession of events—otherwise the emotion would be destroyed—nor will the speech be argumentative, but its only aim is to move the hearer to pleasure or to tears.

11. ON ECPHRASIS

Some who put ecphrasis right after comparison have written as follows: "The sequence of progymnasmata makes little difference, since different people arrange them differently, but there is no reason not to practice ecphrasis right [68] after comparison; for since we said that there was freedom in syncrisis to use the relaxed style, and since in ecphrasis it has been more allowed to use that kind of expression, probably ecphrasis should follow syncrisis." This is what some have said, but following the prevailing custom, we put ethopoeia after syncrisis and ecphrasis after that. And we say that ecphrasis (*ekphrasis*) is descriptive speech, bringing what is described clearly (*enargôs*) before the eyes. "Clearly" is added because in this way it most differs from narration; the latter gives a plain exposition of actions, the former tries to make the hearers into spectators. We compose ecphrases of places, times, persons, festivals, things done: of places, for example, meadows, harbors, pools,[103] and

---

[101] Reading *prosphyê*, as suggested to me by D. A. Russell; cf. Theon p. 74,12, ed. Spengel.

[102] On letter writing as a progymnasmatic exercise, cf. note on Theon, above, pp. 47–48.

[103] This somewhat strange list seems amplified by alliteration: *leimônas, limenas, limnas.*

such like; of times, for example, spring, summer; of persons, for example, priests,[104] Thersites, and such; of festivals, like the Panathenaia, the Dionysia, and things done at them; and, all in all, we use this progymnasma for many things. It differs from narration in that the latter examines things as a whole, the former in part; for example, it belongs to a narration **[69]** to say "The Athenians and Peloponnesians fought a war," and to ecphrasis to say that each side made this and that preparation and used this manner of arms.

Whenever we compose ecphrases, and especially descriptions of statues or pictures or anything of that sort, we should try to add an account of this or that impression made by the painter or by the molded form; for example, that he painted the figure as angry for this reason, or as pleased; or we shall mention some other emotion as occurring because of the history of what is being described. Similarly in other cases also, explanations contribute to vividness.[105] We shall begin with the first things and thus come to the last; for example, if the subject of the ecphrasis is a man represented in bronze or in a picture or some such way, after beginning with a description of his head we shall move on to the rest, part by part. In this way the speech becomes alive throughout.

There being five parts of a speech, as has been said often **[70]**—prooemion, narration, antithesis, solution, epilogue—, ecphrasis will practice us for the narrative part, except in so far as it goes beyond bare description, but what is elaborated in ecphrasis incorporates clarity and brings before the eyes those things with which the words are concerned, and all but makes spectators.

There being three kinds of rhetoric, I mean judicial and panegyrical and deliberative, this progymnasma will be found useful for all; for in deliberative speaking we often encounter a necessity to describe the thing about which we are making the speech, in order to be more persuasive, and in prosecuting or defending we need the amplification that comes from making an ecphrasis, and, of course, in panegyrical subjects the element of ecphrasis is capable of producing pleasure in theater-audiences. For the most part, this progymnasma functions as a part (of a larger whole), but nothing prevents it sometimes being worked out as sufficient in itself for a complete hypothesis, just as it is, for the most part, one of the parts.

[104] Mention of Thersites suggests Nicolaus is thinking of *Iliad,* so an example of a priest may be Chryses in *Iliad* 1.

[105] Cf., e.g., the ecphrases of paintings by Philostratus and of statues by Callistratus.

We need a varied style in it; for the kind of expression we use should fit the proposed subject, whether we make it sweet or render happenings tragic **[71]** or impart some other emotion; for sometimes we wish only to instill good feelings, but sometimes to frighten or amplify feelings, as Demosthenes in *On the Embassy* (19.65) tries by speech to bring the sufferings at Phocis before the eyes.

12. ON THESIS

There has been much dispute in the technical writings about division in what is called "thesis"; we shall, however, take up its division only after first saying what thesis is. Well then, thesis (*thesis*) is something admitting logical examination but without persons or any circumstances at all being specified. It is said to be "admitting logical examination," not because the other exercises are regarded as lacking reasoning, but because this one exercise is exclusively concerned with rational investigation and has no other attribute, since, if a particular circumstance is added, the result is a complete hypothesis. It is in this way, you see, that thesis differs from hypothesis, because the former lacks identification of specific circumstance and the latter is constructed around a circumstance. For example, "whether one should marry" is a thesis; here **[72]** we inquire about the thing in the abstract, not asking if some particular person should marry or anything of that sort, but only asking if the thing (i.e., marriage) is good or not. If, however, we want to imagine, say, that someone who has three sons has rejected them and, after dismissing a wife who is no longer of child-bearing age, considers whether to marry another, it becomes an hypothesis.

This progymnasma belongs to the deliberative species but is divided by careful technical writers into the headings of panegyric. I am not unaware that others have used different headings, some those that are called "final,"[106] some different ones, attributing novel names to them. On this subject, I mean those using novel names, one should realize that all of these things named as headings by some are enthymemes, providing something useful to the subject; for example, what they call "according to nature," or "law," or "custom," or "holy duty" in regard to the dead or in regard to the fatherland. These are the kind of headings they have invented.

Now let us propose that the subject is whether one should marry. If we were to begin with this and inquire whether to marry

---

[106] On final headings, see above, p. 79, n. 26.

on the basis of nature or custom or law, or if it is a holy duty [73] for the fatherland or our ancestors, what are we asking except what benefits would come from marriage, which would be enthymemes of one of the encomiastic headings? If, on the other hand, we inquire who were the inventors and first users, what are we doing other than speaking the enthymemes which we shall adopt in place of origin. Thus, they seem to me to do rightly who divide thesis by the encomiastic headings, in order that the exercise may belong to the deliberative species but use the material and division of panegyric; for in complete deliberative hypotheses, whether exhorting or dissuading, we are accustomed to support our argument with praises and blames. Thus here too those making division in this way seem to me laudable.

Let us include prooemia in it as well, whether one or two or more,[107] the need defining the number for the speaker, containing either a recommendation or denigration of the subject or accomplishing something else of the things that orators are accustomed to do in prooemia. After these, one should go to the heading of origin. In place of mention of ancestors we shall include here those who discovered and first applied the thesis, whether gods or men. After that, instead of the heading of activities, we shall put what results from the practice of the thing, and instead of [74] deeds, the advantages from it, and thus we shall form the elaboration of the thesis.

Panegyrical division in this case differs from the division of the encomion because antithesis does not occur in the latter, unless perhaps resulting from some special material, whereas here antithesis will apply everywhere, with scrutiny of the evils that accompany and follow the thing and rebuttal by use of examples and enthymemes. Rebuttal by example will be drawn from disadvantages that result in other things but are not sufficient to deter those wanting to undertake them, and for this reason choosing what offers more numerous benefits than disadvantages; rebuttal by enthymeme will be drawn from demonstration showing the good result that follows to those who have been most successful in applying the thesis. For example, perhaps, the thesis, Whether one should marry.[108] After saying how many good things come from marriages—generation after generation being born and increasing the cities in population, it may be, individually and collectively [75]

---

[107] On the concept of multiple prooemia, cf. above, pp. 80 and 106.
[108] With the account here, compare Aphthonius' thesis on marriage, above, pp. 121–24.

and creating people who will demonstrate good will in different ways; and after showing that the family line is preserved by these births, and that those who will feed the elderly will be born to the poor and to the rich those who preserve wealth; after many such things we shall place against these benefits what are called *thetika*,[109] the resulting adulteries and effect of loss of children. These will be refuted by the fact that shipwrecks do not keep sailors from the sea, nor do droughts and hurricanes hinder farmers, while added to these are crowns and statues and public maintenance and fame in general, conferred on boys for their acts of heroism, and all the things that reveal happiness to those who have not been tried by ill fortune through a whole lifetime.

Thesis differs from common-place—for amplification of the subject occurs there too and in this respect they have something in common—it differs, then, because in common-place the subject about which the speeches are made is agreed to, but here it is debatable; thus we shall not be prevented from attacking even what we praised. And in common-place we were inciting a vote of judges, but here we shall undertake an evaluation only as advice and with no penalty from the judges ensuing. Moreover, in common-place the person involved is supposed to have done wrong, **[76]** while here there is only a question about something without any specified circumstances.

There are many uses for this exercise and it brings many benefits, in as much as it provides practice in two of the species of rhetoric, I mean the encomiastic and the deliberative, and it is receptive of all of the parts of a speech, I mean prooemia and narrations—those included in scrutiny of the good things about the proposed subject —and antitheses and solutions, which epilogues should follow, containing general advice and exhortation to what is proposed, so that from this the characteristic of deliberation may be preserved.

Thesis is one of the exercises undertaken only as a part of something else;[110] for it is not likely that thesis would be a whole (speech) since it lacks specified circumstance and is, in itself, less than a complete hypotheses, unless one should call it a whole because of including all the parts of a speech.

Some theses relate to nature; for example, whether the universe

---

[109] Thesis-based arguments; cf. above, p. 156. D. A. Russell suggests emending to *antithetika*.

[110] Except, of course, in philosophical teaching.

is spherical, or any other such theological question; some are political, as is the one examined above. Those engaged in philosophical study will be concerned with the division of natural questions, and the division of the political ones has been shown above.

[77]   13. ON INTRODUCTION OF A LAW

Law (*nomos*) is a political decision by a multitude or by an eminent man,[111] in accordance with which everyone in the city is expected to live. Some laws are of general application, some specific; general laws apply to everyone in the city, specific laws apply to contracts between people. Again, some laws introduce rewards for good deeds, some define a punishment for wrongs. A decree (*psêphisma*) differs from a law only in one respect and in all others is the same: a decree is for a particular occasion, a law is ratified for all time.

The exercise in introduction of a law differs from commonplace because in the latter there is an attack on something agreed upon and known to be wrong, whereas here the subject is still in doubt. It is divided into the "final" headings.[112] Those wanting to divide it into other headings did not realize that they were adorning enthymematic demonstrations **[78]** with novel names and were promoting these to the position of headings. Final headings are divided into written and unwritten. "Written" means derived from a law, "unwritten" from a custom. The order of these headings will probably have been already determined in fictitious hypotheses, but in real cases the speaker is judge of the order, as Demosthenes often is, changing the order with the needs of the division.[113]

The exercise includes the introduction of and opposition to laws when they are first proposed, and attack on and defense of laws whenever there is a scrutiny of those passed earlier. Over all, we either attack or support a law that exists, or we introduce or hinder the introduction of one that does not exist.

The present progymnasma is prototypical of judicial oratory.[114] It would also have some relation to deliberative oratory, and some small kinship to panegyric, in so far as by praising or blaming we want to validate or invalidate a law. **[79]** Of the parts of a political speech, it provides exercise only in prooemia and proofs and epilogues; we do not have much need of narration here, in that we are

---

[111] I.e., a "lawgiver" like Solon or Lycurgus.

[112] Possible, advantageous, just, honorable, etc.; cf. above, p. 79.

[113] The classic example is the opening of *On the Crown,* where Demosthenes refuses to accept the order of headings demanded by Aeschines.

[114] Because it is viewed in terms of prosecution or defense of the law.

not concerned with any particular circumstance and the subject before us relates to the future. It is not definitively one of the parts
nor one of the wholes; not a whole because of the lack of specific
circumstances, not a part because more than a part is present. But
it belongs more with the parts than with the wholes.

There is need here for a powerful periodic style, since this is not
a speech looking to the theater nor one inspiring emotion, but one
needing forcefulness and elaboration.

This much should be said for now about these things as an introduction.

Chapter V

Selections from the Commentary
on the *Progymnasmata* of Aphthonius
Attributed to John of Sardis

INCLUDING FRAGMENTS OF THE
TREATISE ON *PROGYMNASMATA* BY SOPATROS,
OBJECTIONS BY "ERISTICAL SOPHISTS,"
AND MATERIAL FROM OTHER SOURCES QUOTED BY JOHN

*This commentary, explaining, expanding, and illustrating Aphthonius'
discussion of progymnasmata and drawing on a variety of sources, is
the earliest of extant Byzantine works on the subject, used in turn by
later commentators. The commentary mentions Nicolaus twice and
draws on his treatise elsewhere, so it must be later than his work, thus
no earlier than the late fifth century after Christ, and it cannot be later
than the tenth century, the date of the earliest manuscript. The author
describes himself simply as John. Quotations from the commentary in
the later compendium by John Doxapatros are attributed to "the man
from Sardis." Hugo Rabe in his Teubner edition (pp. xvi–xx) identified John with a bishop of Sardis to whom Theodore the Studite sent a
letter not long before A.D. 850. If this is correct, John's commentary
dates from the first half of the ninth century.*

*In addition to the work on progymnasmata, John probably wrote a
commentary on the Hermogenic treatise* On Invention, *also cited by
John Doxapatres. This activity suggests that he taught rhetoric,
whether publicly or privately, though where and precisely when cannot
be determined.[1] Sardis is an unlikely place for a rhetorical school in the
early Middle Ages, but John may have taught in Constantinople or
some other intellectual center before going there. Moreover, a Christian
bishop is unlikely to have taught rhetoric, but John's commentaries
might be a product of a time before he became bishop. The name John
certainly indicates he was Christian, but he shows no hostility to pa-
ganism and he never takes an opportunity, as some Byzantine writers
on rhetoric do, to bring in references to Christian orators or to Christian doctrine. He copies from his sources without comment passages that
are clearly pagan in content.[2] His commentary is classicizing, atticiz-*

---

[1] Cf. Kennedy, *Greek Rhetoric Under Christian Emperors*, pp. 275–77.
[2] E.g., references to "the gods" in the list of theses, p. 233,14ff. ed. Rabe; cf.
also reference to gods, below, pp. 183, 208–9, 212, 221, etc.

ing, and anachronistic; one would assume from reading it that not only the rhetorical schools, but the political and legal system of classical and imperial times still existed. In the ninth century rhetorical and philosophical studies experienced some revival after over two hundred years of relative neglect, which had been partly a result of the iconoclastic movement in the Greek church. During these "dark ages" much classical Greek literature and learning was lost.

John cites Theon by name seven times and draws on his treatise on many other occasions. Hermogenes is named five times. More interesting are the passages quoted from Sopatros' otherwise lost handbook of progymnasmata, probably contemporary with Aphthonius. Sopatros is named on eight occasions and probably drawn on elsewhere.³ Of special interest are criticisms of progymnasmata, not found earlier, cited and refuted by John. In introducing the first of these criticism he attributes it (below, p. 182) to "eristical sophists." Their identity is unknown. Some criticisms resemble the method of analysis used by Epicurean and skeptical philosophers in attacks on the teaching of grammar and rhetoric.⁴ It is possible, however, that some of these criticisms are not to be regarded as serious objections by sophists and are what writers on progymnasmata call "antitheses," used as a pedagogic device to emphasize a point, or an attempt to forestall possible objections that had not in fact been made. John replies to the criticisms in the first person, but he is probably drawing on earlier sources here as well. The objections are often reasonable; some of the refutations seem weakly argued.

In addition to these specified sources, and to numerous references to sources that cannot be identified, there are verbal similarities throughout the work to Greek rhetorical texts of imperial times not mentioned by John. Rabe's introduction (p. xxi) and apparatus cite parallels to Pseudo-Dionysius, Anonymous Seguerianus, Menander Rhetor, Alexander, and Romanus. In most, perhaps all, instances the parallels probably derive from intermediate sources—treatises or commentaries on progymnasmata used but not identified by John—and he may have been quite unaware of the original works. There are also a number of similarities to passages in writings by the Neoplatonist philosopher David, who lived in the sixth century (cf. Rabe, pp. xxi–xxiii), also probably coming to John through some intermediate source.

John's work, together with its quotations from Theon, Hermogenes, Nicolaus, and Sopatros, was later incorporated in whole or part by

³ Cf. Hock and O'Neil, *The Chreia*, vol. 2 (2002), pp. 98–112.
⁴ As found, e.g., in Sextus Empiricus, *Against the Grammarians*, and in scholia to the *Ars Grammatica* of Dionysius Thrax.

John Doxapatres, Maximus Planudes, and others into their composite commentaries on Aphthonius. Of the three manuscripts used by Rabe, only Codex Vaticanus Graecus 1408 of the fourteenth century is complete; Codex Coislinianus Graecus 387 in Paris is dated to the tenth century, thus perhaps close to the date of original composition, but it is only a fragment; a version of the text is also incorporated in a thirteenth- or fourteenth-century manuscript of John Doxapatres' commentaries in Vienna.

John begins with a preface, and the chapters on narrative, chreia, maxim, refutation, common-place, encomion, syncrisis, ethopoeia, ecphrasis, thesis, and law have introductory material of varying length, all of which is included in this translation; otherwise, his method is to proceed through Aphthonius' text, quoting a few words as a lemma and then providing comments thereon, often drawn directly from his sources. The translation of the first two chapters given below is complete, in order to illustrate John's method. The translation of subsequent chapters omits John's paraphrases of Aphthonius and comments that seem obvious, repetitive, confused, or unlikely to interest modern readers. The way the material is composed suggests that it may have been dictated to a scribe or to students, with little revision of the text by John, or perhaps that an original version was expanded by insertion of material from other sources. Some things are not very well expressed, and at times the reader may even wonder whether John understood what he was writing. He viewed Aphthonius treatment as the standard teaching on progymnasmata, but he occasionally voices some criticism of it.[5]

This translation is based on Rabe's Teubner, Leipzig, 1928.

A Collection of Exegetical Notes to Aphthonius' *Progymnasmata*, Composed with Much Labor and Zeal by Me, John, Who Have Written It, and Suitably Coordinated with Aphthonius' Phrases

[p. 1 Rabe]   PREFACE

The present account of progymnasmata does not seek to provide a definition of rhetoric; for completeness is uncalled for when the subject is the incomplete. Giving a definition of the whole art is not appropriate for one addressing elementary students about the parts,

---

[5] E.g., he criticizes Aphthonius' definition of refutation for omission of the phrase "through syllogisms" and for calling refutation an *anatropê*.

and the smallest ones at that. Nor is this the place for an examination of the kinds of rhetoric. That would be to diverge from the subject before us, since comprehension of the whole of rhetoric is impossible for those content to learn about the parts. For since [2] in these discussions we make visible to those beginning the exercises the footprints and shadows, so to speak, of judicial oratory, by which we prove a charge and by which we make the judges keen for punishment, and of deliberative oratory, by which we confirm theses while advising choice of some actions and avoidance of others, it is clear enough, I suspect, that it is not fitting to combine with the discussion here an account of the kinds of oratory, nor to alarm the hearer by the greatness of the task.

We ought first to look at the nature of progymnasmata in that we said they were incomplete. They are incomplete in that none of them is introduced into a court of law or political assembly, for that is the special province of complete hypotheses. If something is principally confirmed by a few epicheiremes and not by the final headings,[6] it is incomplete and makes a part of something else. Further, we know that a complete hypothesis is cut up into the four parts of a speech: prooemia, narrations, proofs (*agônes*), epilogues. We find, however, that none of the progymnasmata consists of these parts of a speech; rather, each progymnasma in itself bears, as it were, an image and shadow of such parts: the narrative (is an image) of statements of a case (*katastaseis*); refutation and confirmation of proofs; and the common-place offers a footprint of epilogues; and the opening thoughts everywhere of progymnasmata that admit such thoughts do the same for prooemia. [3] The goal of progymnasmata is multiple because those who busy themselves in writing use maxims here, chreias there, here ethopoeias, there common-places. Wherefore, there is need for the practitioner to use them as parts of a speech and not as complete speeches.

You should know[7] that progymnasmata are miniature rhetoric. Just as in learning handicrafts there are things to learn before getting a complete understanding of the art—in the case of metal workers, for example, how to light the coal and work the bellows, in the case of shoemakers, how to make a last (?)—so in the progymnasmata one should begin first from the easier ones, and this is the

---

[6] Or headings of purpose: the just, honorable, advantageous, etc; cf. above, p. 79, n. 26.

[7] This phrase, recurring throughout the text, seems to mark the turn to a different source.

fable. And as those making the transition from study of the poets, by whom fables are begotten, to study of rhetoric can first become acquainted with what is closest to what they know, using this as a rule of teaching, and as our nurses and pedagogues allure us and teach us our duties with fables, so what is needful for those advancing into rhetorical studies must be suggested through fables. **[4]** And in addition, because deliberative is by nature the first of the species of rhetoric—because a need for counsel comes on us first—, for this reason fable is made the first exercise as being of the deliberative sort.

I. ON FABLE

Fable originated with poets but has come to be used also by orators in giving advice.

Aphthonius is saying that fable was invented by the poets for the sake of enchantment (*psychagôgia*),[8] and the orators adopted it for giving advice (*parainesis*) and to make their subjects credible. Since fable is attributed to the deliberative species of rhetoric, and the end of that is the advantageous, Aphthonius added that it came "from" (*ek*) giving advice rather than "for the sake of" (*heneka*) or "through" (*dia*) giving advice. Fable is of two sorts, either altogether fictitious or credible. Fable differs from chreia and maxim because in them advice is derived from true things, here through fictitious ones, and we practice refutation of them but never of a fable.[9] We construct chreias and maxims from what is believed and defined, praising or blaming the speaker, but here, attributing the story to no one, we give advice by means of the fable as our own opinion, unobtrusively introducing something useful to a young man. **[5] Fable is a fictive statement, imaging truth.** He says *mythos* is, as it were, a kind of *logos,* since the ancients used *mythesthai* to mean *legein,* but fable is not so called, as some have thought, because it is simply a *logos,* but because it is fictive in nature. This is the characteristic of fable, and lacking that it will not be called fable. *Logos* is the genus in the definition, and the rest is the difference separating it from true stories. The words "fictive statement" are there since it is generally agreed to be composed of fictions. "Imaging truth" stands for "having an image of truth." Fable has an image of truth since it would not do its proper job unless it had some similarity to truth. It becomes similar to truth from

[8] Cf. above, p. 135, n. 18
[9] Cf. Nicolaus, above, p. 141.

the credibility of its invention; thus, false in nature, credible in principle. We must consider the source of the credibility: from places where the creatures involved are accustomed to spend their time; from words fitting the nature of each; from actions which do not exceed the ability of each; for example, do not say that the mouse was deliberating about the kingdom of the animals or that the lion was overcome by the savor of cheese; and if there is need to add some speeches, **[6]** let the fox speak misleading words (*poikilia*), and the sheep simple things full of naïveté; and let the eagle be aggressive toward deer and lambs, and the jackdaw not at all, not even thinking about them.[10]

Sopatros[11] defined fable as follows: "Fable is a fiction (*plasma*), persuasively composed for an image of things that happen in reality, creating some counsel for men or a sketch of action. It is a fiction because it is formed (*plattetai*) so that the thing seems to us to be true; it becomes persuasive because we form the speeches or action in accord with the nature or reputation of each of the animals: since the lion is kingly, we attribute a kingly mind to him, and since the fox is villainous we make up a villainous intention for him, and similarly we represent the deer as cowardly and slow witted. As a result, if we depart from any of these stereotypes, the speech will become incredible. It gets its composition from things that happen in reality, because while looking to the things that happen to men we compose the fable as an image of those things. For example, having seen that many men do something excessive for profit and lose what they have and out of pleasure betray **[7]** their own safety, we made up the fable of the dog carrying the meat along the river and the fable of the lion falling in love with the girl. It creates a representation or recommendation of things, by which we urge action or no action, or we suggest what sort of things happen to people; for example, how many people are deceived by a bare report, as in the case of the bird-catcher chasing the cicada, and by persons putting on a terrifying and commanding act, as in the case of the ass dressing himself up in a lion skin."

It is called Sybaritic and Cilician and Cypriot. Sybaris is a city of Sicily[12] much given to extravagance in consuming food, from

---

[10] Cf. Nicolaus, above, p. 134.

[11] Either the Athenian rhetorician of the late fourth century after Christ, author of a long treatise on declamation (ed. by Walz, *Rhetores Graeci* vol. 8, pp. 1–385), or another rhetorician with the same name, author of a commentary on Hermogenes' *On Staseis* (Walz, vol. 5, pp. 1–211). For Sopatros' work on progymnasmata, see Rabe's edition of Aphthonius, pp. 57–69.

[12] Actually in southern Italy.

which comes the proverb "a Sybaritic table." Fables are called
Sybaritic and Libyian and Cilician and Cyprian, also Egyptian and
Carian. **Varying its names with its inventors . . . :** He is saying
they are clearly named in this way from the inventors. **Calling it
Aesopic has largely prevailed.** Among all of these, he is saying,
there is a single difference, the specific source attributed to each; for
example, "Aesop **[8]** said," or a Lybian man or a Cyprian or a Sybarite. If, he says, there is no adjective signifying the source, we
commonly call such a fable Aesopic. Overall, they are named Aesopic, not because Aesop was the first discoverer of fables—for
Homer and Aeolus[13] and Archilochus and others who lived earlier
seem to have known them—but because Aesop used them to a
greater extent and cleverly, as we speak of Aristophanic and Sapphic and Alcaic meter, not because these poets first or only used the
meters, but because they used them the most. **Some fables are rational:** Those involving only a human being, maybe a farmer or an
unfortunate old man, choosing to die but then begging to be spared
out of love of life. **Some ethical:** Like the fable of the ant and the
cicada. **Some mixed**: Like the fable of a man and a horse. **Rational when a human being is imagined doing something:**
"Doing" instead of "having done."[14] The diction is Attic. **Ethical
when representing the character of irrational animals:** By
character (*êthos*) here he means temperament (*tropos*); for example,
the nobility of the lion, the deer's silliness, the villainy **[9]** of the
fox, and the hare's cowardice, the greed of mice, hawks' rapacious-
ness, the shamelessness of dogs, the simplicity of sheep. **Mixed
when made up of both, irrational and rational.** Like the miller
who beat the old horse at the mill, and it turned and addressed the
man. **When the moral for which the fable has been assigned
is stated first, you will call it a promythion, when at the end
an epimythion.** After a statement of the fable, necessarily we
briefly reveal its purpose; for the intent of the fable should be understood by the young man after hearing it. This is called
epimythion, receiving its proper name from its place. This same
thing becomes a promythion from its position when we put it before an account of the fable, which does not seem to me a good thing
to do. For if we make up the fable to catch the young man, choosing to lead him to good advice, so that thus, as it were, drawn by the
bait, we shall subdue him by persuasion, clearly, if we prefix some-

---

[13] Probably a mistake for Hesiod; cf. Theon, above, p. 24.
[14] I.e., Aphthonius used the present rather than the aorist participle.

thing of this sort, the rest of the fable is unnecessary; and again, if
we form the fable for the sake of the epimythion, whenever we an-
nounce the purpose of the fable ahead of time, the fable is hence-
forth unnecessary.[15] For if the youth knows our advice, what occasion is there for the fiction?

[10]   **A Fable of the Cicadas and Ants.** To some, the tale of
the cicadas and ants has not seemed to be a fable but to be the truth,
whereas it is characteristic of a fable to be false. We say that there
are two kinds of fable; one is allegorical, the other political. It is allegorical when the apparent fiction has one meaning but seems to
say something else; for example, the fictions in Homer, such as "She
grabbed the son of Peleus by his yellow hair."[16] The fable disguises
"the mind" (*nous*) by calling it Athene. This is, for the most part,
the nature of poetic fables, and thus they are not useful for rhetoric,
since they are dismissed as only fables by one encountering their es-
sential falsehood. Of the political fables, some are fictitious, some
historical. Those are said to be fictitious which contain in then
much indication of being invented, like the one about the lion who
had grown old and was feigning disease, or the one about the horse
and the tortoise. The fictitious nature of these and others like them
is easily perceived. Historical fables are those that seem to be the result of inquiry and to have been witnessed, although these too are
acknowledged to be false; but by the nature of the material they di-
vert attention from their ficticity, as does the present fable and the
one about the dog that grabbed the meat and the one about the bird-
catcher who was deceived by the voice of the cicada; [11] for fables
like these, on the surface giving an impression of truth, disguise the
falsehood in them.

      You should know that by beginning study with fable we are nei-
ther trying to enchant the minds of the hearers, as some have said,[17]
and certainly not to demonstrate that the student encounters in
rhetoric something akin to his poetical studies. Rather, we start with
fable because we are introducing the young to the great mystery of
rhetoric, by which I mean what is persuasive; for if in fables we succeed in teaching how to form speeches and actions appropriate for
the characters, it is clear that we shall become competent for the
rhetorical task of composing speeches worthy of the persons in

      [15] Cf. Nicolaus, above, p. 136.
      [16] *Iliad* 1.197; cf. Heraclitus, *Homeric Problems* 20.1–2.
      [17] Cf. Nicolaus, above, p. 135; but at the beginning of the chapter John raised
no objection to this.

complete hypotheses. And in addition, fable has combined a glimpse of the three species of rhetoric: of judicial, by which we prosecute people, of deliberative, by which we exhort or dissuade, and of encomia, by which we blame or approve. Thus, fable is assigned first as being something encompassing the seeds of all the art. **It was the height of summer . . . :** Instead of "the hottest and mid-most part." **[12] And the cicadas were offering up their shrill song:** *Aneballonto,* instead of "were sending up, were singing," or "were striking up," from the metaphor of cithara players. *Aneballonto* also signifies "they postponed;" for a postponement is an *anabolê*. *Syntonon* ("shrill") instead of "much strained;" or because it is a kind of musical sound, like the barbiton and organon and psaltry. **But it was the task of the ants to toil . . . :** This kind of fable is ethical; for the cicada sings in summer and the ant toils about the collection of food. *Epêiei* ("it occurred to them") instead of "they felt eagerness." **When the winter came on:** For in winter, the cicada, ceasing its song and disappearing, is supposed to suffer thus from lack of food, while the ant takes its leisure from its toils for pleasure. The credibility of the fable derives from the occasion and the actions and the habit of each animal. **Similarly, a young person who does not want to toil fares badly in old age.** The epimythion is paradeigmatic; for the orators used fable for proof by example. An epimythion is a statement added to the fable and revealing what is useful in it. They apply the moral in three ways, either paradeigmatically or enthymematically or prosphonetically. Paradeigmatically, for example, **[13]** "This fable teaches us not to do something," and again, "Thus a young person who does not want to toil fares badly in old age." Enthymematically whenever we say, "For one who does not do something deserves rebuke." And prosphonetically, "You too, my boy, refrain from this or that."[18] An epimythion takes the place of an epilogue; for it is possible to provide a conclusion in this way whenever, after the fable has been stated, we venture to bring in some gnomic statement fitting it; for example, "A dog was carrying a piece of meat beside a river, and having seen his reflection in the water, he thought it was another dog carrying a larger piece of meat. When he dropped what he had and jumped into the river to seize it, he disappeared under the water." We shall compose the epilogue as follows: "Thus, then, often those hankering for greater things destroy themselves as well as losing what they have."[19]

[18] Cf. Nicolaus, above, p. 135.
[19] Cf. Theon, above, p. 26.

Some of the eristical sophists[20] raise doubts about the use of fables, saying, "Things that are acknowledged to be false are not useful to orators; for it is impossible to practice rhetoric (*rhêtoreuein*)
with them. A fable is acknowledged to be false; therefore it is useless to an orator in speaking." We solve this problem as follows: To
practice rhetoric is to support the speech with enthymemes and examples. If then we join in a debate arguing by means of a fable, [14]
it really is useless for rhetoric; for proof is characteristic of a rhetor.
But if we set out the fiction in a simple way, teaching something
credible from the fable while desiring only to give advice, the exercise is a useful invention for the young. Again, they say, "If the beginnings of things are useless, the endings are useless as well. Fable,
which is a falsehood, is the beginning of exercise in rhetoric. The
end is therefore useless." And we say that fable is the beginning of
rhetorical exercise and falsehood is a feature of it; one should, however, not pick out one little bit and overlook a rather large number
of good things: teaching how to be persuasive and how to invent
even falsehoods persuasively, which is the greatest topic of rhetoric;[21] and also the moral advice that comes from fable and the correction of habits. By means of its influence on the mind, fable bestows on us the greatest of things useful for life. So we should not
overlook other benefits from fable because of falsehood, a thing
which is acknowledged to be useless.

2. ON NARRATIVE

He has put narrative after fable since fable is false in a simple way
and fitting for the young when just being introduced to composition, while narrative shares both features: sometimes it is [15] false,
sometimes true. Thus, **Theon** says (above, p. 25) that since fable
and narrative are intertwined, "after having stated the fable, we
bring in narrative, or conversely we put the narrative first, the fable
second; for example, having imagined that a camel who longed for
horns was deprived even of his ears, after stating this first, we go on
to the narrative as follows: 'Croesus the Lydian seems to me to have
suffered something similar to this camel,' followed by the whole
story about him."

[20] This is the first of the passages in which John quotes criticisms of progymnasmata, drawn from sources unknown to us. The arguments resemble attacks
on grammar, rhetoric, and other liberal arts by Sextus Empiricus and skeptical
philosophers in general.
[21] By late antiquity "rhetoric" meant first and foremost the practice of declamation, in which the hypotheses were often imaginary.

Narrative is an exposition (*ekthesis*) of an action . . . : Instead of a report (*apangelia*), publication (*prophora*), or narration (*diêgêsis*). **That has happened or as though it had happened.** "That has happened," through being historical and truthful; "as though it had happened," through being fictitious and false; for narrative is a recounting (*aphêgêsis*) of things that really happened or of things seeming to have happened. Some things are true by nature, some false; the orator judges the true by looking not only at the nature of the things but also at the prestigious person of the speaker. Acknowledged truth is seen in these two things: either when something seems to be so to all, or when it satisfied those of repute among the ancient philosophers or poets.[22] Thus we do not avoid fabulous narratives, even if they are false by nature, but **[16]** we accept such things as true on the evidence of the wise men who have mentioned them as true, receiving the judgment of truth from those who have recorded it. Also among the orators, many things will be found that do not have the nature of truth but are honored as true because of the reputation of those who recounted them, as the story of Kore and Demeter in the *Panegyricus* of Isocrates (4.28) and in Demosthenes (23.65–66) what is said about the Areopagus, and the stories in the poets about the gods. When once such things seem so to the many or the wise, those of the orators who tell them no longer take any trouble about them but receive them as true. This is a characteristic element of the art of rhetoric. **Narrative differs from narration as a piece of poetry differs from a poem.** He says that *diêgêma* differs from *diêgêsis*; for a *diêgêsis* is exposition that is comprehensive of many things, whereas *diêgêma* is a exposition of one thing. **Some narrative is dramatic, some historical, some political.** False narrative is dramatic, and is also called fictitious; historical narrative is the truth, for example, that of Herodotus; persuasive narrative is political, for example, that of the orators, which they also call "private" (*idiôtikon*).[23]

You should know that they say some of these are mythical, some possible (*endekhomena*), some true. Those that are false by nature are said to be mythical, those that did not happen **[17]** but are capable of happening are called "possible," like the dramas of the comic poets. Some have said these are "doubtful," as if inclining to either opinion and seeming true to some and thought false by others. Narrative from history, as that of Thucydides and that in courts

[22] An adaptation of Aristotle's criterion for dialectic; cf. *Topics* 1.2.
[23] I.e., as in the "private" orations of Demosthenes, dealing with ordinary life.

of law, is true. Whatever, in addition to truth, has some other features, including arrangement and order and forcefulness, these we
call "a statement of the case" (*katastasis*) and not narration.[24]

Imagined narrative is dramatic. Imagined and fabulous
narrative is dramatic. We call dramatic all those things that are not
reported by the composer of the work but by the characters involved. **Narrative giving an account of early events is historical.**

This is sometimes derived from one who witnessed it, sometimes from other persons. *Historia* differs from *syngraphê* in the
time with which it deals; for narration of early and ancient events is
called *historia,* and exposition of events contemporary with the author is *syngraphê.*[25] **What orators use in their contests is political.** Whatever is spoken only in the voice of the narrator, what happens in constitutional states, and what we make use of in political
life is called "political." This includes deliberating and rendering
judicial decisions and speaking at festivals. **[18]** Therefore, the sort
of thing that happens to private individuals in daily life and in the
changing course of events is called "private" (*idiôtikon*). **There are
six attributes of narrative: the person who acted; the thing
done; etc.** For example: who? what? where? how? when? why?
These are said to be attributes (*parepomena*) and elements (*stoikheia*) and circumstances (*peristatika*) of the narrative. Elements are
the things from which it is composed and into which it is analyzed,
and things are said to be circumstances that surround and contain
the whole action and the whole hypothesis. Since narration is a clarification of actions, the judge needs to know about the act: that it
happened and how and when and in what way and who were the
doers and where, and whether it had been planned ahead of time or
not, and the reasons why it was done in one way and not in another.
Elements of the narration, therefore, are the person, whether one or
more, and the thing done by the person and the place in which the
action took place, and the time at which the action occurred, and the
manner of the action and, sixth, the cause of these things. Since
these are the most general elements of which narrative is composed,

---

[24] *Katastasis* was used by some rhetoricians to mean the statement of a case
and may include proposition, definition of the issue, partition, narrative, anticipa-
tion of objections, and other features of an oration.; cf. Anonymous Seguerianus
112 and Apsines 3.23.

[25] Compare, e.g., Herodotus' *historiês* (1.1) with Thucydides' *xynegrapse* (1.1).
It is characteristic of John, as of other teachers of rhetoric, to take no account of
any post-classical narrative history.

a complete narration contains all of them, as well as things directly connected with them, and a narration is deficient that is lacking any of these.

The attributes of the person **[19]** are origin, nature, rearing, disposition, age, fortune, morality, deed, word, death, what follows death; of the action, whether great or small, safe or risky, possible or impossible, easy or difficult, necessary or not necessary, beneficial or harmful, just or unjust, honorable or dishonorable; to time belong the past, the present, the future; what was first, second, and subsequent; what pertains to life in our time, what to antiquity; then, whether in winter or spring or summer or fall, at night or by day; whether the action took place at an assembly or a procession or a festival, and whether at weddings or a reception of friends, or in circumstances of grief or any other of life's occasions; to place belong size, distance, near a city or town, whether the place was sacred or secular, private or belonging to another, deserted or inhabited, defensible or weak, level or mountainous, dry or wet, barren or wooded, and all similar things; to manner, whether willingly or unwillingly, each of which is divided into three: unwilling into by ignorance and by accident and by necessity, willing into whether acting with force or stealth or deceit; and to the cause of the actions belongs whether they were done to acquire benefits or to escape from evil; or because of a lover or wife or children; or because of the emotions: anger, love, hate, envy, pity, drunkenness, and things like these.

The virtues of narrative are clarity, conciseness, credibility, and hellenism. *In the following account, John draws, without acknowledgement, on what Theon had written about narrative, and also on discussions of the virtues of narration in oratory as found in rhetorical handbooks such as that attributed to Anonymous Seguerianus. Some of what is included does not much apply to progymnasmata. There is some repetition (e.g., about conciseness), resulting from use of a variety of sources.* Clarity: **[20]** that is, a pure and unadorned and careful style; for purity and good judgment are kinds of clarity. Vices of narration are obscurity (*asapheia*), verbosity (*makrologia*), lack of persuasiveness (*apithanon*), and barbarism (*barbarismos*) in choice of words. Thus, the use of words in their proper sense and avoidance of hyperbaton and long sentences is a feature of clarity.

Since there is occasion to speak of clarity, something should be said about obscurity; for by avoiding its tropes we shall be able to make speech clear. Obscurity, then, in general, occurs in two ways; for doubtful clarity occurs in word choices or in contents, and often in both. Obscurity comes about in contents whenever the things being said depart from common understanding; for example, things in dialectic and geometry. Also, whenever we mix up the order of events so that first things are last and last things put earlier. Such things often fulfill the needs of arrangement, but they make a speech hard to follow and unclear. Repeated mentions of the same things also make a speech unclear; it becomes long and tiresome unless we vary it with different constructions and at one time speak as knowing the facts, again as summarizing them, and at another time as something we are reminding the audience of. Thus the tiresome quality is avoided. A fourth cause of obscurity is when we leave out some of the things. Fifth, when [21] we bring in long digressions from the subject. Obscurity arises from diction as follows: when one uses foreign words and tropes and ambiguities and strange words, and composition that is not simple and natural but employs hyperbata and long periods and allegory. Word coinage also makes for obscurity, like "his eye sizzled" in Homer (*Odyssey* 8.394) and *kelaryzei*[26] and such like. You will create obscurity also if you violate sequences with illogical accounts and jump over some things and insert others out of order. That is what someone does when he wants to deceive the judge by the sequence. These and more than these things create obscurity. Clarity is vivid teaching about subjects that leaves nothing doubtful from its expression.

Conciseness similarly comes about in both word choice and contents. You will make the narration concise from treatment of the contents if you do not begin from the distant past, as Euripides did in many cases, and do not waste time on redundant matters,[27] as those usually do who narrate things (long) after the fact; for it perhaps suits historical writing to lengthen the account and begin far back and elaborate some of the things that seem incidental, but anyone who is speaking a narration should look to the chief point of the whole subject that he has proposed, [22] including in the narration only those things that contribute to this; for conciseness is speech signifying the most important features of the subject. Thus, you will make a speech concise by not speaking at length, as do those who narrate other things after the fact, and if you omit things distressing the hearers and which cannot help the debate and can be said elsewhere, and if you do not use digression nor episodic passages and do not wander from the subject; further, if you excuse

---

[26] "Murmur," of flowing water, *Iliad* 20.261; cf. Theon, above, p. 30.
[27] Reading *eis ta parelkonta,* as suggested to me by D. A. Russell.

yourself from tautology and express things that took long in brief space. Conciseness occurs in word choice if you do not use synonyms, like "thick and crowded" or "sword and blade;" for each of these is adequate for clarity. And if you choose words with few syllables from among synonyms, call a sword *xiphos* instead of *makhaira,* for example; and if you do not add unnecessary adjectives to nouns, like the poet's "moist oil" (e.g., *Iliad* 23. 281), and if you avoid periphrasis, like "Herculean might" (e.g., *Iliad* 11.689), and if you do not substitute a phrase for a word, such as "he departed this life" instead of "he died," and things like that; and if you use some metaphors in a proper sense, as Demosthenes (2.9) used "bucked off." By choice of one word he filled out the whole thought. What is called ellipsis creates conciseness; for example, "You love him and he you," where repetition of "loves" is implied. **[23]** Asyndeton too gives an impression of conciseness; for example, "When the ships had been stripped bare, the Chersonese had been plundered," and what follows (Demosthenes 18.139). Nevertheless, care must be taken lest unawares you fall into colloquialism or obscurity in desire for conciseness.

Credibility is an impression of truth. A narration becomes credible if one tries to make everything one says resemble the truth; this will occur if we do not set out the facts in bare form but include the parts. The parts (*moria*) of a narration are person, act, place, manner, time, cause, instrument. Person is the doer and the sufferer; act is an insult, blows; place, as Demosthenes says he was beaten "in the theater" (21.1, 18); manner, as by persuading, by deceiving, by forcing; time is, for example, at night, during the day, at a festival; cause is hatred, love, profit; instrument is with a stone, with a stick; these are said to be the parts and sources of a narration. In addition, it is credible if each thing that is said is consistent with the others and there is no discord or conflict; then, if we do not just set out the bare parts but describe each accurately, like the words "strong, great" in *Against Meidias* (§71). One must add the cause to all of these things; for this is most productive of belief. The character and emotion of the speaker also create credibility; character if it seems not affected, and emotion not only persuades but even moves. It also creates credibility **[24]** to say some small criticism of oneself and something acknowledged as good about the opponent, as Aeschines said (3.171), "His father was a freeman; for there is no need to lie." Vividness (*enargeia*) also contributes to persuasion. Vividness is speech bringing what is described before the eyes. Unpracticed language, revealing improvisation, also creates persuasion.

You will create credibility also if you do not say everything with confidence but add such things as "I think" and "perhaps" and "probably"; for since that which has some attractiveness and tendency to encourage agreement is persuasive, the orator is obviously aiming at the persuasive. Since his purpose is to persuade, he cannot attain it without what is persuasive. If his words were always addressed to an urbane audience, or something close to urbane, he would always make his speech persuasive by keeping to the truth, but since for the most part he addresses common people, for whom it is natural to suggest the truth in many words, it is clear that he will not only use valid arguments but also false ones, as though he were addressing children. There is nothing to hinder use of falsehood as bait, revealing some of the truth like a physician and a general; for it will be an orator's task to foresee if it is possible to persuade without deceit, but the "second wave,"[28] as they say, in the use of persuasion is by deceit and trickery.

To conclude about the narration being credible, [25] one must adopt a style suited to the characters and the subjects and the places and the occasions, and as for the contents, these should all be probable and consistent with each other. One should also briefly add reasons to the narration and say what is unbelievable in a believable way; and simply put, it is appropriate to aim at what is fitting to the person and the other elements of the narration.

To repeat what we are saying, using proper words creates great clarity, but so sometimes does the use of metaphors sometimes for a vivid picture of the subject; for periphrasis makes for obscurity, which also results when we stretch out the length with long periods; and hyperbata and digression beyond what is needed and words meaning something other than what they say (*allêgoriai*) create obscurity.

Conciseness comes about in both word choice and contents, and these are concise if we do not digress. One ought to offer an excuse for long digressions when inserted in a narration—though there is no need to apologize for all, for a digression gives the hearers' mind a rest—, a digression of such length, that is, that alienates the attention of the hearers so that they need a reminder of what has been said earlier, like the digressions of Theopompus in his *Philippic Histories*. There we find two or three or more whole histories inserted as digressions in which there is no mention of Philip nor of any other Macedonian.[29] We shall, thus, have conciseness in mind if

---

[28] "The next best way."
[29] Cf. Theon, above, p. 30.

we do not digress and if we do not begin far back in time; for not to begin **[26]** with the proper subject but to prefix some things and then come to the pertinent actions is not characteristic of conciseness. For example, if a soldier left his proper place and came into sight of his commanding officer, he might be reproached thus: "What good luck that you are here! You yourself will enjoy some reward from those bringing a reward, and you will make those seeing you happier, and you would give us a fine subject for speeches, the very subject I particularly want in order to fashion my commendations of the brave, coward and unmanly as you are, and deserving not one but many deaths for giving your fellow soldiers, as far as was your intent, over to destruction. For what else is it than to destroy your fellow soldiers as much as you can if you leave your post and turn your back to the enemy? How have you had the nerve to come into my sight?" All these statements preceding the subject confuses the mind of the hearer; for he doesn't know what the person who says these things is getting at. But if he began with the action and said "coward and unmanly" and what follows, and then said "What a fine example you have set!" the hearer would not miss the point. Lengthening something out and beginning far back in time and bringing in things that seem to be incidentals may perhaps be appropriate in a history, but one speaking a narration ought to look at the main point of the whole matter which he has proposed and **[27]** include in his narration only what contributes to this. Take what is said about Cylon, for example. If one is composing a history about him it is appropriate to say who his ancestors were and name his father and mother and mention many other things, including the contests which he won at Olympia and how many victories he had, and to identify the Olympiads at which he won prizes. But one who is speaking a narrative (*diêgêma*) about him should not go into any such details and should follow the model of Herodotus and Thucydides when they described the Cylonian pollution.[30] Further, one should narrate things that will distress the audience as briefly as possible, as Homer says (*Iliad* 18.20), "Patroclus lies dead," and dwell on pleasant things, as the same poet made Odysseus narrate his adventures with much detail and leisure to the story-loving Phaeacians.[31]

A report is concise if, for example, a king who has provided the public with some benefit urges them, in return for the benefit, to

---

[30] Cf. Theon, above, p. 33.
[31] Cf. Theon, above, p. 34.

demonstrate good will toward him: "Our policy, even if we do not say it, you know. I want to be able to know some such thing about you. And probably this is not unreasonable; for I should enjoy from you the same disposition that you enjoy because you know my attitude."[32] Do you see how quickly he moves on and does not linger on the thoughts? If he had wanted to be careless, he would have said, "As for our policy, you know, even if we do not say it, how good it has been for you. I want to recognize **[28]** a similar attitude proceeding from you to me. And I do not wish anything inappropriate if I want this; for I should enjoy from you the same disposition that you enjoy from me."

There is conciseness in language also if we avoid periphrasis. It is periphrasis when, instead of adopting one noun or verb, you extend the construction with more; for example, instead of saying, "I think," you say, "I have an idea," and instead of saying, "I agonize," you say, "I am brought into agony," and instead of "I practice," "I compose a practice exercise." Further, by use of a longer explanation; for example, instead of saying, "The subject being a happy one, happy words rightly accompany it," it would be periphrasis if you were to say, "Since there is a happy quality present in the subject, there is an obligation for there also to be a happy quality present in the words"; and instead of, "Since, therefore, the festival is now brilliant, come let us as much as possible display brilliance in the words," if you were to say, "Since, therefore, the circumstances of the festival shine brilliantly upon us, come, as much as possible let us demonstrate brilliance in the joyousness of words." This kind of periphrastic expression belabors a prepared speech; one who cares about conciseness should, thus, avoid periphrasis and also not use synonyms; for words having the same force make the statement longer when it is unnecessary, as in Demosthenes' *Second Olynthiac* (§1), **[29]** "This seems in all respects the work of some superhuman and divine beneficence."

Asyndeton has some of the effect of conciseness; it occurs when we leave out the conjunctions that tie the statement together; for example, "A little more than three hundred men of Thebes entered about the first watch with arms into Platatea in Boeotia, although an ally of Athens; Naucleides opened the gates for them; they placed their arms in the marketplace," and so on.[33] And in Demosthenes (18.69), "Amphipolis, Pydna, Potidea, Halonnesus," and

---

[32] The source is unknown, possibly Sopatros.
[33] Paraphrase of Thucydides 2.2; cf. Theon, above, p. 38.

(9.27), "But he goes against Hellespontus, earlier he came to Ambracia, to Elis, that great city in Peloponnesus, recently he was plotting against Megara."

There is need to chose shorter words. And one should use simple words rather than compounds and shorter rather than longer, whenever they signify the same thing. Let us avoid epithets and redundancies and repetitions, if we care about conciseness. Often ellipsis creates conciseness, and the figure of speech called epizeugma, when one thing is made to apply to many similar things; for example, if we say, "He[34] commended the Athenians for fighting well at sea, the Lacedaimonians for fighting enthusiastically by land, the Plataeans for aiding the Athenians, **[30]** and the Tegeans for sharing the common contest." The word "commended," placed once for sake of conciseness, has yoked (*epezeuxen*) together many things. Conciseness means to give an account of necessary preceding events without extending the speech by too many of the circumstances.

Credibility is treatment of the subjects leading the hearers to persuasion.

It is hellenism (i.e., pure Greek) if you do not use solecisms or barbarisms or depart from the dialect that you have chosen, [and if you aim at what is appropriate to the proposed persons and things and whatever character and age and fortune is considered.][35]

They say that credibility is the characteristic virtue of a narrative and that the others belong to the whole speech.

Some narratives are told for their own sake, some in relation to something. Those told for their own sake are ones containing simply an exposition of the contents, like this narrative about the rose or the story of Daphne or how Xerxes crossed Athos and the Hellespont, while those in relation to something are the ones used in the lawcourts; for it is something effective and the speaker makes his exposition with a view to this. This progymnasma is useful preparation both for statements in the law courts and for compositions of the historians; for one who has written a narrative well will be able also to compose a history well. History is, in fact, an exposition of one narrative after another.[36]

[31] But someone will say, "Isn't it the fact, then, if narrative is an exposition of events and fable contains an exposition of events,

[34] Herodotus, cf. Thucydides 9.71.
[35] This comment seems inappropriate here and should perhaps be deleted.
[36] Cf. Theon, above, p. 4.

that fable and narrative are the same? What then is the difference between these progymnasmata?" We say in reply that the names differ either by nature or in actualization. Each has its proper modifying term from nature and from actualization; for fable, being fictitious by nature, when activated for advice, looks to what benefits the hearer, while narrative, by nature subsequent to the sequence of events that have happened, has the actuality of teaching the hearer what has resulted. The purpose of a narrative is the teaching of the narrative, the purpose of a rhetorical fable is not the teaching of the fable but the deduction of the moral. The exercises differ, then, in the way each has a different function.

Again, they say, "If falsehoods are useless to the orator, and if mythical narratives are by nature false, they are useless to the orator; for they do not persuade the hearer." And we say that probabilities (*endoxa*) are material for the orator and he accepts these as truths; for this is an element of his art, and thus the orator does not busy himself with nature, which is the special possession of philosophy, and if he were to do so, clearly he will be going beyond the limit of his art. Thus, then, we construct and refute mythical narratives, **[32]** realizing in each case that we are treating what is debatable. Falsehoods inhere in the nature of the material, but because of the reputation of the speakers they are taken as true by those who say and those who hear them. There are various treatments based on need; for when there is occasion to teach, what is commonly believed is taken as true, but when the occasion is for argument, we offer falsehood; so there is always a treatment in terms of need.

Let one who admires the rose for its beauty . . . : (Literally, "of its beauty," in the genitive,) instead of "concerning" (*peri*) or "because of (*heneka*) its beauty." Some insert the word "to be" after "beauty." **The goddess was in love with Adonis and Ares was in turn in love with her.** The form is direct discourse. The narrative begins with "the goddess was in love." What precedes take the place of a prooemion. Persons are Ares and Aphrodite and Adonis, actions are loving and loving in turn. The myth is as follows: A certain maiden was in love with her own father. Clearly at a loss, she had intercourse with him in disguise. When the father learned what had happened he was angry at his daughter. Neither able to live, because of her father, nor to die, because she was pregnant, she prayed to Aphrodite, who changed her into a tree. In the ninth month after she was turned into a tree she broke through **[33]** the tough bark and gave birth to Adonis. Aphrodite took him and raised him and fell in love with him when he came to manhood. **The goddess was to Adonis . . . :** He is saying that what Ares was to Aphrodite, since Aphrodite was obviously in love, this she was to Adonis. Instead of Ares was in love with Aphrodite, Aphrodite was in love with Adonis. **Ares, being struck with jealousy . . . :** This is the manner, and the cause is "thinking the death of Adonis would be the end of love." **Hurried to the rescue . . . :** Instead of "rushed to help Adonis." "Going out to him" is included in "to help." **And in her haste, falling on a rose, she stumbled among the thorns.** Here is the place, place-in-which instead of place-to-which, in order to show her having fallen and having arrived. "Stumbled" is used instead of "deflected" or "struck." **And pierces the bottom of her foot . . . :** Instead of "is struck" or "is pricked." **Changed to the now familiar appearance . . . :** That is, of blood, because it is dark red. As the bottom of her foot was white before but bloodied after this, so it happened to the rose.

3. ON CHREIA

[34]   Aphthonius put fable first because it carries an image of all rhetoric and confers a faculty of speaking. It is an image of the art because, in itself, it bears and reveals the three species of rhetoric; for by it we praise fine things and condemn evils and exhort or dissuade, with the result that from these the young man perceives a trace of the three species of rhetoric. It contains the whole faculty of rhetoric in teaching us how to handle credibility. We know that credibility results from the young learning how to make speeches suitable for the supposed characters in a fable: to attribute to the lion, as king of beasts, a kingly mind, and to give the fox, being villainous by nature, an intent full of villainy, and we shall make the deer, being silly, think simple-minded thoughts. It is clear that if we alter such a quality in the animals, we shall make the fable unbelievable. Thus, clearly, starting from this introduction, students will maintain characters appropriate to persons also in their declamation and will make their speech persuasive.

Here, some are skeptical, saying that, "If what is acknowledged to be false is contrary to what is persuasive—for something persuasive is what can persuade, thus it is called "persuasive" from its persuading the opponent—the falsehood that is a natural part of fable is, as a result, contrary to the persuasive. **[35]** Who will be persuaded that something is true which is not true by nature? For example, that the horse is rational and the tortoise too, or that the lion desires marriage or the ass wants to seem to be a lion, when these things are against nature and false." We shall reply that, just as in practicing hypotheses, by agreement we grant a premise that is false,[37] similarly in fable, starting with the title, we grant as a given that dumb animals are doing or saying something, since if this is not granted there is no fable to start with. When this is agreed, just as in fable, starting with the title, it is agreed that dumb animals are rational or say or do something, in the rest of the account we are seeking what is credible if the fiction conforms to the character of the participants and if the account of the circumstance fits the participants. In this alone is credibility seen. For these reasons fable was assigned the first position, and also because fable is a ready tool of moral instruction for a young man by means of the fiction and the simplicity of the style and the brevity of the exposition.

Narrative is second. Of the five parts of a speech, one consists in prooemia, another in narratives, another in antitheses, another in solutions, and another in epilogues. Now fable, even if it sometimes contributes to belief, nevertheless occupies the place, so to speak, of prooemia, by which it both confirms and attacks something—this is the function of prooemia—[36] and it requires that narration come second.[38] Further, fable is by nature false, and the false lacks substance; but narrative has something true about it, something that actually exists. From not-being becomes being. Thus, quite reasonably, fable has been put first and narrative has second place. Further, fable is always false, whereas narrative is sometimes false, sometimes true. Since, then, progymnasmata advance little by little to the greater, it is reasonable that we come second to narrative as having some more truth than fable.

We set the chreia as the third progymnasma; for the progymnasmata rightly follow the order of the parts of a speech. Just as the agonistic part comes third in a speech, so here after narrative the agonistic part is third in the sequence of smaller parts; for in chreias we confirm whether a statement is true, whether an action is well done. All confirmation belongs to proofs.[39] Further, all art ordinarily advances, beginning from the simpler, toward the more complete. Thus, we have observed this fact in the case of the progym-

---

[37] Traditional themes for declamation in rhetorical schools contained many historical and legal falsehoods.

[38] John, or his source, is confused about the traditional function of prooemia, which is to gain the good will and attention of an audience.

[39] *Agônes*, the proofs as a part of a speech.

nasmata; for the fable and the narrative were rather simple, whereas it is more complete to be engaged in debate to confirm something else, even if this happens to be something rather small; for, as I said, [37] we confirm a single saying or a single and brief action. Further, to speak in support of someone else has rhetorical force. Thus, in a chreia we speak in support of those who have said or done something on the ground that they spoke or acted well. This is more difficult than expounding a fable or narrative. For those things are simpler and involve unforced language. Further, since a fable is rather simple, it delights by its invention and contributes to great things, while a chreia, even if it benefits the hearers the same as does fable, yet has some more agonistic quality and contains a confirmation; for it is not only a chreia[40] but also a confirmation of a chreia. To have joined in debate with someone requires a more complete grasp; for if Aphthonius had regarded the exercise as concerned with inflections and numbers, as in grammarians' schools,[41] it would really have been just a chreia, but if it includes an argument from epicheiremes and paradeigms, as we do in confirmation of the chreia, moving after the prooemion and statement to support of it, this is no longer only a chreia but confirmation of a chreia.

***

At this point, John quotes Aphthonius' definition of a chreia and proceeds to phrase by phrase analysis of his description, omitted here. John's commentary incorporates considerable material taken from the accounts of the chreia by Theon and by Nicolaus, although neither author is named. At 47, 10 John is commenting on Aphthonius' list of topics for elaboration of a chreia. One topic is citation of a paradeigma, *or example:*

A paradeigma is a similar thing attributed to a similar person, something known offered in support of something unknown; for example, "Do you want to see the beauties of rhetoric? Look to Demosthenes." Comparison (*parabolê*) differs from paradeigma in that a comparison is drawn from unspecified things, a paradeigm from what are specified; and a comparison may be drawn from lifeless and unreasoning things; for example (Demosthenes 2.10), "Just as, I think, in the case of a house and a boat," and (*Iliad* 6.506), "As when a stabled horse, having fed his fill at the manger," and (*Iliad*

[40] I.e., a statement of what was said or done.
[41] Cf. the remarks of Nicolaus, above, p. 139, and the treatment of the chreia by Theon, ch. 3.

11.558), "As when a lazy ass, going by a field, gets the better of boys." **[48]** A paradeigma is drawn only from men or gods. And a comparison is often from things of the past, a paradeigma from those of the present. A paradeigma is a demonstration by means of a narration that is similar and known to something in doubt and unknown. . . .

***

At 54,18 John is commenting on the example of Demosthenes, offered in support of the chreia recommending toil:

(Aphthonius) is saying that (Demosthenes') zeal so exceeded the zeal of all others as to cause trouble to his head and to deprive it of its ornament[42] rather than that his thoughts should be confused and lead to nothing. **[55] And he expended in toils what others lavished on pleasures.** Either he is speaking of his wealth, which he used up in buying books, or what he spent on oil for his lamps.

***

[55,16]   4. ON MAXIM

Aphthonius put the maxim after the chreia, both because it uses the same division of topics—wherefore many technical writers have not given it special treatment, thinking it to be included in the chreia—and because the arts advance from the lesser to the greater. Now the chreia, **[56]** even if it has close relationship to the maxim, is by its nature a lesser exercise because it states particulars. After having been exercised first in particulars we move to the general statement, which is the maxim. The maxim in its perfect form requires greater thought and skill, since it is more general and in that respect more complete. It is called maxim (*gnômê*) because it contains knowledge (*gnôsis*) of what naturally characterize things.

Maxim is a summary statement in declarative sentences, urging or dissuading something. He said "statement" (*logos*), since maxim is always in words and not, like the chreia sometimes in deeds. "In declarative sentences," since the chreia often takes the form of question and answer, while the maxim is only cited as a declarative sentence. "Declarative sentence" (*apophansis*) is a generic term including negative and affirmative statements. Thus, since maxims are spoken in negative and affirmative statements, Aphthonius for this reason includes both in the generic

---

[42] See note on this passage in the translation of Aphthonius, above, p. 99.

term, saying "in declarative sentences." "Summary," (*kephalaiôdês*) instead of brief and curtailed, or instead of recapitulated. A recapitulation (*anakephalaiôsis*) is language recounting in brief form what has been said in greater detail in the narration and other parts of a speech. "Urging," clearly something good, and "dissuading," clearly something bad.

[57]   **Sopatros** defined the maxim as follows: "A maxim is a declarative statement, in universal form, concerning the quality of persons or things or both. It is a statement about persons whenever one says, (for example,) 'I never asked who a man is / Who enjoys bad company, knowing that / Such he is as those with whom he likes to be.'"[43] Or like, "The majority of men are bad.' Concerned with things, as (Demosthenes 2.12), 'Every speech, if deeds are lacking, seems vain and empty,' or (Isocrates 1.6), 'Wealth is more a minister of vice than of nobility.' There are many other declarative statements about things said by the ancients. By 'both,' I mean a thing and a person, as when Demosthenes says (18.192), 'What is past is always dismissed by everybody, and no one proposes any care about any of it.'" *The quotation from Sopatros ends here.*

***

[60,19]   So much for the distinctions, and you should elaborate it with the headings for the chreia. The maxim, he is saying, is divided into the same topics as is the chreia. But someone might object in this way: "If the maxim contains knowledge of what characterizes things in accord with nature, it is true and acknowledged so, and being acknowledged it has no need of confirmation. Thus, it was unnecessary for him to say to confirm the maxim." This **[61]** is a strong objection, but we refute it as follows. Many maxims are persuasive, but what is persuasive is not true at all times; for example, (Hesiod, *Works and Days* 763–64), "Talk never utterly fades away, / If many folk speak it." This is not true at all times. Then too, truth needs advocacy in order to persuade the hearer; for the maxim is not always by itself appealing to the hearer. "Make a promise, and disaster is neigh"[44] is not always true, nor is "One wise thought defeats many hands."[45] So they always need confirmation to persuade the hearer.

Again, someone might say, "If the elaboration of a chreia and a

---

[43] Cf. Hermogenes, above, p. 78.
[44] Attributed to Thales of Miletus in Stobaeus 3.1; frag. 215, ed. Diels-Kranz.
[45] Euripides, frag. 200, ed. Nauck.

maxim is the same, there is no need to practice oneself on the
maxim." But we have already stated the difference: in the chreia the
saying that is being confirmed is a particular one, whereas in the
maxim it is a universal; and in the chreia all the confirmation is directed to praise of the speaker, whereas in the maxim it is naturally
confirmation of the saying itself. The following too should be said
about the maxim. Let it be granted that it has a shared feature with
the chreia, since the exercise is one of the double ones that involve
arguments on both sides and not one of the simple exercises dealing with one side only, as are the fable and the narrative and the
ecphrasis; for in these there is simply a recounting of things, but in
the maxim and in the chreia there is not simply a recounting of
things but there will be a positive and negative part,[46] as also in
refutation and common-place and encomion and the remaining exercises. If then we can argue in support of a chreia and a maxim,
clearly we can also argue against them, but because of their benefit
to the young **[62]** we do not refute chreias and maxims but we practice argument in support of them in order to urge the young to in-
dustry and that they may reap the advantage of what is being said
or done.

***

**[62,23] A chreia differs from a maxim in that a chreia
sometimes indicates an action:**
    He says this because the chreia **[63]** consists in words, but
sometimes also in actions, whereas the maxim always consists solely
in words. **And in that a chreia needs to indicate a person.** The
chreia is always attributed to a person, whereas the maxim is a universal statement and not always attributed to a person. Aphthonius
mentioned two differences, but we add the following that have been
identified by others: We are able to do what is said in the maxim,
for example, "There is no need for the strong to act violently toward
the weak," but it is not in our power to fashion a chreia without a
person; and the maxim only states a universal, the chreia sometimes
a universal, sometimes a particular. Further, they differ in that a
maxim is always something useful in life, whereas a chreia is sometimes a pleasantry with no practical application.

***

---

[46] The reference is probably to the raising and answering of objections (antithesis and solution).

[63,25] Theognis did not allow his poetry to be attacked.
The first heading here is the *prokatarktikon,* **[64]** which is praise of
the speaker. This needs to be specific to the man of whom we have
made mention and of the subject. We must laud both the one who
spoke and the one who did the deed. Demosthenes did this in
Against Aeschines (19.297); for when he is going to read an oracle
telling the leaders to take care, he says, "I shall read to you an oracle of the gods themselves, who always save the city much more
than do its leaders." Aphthonius has done this here by speaking
praise of Theognis who proposed the maxim, separating him from
all the other poets as liars because of their use of many myths and
accepting his poetry as containing abundance of counsel and advice
about things useful to our daily life. . . .

***

[67]   5. ON REFUTATION

Refutation and confirmation have been rightly put after chreia and
maxim; for these exercises are of an argumentative kind. But you
see that here again we proceed to the greater, combatting or supporting by means of a complete narration and **[68]** many words and
subjects.

They[47] ask, "How is it possible for refutation to precede confirmation; for how can we refute when we do not yet known something
about it?" And we reply that refutation is concerned with known
and evident things. And (we ask in turn,) How is it possible to confirm things not previously refuted? For these things have their support from themselves and have no need of confirmation. For this
reason, attack on and fair words about the speakers precede the
statement, as already known and evident; for he teaches it in the
narration.[48]

Refutation is an overturning of some proposed subject.
He ought to have added "by syllogisms" to the definition so that it
becomes "an overturning by syllogisms of some proposed subject,"
since there is an overturning also by witnesses.[49] Further, commands of tyrants overturn things but certainly the order of tyrants
and despots is not a refutation for this reason. He is saying that the
overturning of the proposed subject is a speech of rebuttal. There

---

[47] I.e., the eristical sophists; cf. above, p. 182.
[48] Or perhaps better, "in the chreia," as suggested to me by D. A. Russell.
"He" is Aphthonius.
[49] John may have found this criticism of Aphthonius in one of his sources.

was no need for him to say "overturning" (*anatropê*) but he should
have spoken of a "testing" (*elenxis*) of the proposition; for we remove belief in it rather than remove the subject; for surely we do
not make it utterly vanish nor do we bring it into not being. **One
should refute what is neither very clear nor altogether impossible:** We refute, he says, and confirm **[69]** things neither true
nor false by nature; for refutation and confirmation are a waste of
time when belief for or against something is already held. All such
efforts are a waste of time where the hearer has a previous belief.
For this reason we do not refute or confirm fable; for belief that fables are fictional has been predetermined and it is a waste of time
for one refuting them to say they are false—it has already been
agreed—and for one confirming them to say they are true is a useless statement; for it has been previously determined that they are
false. **But what holds a middle position.** By "position" (*taxis*) he
means nature (*physis*). Since some events have really happened and
are true and some have an appearance of having happened, we shall
omit those that have happened and are of a true nature; for it is not
possible to provide demonstration to undo them. But we shall try to
refute those of the other sort. Aphthonius says this because we do
not refute or confirm all narrations but only those that are capable
of having happened but which did not. These are those where opinion is in doubt, of which there is an especially large crowd in mythical narratives. These are to a great extent receptive of treatment for
or against. **[70] Those engaged in refutation should first ver-
bally attack those who have said something is so.** Attack (*dia-
bolê*) on those who have alleged something should come first, but
there is no need to use intemperate rudeness; one should suit the
words to the quality of the supposed persons, since perhaps, if the
speaker is young, he lacks confidence for speaking boldly; and even
if he is older, one ought to compose the argument in a way that is
restrained and indicative of character. **Then add an exposition of
the subject and use these headings.**

Let there be, he says, at the beginning an attack on those who
have alleged something as a simple prooemion, then an exposition
of the subject, then in turn the headings from the beginning
through each of the parts.

But someone might say, "If a rhetorical speech is quadripartite,
made up of prooemia, statements (*katastaseis*), proofs, epilogues,
and if the refutation has a prooemion, statement, refutation or confirmation, by which we try to show that the narrative as proposed is
false or true, and a conclusion, which is equal to an epilogue, then

the refutation is a complete hypothesis, or complete hypotheses are refutations of what is being claimed by the opponents." We shall reply that what is being said[50] is very silly; for **[71]** we have not used final headings—the just, legal, advantageous, possible—but three or four or fewer epicheiremes, however the material provides treatment. These do not constitute a heading and the epicheiremes are being practiced for their own sake and not included in a heading. But look, he says, "The possible is included in the confirmation." Not, however, in the form of advice but in scrutiny whether it is possible to happen or not in nature, which creates an epicheireme. The heading is made up of many epicheiremes, whereas the epicheireme itself is, in itself, simple.

John continues with material from Nicolaus, without acknowledgement. Subsequently (pp. 75ff. Rabe) he incorporates Theon's discussion of the sources of epicheiremes, and then proceeds to line by line commentary of Aphthonius' text.

***

[84]   6. ON CONFIRMATION

Confirmation is the corroboration of some matter at hand. He is saying that the confirmation is constructive language, corroborative of the matter at hand, showing that it is true.

The chapter continues with a brief line by line explication of Aphthonius' text.

***

[89,15]   7. ON COMMON-PLACE

There are four parts to a complete hypothesis: prooemion, narration, proofs, epilogue. Fable and narration occupy the position of prooemion and narration. Chreia and maxim **[90]** and refutation and confirmation are in the place of proofs, and common-place, being an epilogue, logically follows these; for it amplifies what precedes, having the force of an epilogue and sharpening the interest of the judges after the demonstration. Common-place differs from encomion in that common-place applies to every person and in every place when viewed in terms of the subject, but an encomion is not the same everywhere; one will not praise an Athenian in the same words as a Theban.

---

[50] The theory just stated.

A topos is a starting point for an epicheireme or a starting point for a proof. The *Topics* of Aristotle shows that the epicheirme[51] is called a topos; for those books contain only the starting points of epicheiremes. It is called topos because, starting from it as from a 'place,' we easily construct an argument against those acknowledging wrong-doing. For this reason, some have defined it as the starting point of epicheiremes. An attack on a violent bully applies to all such in common and is not open to question and is called a topos. Starting from this, as from a place, we easily have a supply of things to say against Meidias and his ilk. So it is a topos, because one can use it as a base to find an epicheireme. It is called "common"-place by a metaphor from those standing in their own place **[91]** and ready to contend in strength with rivals.

A common-place is a statement amplifying inherent good or bad things. Topos, he says, is of two sorts, one directed against those who have done wicked things, for example against a tyrant, a traitor, a homicide, a profligate, the other on behalf of those who have accomplished some good thing, for example for a tyrannicide, a war hero, a lawgiver. Thus topos is double and rightly includes argument pro and con. For if it is a part of a speech, and every speech involves two sides of an issue, this too should go in both directions. He says common-place "amplifies"; for it is not an investigation and test of the fact but amplification and enlargement (*ongkos*) and forcefulness. Amplification suits an advocate's speech in a trial;[52] Aphthonius did not make the same mistake as others,[53] since he defined it as a tirade and an assault and something that fills the place of an advocate's speech.

Sopatros defined common-place as follows: "Common-place is an amplification of an acknowledged crime or error. A crime (*adikêma*) is something having a definite punishment by law and (involving) some unacceptable action of someone toward another, such as killing, wanton insult, adultery, grave robbing, and the **[92]** like; an error (*hamartêma*) has no penalty defined by the laws but is nevertheless detested by everybody when done against us and by us, such as wastefulness, drunkenness, fornication, sloth, and things like that." *The quotation from Sopatros ends here.*

Some say, "If common-place sharpens the judges for punish-

---

[51] Enthymeme, in Aristotle's terminology. John's statement shows some confusion.

[52] I.e., a second speech, after the litigant has spoken on his own behalf.

[53] These "others" apparently included proof that the person attacked had committed the act.

ment, in the case of errors such as profligacy, laziness, drunkenness, and the like for which there is no penalty, what is the purpose of sharpening them?" And we say that its purpose is the proper attitude toward error, that is, hatred and dissuading one who does such things. This is the judgment against such things, and one should everywhere keep to the goal of the topic.

And again some ask, "If common-place is an amplification of an acknowledged crime or error, is an account of it unnecessary? For it is always unnecessary to make a speech about things that are acknowledged." And we say that such people have already giving a refutation in their premise; for they said amplification was a property of the topic, and so common-place has as its goal to make an amplification of what is acknowledged.

John then draws, without acknowledgement, on Nicolaus, and subsequently incorporates material from both Theon and Nicolaus, again without attribution.

***

[94,5]   It is like a second speech and an epilogue. It has a similarity, he says, to the second speech (*deuterologia*) and the epilogue.

There are four kinds of *deuterologia*. There may be two speeches by the same speaker on the same subject, as in Antiphon's *Tetralogies;* for there were two accusations and two defenses by the same person and on the same subject. The prosecutor accuses and the defendant replies, then the prosecutor accuses again, refuting the defense, and the defendant defends himself against the second attack. Or the speaker may remain the same but the subject under discussion may differ; and this is found in almost every case receiving judgment; for we make the first speech about the complaint and the second about the penalty.[54] First it is necessary to demonstrate that he has been a traitor, and finally to say what penalty fits it. The speaker remains the same in such cases, but the subject is different. At one time we are making a speech about treason, perhaps, or tyranny or some other charge, and at another about the penalty to be paid, as we find in *Against Aristocrates*. And it is possible for the speaker to change his ground after delivering the earlier speech. **[95]** Or, in contrast, the subject can remain the same while the person changes, as in the case of what are called first and second plead-

---

[54] As seen in the trail of Socrates; cf. Plato's *Apology* 38c–41d.

ings. This happens when two persons share one case and one speaks first and the other second. The person differs, but the subject is the same, as in *Against Androtion,* where Euctemon and Diodorus shared the case and Euctemon spoke first on the subject and Diodorus second. Similarly, in *Against Aristogeiton,* Lycurgus was first and after him, Demosthenes.[55] So it is also in *Against Leptines,* for two speakers shared the case there as well. And the speech *Against Aristocrates* is similar. The word *deuterologia* is also used to mean *dittologia,*[56] as in common parlance. For we say to repeat oneself is to say the same thing twice (*deuterologein*). *Deuterologia* is used in this meaning when, after the subject is demonstrated, we make a recapitulation of what has been said earlier and say this, as it were, for the second time. This much about *deuterologia.*

***

[98,4] We make up a form of prooemia for the sake of practice for the young. Since the form (*typos*) of prooemia alone is not taught elsewhere, Aphthonius put a species or form of prooemia in common-place, although contrary to its nature, so that we exercise ourselves in each part as we advance through the previous exercises to a complete hypothesis. Thus the authority on the art says that prooemia do not naturally belong to the common-place, but for the sake of exercise and so the speech does not seem lacking a head, we make up some kind of prooemia. He rightly incorporated a "form of prooemia" in order that the whole discourse not be gaping and lacking a head.

***

[105,4] It is necessary for us to say how many things are connected with common-place. Eight things are connected with it: definition, for example, "common-place is speech amplifying inherent goods and evils"; cause, for example, "it is so called from fitting all in common who take part in the same deed"; similarity to *deuterologia* and epilogue, for example, "it is like a second speech and epilogue"; after the prooemia statement of the heading derived from the opposite; comparison; criticism of intent; digression containing accusation against his previous life; rejection of pity because of the six headings called "final."[57]

---

[55] See above, p. 154, n. 59.
[56] Saying something twice.
[57] As listed by Aphthonius: legality, justice, advantage, possibility, honor, result.

You should know that fable has some resemblance to common-place; for in fable one factor is exhortation to hatred of the wicked; for example, hatred of tyrants, as when we tell the fable of the wolf making himself tyrant over the animals and the lion plotting to take over the kingdom; or hatred of thieves and those sinning against the gods, as when we describe all the other animals fleeing from Apollo and Artemis and insulting them, but only the dog flattering and making up to them. The difference is that common-place has an exhortation to punishment, as for an acknowledged crime, while fable is advice to avoid such things. And fable shows those who put their hands to wicked deeds as having been chastised **[106]** —for otherwise it would not perform its function—and is a deterrent from worse things, whereas the purpose of common-place is to make the wicked receive punishment. Also, common-place proceeds through a series of headings—for example, prooemia and the rest—while fable takes a simple form. Similarly, narrative resembles common-place, and the other exercises; for it occurs as a small part in all of them. In common-place we shall give a narrative in accord with what is called *diatypôsis*,[58] and in introduction of a law we narrate things about the law, and also in thesis, where we discuss nature or a constitution or marriages or any of such things.

***

[112,14] Now all other men . . . : Nicolaus[59] calls this heading "before the fact," which he says is not introduced for the sake of the facts but as a reminder to the judges of what they know. Here he says it is necessary to take up "homogenious things"[60] as giving life to the speech. Whatever is taken from similar things are said to be homogenious; "For," he says, "while conjecturing about what has been done earlier and saying that after many other things **[113]** the defendant did what he is now accused of, we ought to provide credibility to our words from the examination of things like to those now being judged; for example, we shall say against someone being tried for temple robbing, that it is probable, after committing many earlier thefts, that he finally turned to this source of profit."[61] When someone desired a tyranny, he is supposed to be rich and to have done many violent things. It is good here to consider homogenious

---

[58] Vivid description.
[59] Cf. above, p. 151.
[60] Cf. above, p. 152.
[61] Cf. above, p. 152.

things, since it is not possible for one to proceed to tyranny without having been practiced previously in a reckless way in each of its parts; for when in authority, in his pride he indulged his audacity, regarding all others as beggars, dirty objects rather than men. Therefore, in due course he came to the pinnacle of his crimes." This is what Nicolaus says, consistent with Aphthonius.

Sopatros, on the other hand, says that the epicheireme "before the fact" is of the following sort. "A fact," he says, "is the subject on which we are making the speech; for example, tyranny, desertion, adultery. Now what was before these? Before tyranny there was democracy, government by law, everything in a state of peace, no use of force, nothing illegal, and so on. Before the man deserted, all were ready for war, there was good order for battle, valor among the men, successes, and such like. Before adultery there was modesty among women, good will in the household, unsuspecting cohabitation of husbands, and such like."

***

[116,1] Note that Aphthonius omitted the honorable and the result; for not all headings apply in all cases, nor do they have a definite order. One should use those that suit the case at hand, since there is no necessity at all to go through all.

8. ON ENCOMION

The exercises described up to this point preserve a partial image of complete cases, but encomium is complete in itself and contains a full hypothesis. This is because, of the three species of rhetoric, one is encompassed here, I mean what is called panegyrical. Because of the variety in the epideictic species, it is equivalent to speeches on great causes and needs complete control of its internal arrangement and division.

Encomion is speech expressive of inherent excellences. Aphthonius gives the definition first so that, knowing what encomion is, we may understand the division. "Expressive," instead of narrational, reportive, revealing the greatness of virtuous deeds and other excellences.

Some[62] object, "If rhetoric is tripartite, and the species are equal to each other, **[117]** it is very strange for the judicial and deliberative species to consist of complete hypotheses, while the encomiastic is found in an incomplete one; for progymnasmata are incomplete."

---

[62] The "eristical sophists" of p. 182, above?

We reply as follows. On the one hand, in terms of the division of rhetoric on the basis of species, the three are equal to each other, but on the other, in terms of a complete speech encomion is incomplete; for it is part of a complete speech, and in judicial speeches there is often need of encomia, as in *On the Crown* and *Against Leptines,* and in deliberative speeches too. As a result, sometimes it is included as a part and sometimes it contributes to the hypothesis, functioning like a kind of epicheireme; for on these terms it is time to call the epicheirematic topics also "a complete hypothesis." This further must be said. If by dividing up a complete hypothesis we put each part among the progymnasmata—for example, narration, refutation, confirmation—, clearly encomion also is put among the exercises as something that occurs incidentally in an hypothesis as a part of it. Further, a complete hypothesis is divided into "final" headings, and "final" headings are the legal, just, advantageous, possible, of which each heading can make a complete hypothesis. What do I mean by this? (They make a complete hypothesis) whenever only the just or only the advantageous or the possible is in question. Speeches divided into "final" headings are themselves complete, but encomion has topics, that is, epicheiremes, instead of headings. These are properly called headings when found in an hypothesis. But if encomion is not divided into any of these [118], it is not a complete hypothesis and remains rightly put among the incomplete. Further, a complete hypothesis is one that contains something discussed in a lawcourt or assembly or council chamber, and none of this is discussed in encomion. It is devoted to amplification of acknowledged goods; thus encomion is not a complete hypothesis.[63]

Others speak of its common features with narration and contend that it is a complete hypothesis; for they say that in narratives we also praise either some grove or watery place or some strikingly attractive young man. But in narrative this is not always the case, and if sometimes we have need to praise, we do it for the benefit of increasing persuasiveness, whereas in encomion the goal is to celebrate. And in narration we praise with few words, but here throughout all the headings of the encomion. The narration is a part of the speech, but an encomion is a self-contained and complete logos.[64]

[63] The distinction between headings and epicheiremes may derive from Sopatros; cf. below, p. 227.

[64] This is inconsistent with what is said in the previous paragraph. Drawing on different sources, John has apparently become thoroughly muddled. Some of the problem results from using encomion to mean both an epideictic oration and a progymnasma.

Another reason why encomion is included among the progymnasmata is that often we require the young to address a governor.[65]
**It is so called from singing in villages in ancient times.
They used to call narrow passages _kômai_.** The poets, he is saying, sang hymns to the gods in the villages. They sang in villages
[119] and not in cities, either because in ancient times the inhabitants of Hellas lived in villages, as Thucydides says (1.10), and not
in cities; or because hymns to the gods were most favored among
pious farmers and at gatherings of those dedicating the first fruits
of the harvests to the gods: at the Thalysia and Epilenia and such
festivals. But others say it was not in villages (_kômai_) but in revels
(_kômoi_) and drinking parties (_symposioi_) that the poets sang, and encomion got its name from that because the ancients composed eulogies of men at a revelry and, as one might say, at a game.[66] A eulogy
(_eulogia_) is a form of praise that can be spoken in poems and lyrics
and not always in prose. The species of encomion is called panegyrical because for the most part the ancients celebrated people at
festivals. **It differs from a hymn and an _epainos_ in that a hymn
is a celebration of gods, an encomion of men.** Some think
there is no difference between saying _epainos_ and encomion on the
ground that both words mean the same thing; however, Aphthonius
says encomion differs from hymn and epainos; for hymns and
paeans and processionals and dithyrambs are customarily addressed
to gods, and encomia to men. Hymns are distinguished on the basis
of each god: those to Apollo are called paeans and hyporchemes,[67]
those to Dionysus **[120]** are dithyrambs, those to Aphrodite _erôti-
koi_. Those to the other gods they call hymns generically, though the
term is more generally used of those to Zeus. Paeans are specifically
hymns sung to Apollo and Artemis; on occasions of suffering from
pestilence the ancients appeased these gods with the paean, thinking that Apollo was the same as the sun and Artemis as the moon,
and that droughts and pestilences were caused by the sun and
moon, but later they sang paeans to all the gods. They called processionals (_prosodia_) by that name because those who were ap-
proaching temples or altars sang to the accompaniment of the flute.
Hymns, in contrast, were sung while standing still and accompanied
by the cithara. Hymns to Dionysus are dithyrambs, since he was
called Dithyrambos because he went through two doors (_thyrai_) and

---

[65] I.e., compose a _prosphônêtikos;_ cf. Menander Rhetor 2.10.
[66] Cf. Theon, above, p. 50.
[67] A choral hymn in cretic verse.

bellies; for he was born after being snatched from the belly of Semele by Hermes when she was struck by a thunderbolt, and from the thigh of Zeus, where he was afterward sewn up. From that he was called Eiraphiotes.[68] He is Dithyrambos from going through two 'doors,' the womb of his mother, Semele, and the thigh of Zeus; or because he was raised in the two-doored cave of Nysa.

***

[123,1] Now Aphthonius has stated two differences between encomion and *epainos,* but there is a third to be added, because *epainos* is concerned with true things, encomion with what is believable.[69] Those who express themselves with praise of people in accordance with their real thoughts are speaking *epainos,* not only bearing witness to their subject's possession of virtue by their words, but also adding the assent of their mind. Of course, the ancients called *epainos* only what was agreed to, as in Homer (e.g., *Iliad* 4.380): "And they praised." Encomion imitates the sincerity of *epainos* but it does not imply an acknowledgement in the mind of the speaker of the encomion that what is said is true. Of course, whenever we extol pots or potsherds, as Polycrates did,[70] or baldness or a fly,[71] we are not at all praising out of pure admiration but exercising ourselves in credible speeches. Opinions and reputations are proper to encomion, fame and glory to *epainos.* Those giving an encomion rightly use the opinions of the many, since they are concerned with the believable, not with the truth, and *epainos* has been judged as fame by serious people and glory is an extension of what has been said earlier. Those delivering an *epainos* praise what is true and they are confirmed by the judgment of serious people.

***

[139,5] **After these a comparison, attributing superiority to what is being celebrated by contrast . . . :** Theophrastus in his *Technai*[72] divided encomion into two kinds; for he says that some encomion is qualitative, some quantitative. The qualitative consists

---

[68] Of doubtful etymology, but often taken to mean "unsewn," cf. *Homeric Hymn to Dionysus* 2.

[69] In *Rhetoric* 1.9.33 Aristotle says epainos praises virtue, encomion praises deeds.

[70] Cf. Alexander in Spengel, vol. 3, p. 3, and Radermacher, pp. 130–31.

[71] There is an encomion of baldness by Synesius and of a fly by Lucian.

[72] Frag. 678 in W. W. Fortenbaugh et al., eds., *Theophrastus of Eresus: Sources,* Pt. 2 (Leiden: Brill, 1992).

of showing by means of his origin and education and deeds what sort of person someone is, whether good or bad, and the quantitative consists in comparisons; for whenever we have established the quality, then we demonstrate how much greatness he has by contrast to another. And encomion of quality is examination concerning substance, of quantity examination of an accident, which is shown by contrast with another. Comparison is like a measure of the reputation of those being celebrated, from which measure we comprehend the greatness of their virtue; for example, so-and-so is admirable, for he has done such and such. From this we admire him only to some extent, but how great he is we do not know. But if we add that he is comparable to somebody, we are teaching how great is the virtue of the subject from comparison with the one brought into the discussion. This clarifies the magnitude and adds an opinion.

***

[142,6]   Some have asked, "If the end of encomion is the honorable, and the end of invective is the base, what is the end of a speech bidding farewell to one who is departing (*propemptikos logos*)?" We reply as follows. A farewell speech is divided into two parts, into invective and encomion; for at the beginning we castigate the one departing as abandoning his friends and we call him unsettled and forgetful, but at the end we praise him, taking from encomia the reasons why we bear his departure heavily. Thus, the purpose of a propemptic speech at the beginning is the bad, at the conclusion the honorable. And to sum up in a word, the purpose of the ceremony of farewell is the panegyrical species.

***

[167]   9. ON INVECTIVE

This chapter lacks any introductory material.

Invective is a statement expressive of inherent evils. The definition of each exercise is put by Aphthonius and Hermogenes before its species and division because the definition is analogous to unity, division to plurality. The smallest division is into two. Since, then, the singular precedes every other number, for this reason definition, analogous to it, precedes division. Each rhetorical species being divided into two—judicial into accusation and defense, deliberative into what is to be chosen and what is to be avoided—it logically follows that the encomiastic species, which the ancients called panegyrical, is divided into what is called by the same name, encomion, and its opposite, invective (*psogos*). And so, invective, falling under the genus encomion, will be called "encomion" generically. Since invective and encomion are species of the encomiastic part of rhetoric, the species are rightly called by the same names as the genus is called. For this reason, Isocrates' speech *Against the Sophists,* which happens to be an invective, has been included among encomia. A thing does not always have the same nature because it illegitimately shares the same name; (for example,) vinegar is euphemistically called sweet by some people. Is it, for that reason, the same thing as honey? [168] Not at all. Nor if invective is euphemistically named encomion will it have any close affinity with encomion. Just as encomion is an amplification of the virtuous qualities of a person or thing, in the opposite way invective is an amplification of the evil qualities of a person or thing. And if one amplifies evils in common-place and there is, similarly, an amplification of evils here, is invective superfluous? No, since there punishment follows from the amplification, while here there is only an attack.

***

In his commentary on Aphthonius' invective against Philip of Macedon, John incorporates an extended passage on Philip's death from Diodorus Siculus 16.92–94. The following story can be compared with one in Aelian's Varia Historia *3.45.*

[179,11] But others say that when an oracle told Philip to beware of *to harma* ("a four-horse chariot"), he thought this meant Harma, a fortress in Boeotia, which Homer mentions (*Iliad* 2.499): "Those who live around Harma and Eilesios and Erythra." He kept away from there and did not visit it. As things turned out, however, the oracle had a different fulfillment. When a festival was being held in Aegae in Macedonia, since Philip was in the city at the time he joined in feasting and celebrated the games, taking his seat in the theater. A Laconian named Pausanias, joined by three sworn confederates, was plotting against Philip and, running into the theater with his confederates, killed him. This seemed to be the fulfillment of the oracles since there were four plotters, filling out the number required for a four-horse chariot. [180] But some say that a chariot had been engraved on the handle of Pausanias' sword.

***

10. ON SYNCRISIS

[180,16] The seeds of syncrisis have been found earlier in common-place and encomion and invective. For this reason Aphthonius
rightly gave an account of it right after them. The first thing to be
said about syncrisis is that this term is not current among the ancient writers;[73] instead of *synkrinein* they said *krinein*, **[181]** as in
Against Meidias (154), "I shall justly test him, comparing (*krinôn*)
him to myself." Phrynicus the Atticist, saying that *synkrisis* is the
opposite of *diakrisis,* wants to use the words *antexetazein* and *para-
ballein* (to mean 'compare').[74] Since the technical writers are not
very precise about words, but present a clear account in whatever
words they can, probably Aphthonius was following earlier technical writers in his use of the word.

***

**[191,16] (Peleus was granted) marriage with a goddess as a
prize of valor for slaying the Lapiths.** Some say he was not
granted marriage for this reason but because of his self-control; for
Peleus had the greatest self-control. Once, when Hippolyta, the
wife of Acastus, had fallen in love with him but was unable to persuade him, she slandered him as having tried to use force against
her.[75] When Acastus learned this, he took Peleus to a deserted place,
stripped him of his weapons, let him go, and departed, after saying,
"If you are innocent, you will be saved." The gods were happy to
send Hermes to him with a dagger made by Hephaistus, and so he
escaped danger. **[192]** Now Zeus had been planning an affair with
Thetis, daughter of Nereus, but learned from Prometheus that a
child born from her would be much greater in power than his father
and would take away his kingship, and frightened at a plot, he gave
her to Peleus, the son of Aeacus, in marriage.

***

[73] *Synkrinein* meaning "to compare" is found in Aristotle, *Rhetoric* 1.9.38, and
the noun *synkrisis* occurs in Aristotle, *Topics* 1.5.102b16. The exercise in comparison was called *synkrisis* at least by the time of Theon.

[74] Phrynicus was a lexicographer of the mid–second century after Christ. Apparently he regarded *synkrinein* as properly meaning 'to bring into combination,'
contrasting it with *diakrinei*, 'to divide,' and preferred the other two verbs cited
here to mean 'compare.'

[75] This story, from an unknown source, seems modeled after that of Hippoly-
tus and Phaedra.

[192,19] The one was reared by Cheiron . . . : Thetis, having been forced by Zeus to marry Peleus, threw her offspring into the fire, thinking mortal flesh would be consumed by the fire and what was immortal would survive.[76] In this way she destroyed six children. Achilles was the seventh to be born, and she threw him into the fire in the same way, but Peleus saw it and snatched the boy away, took him to Mount Pelion, and gave him over to Cheiron. Cheiron was a centaur, inhabiting a cave in Thessaly. After he had taught him medicine and lyre playing **[193]** and music, he gave him back to his father, who fed him on the marrow of lions and bears and called him Achilles. When Achilles was about to join the expedition to Ilium, Peleus told him that if he fought the Trojans he would have only a short life, but the greatest glory, while if he refrained from battle he would have a long and undistinguished life. Achilles, when he learned this, chose eternal glory with short life and joined the expedition in Troy.

***

[194]   11. ON ETHOPOEIA

Ethopoeia (or speech in character) is suitable in all parts of a speech and especially in the proofs; for it makes the language alive and moves the hearer to share the emotion of the speaker by presenting his character. Ethopoeia has been included among progymnasmata so that a young man may be practiced in it and not be unprepared in his declamations. Ethopoeia occurs in almost all the previous exercises and is a part of each, starting with fables. If we want to extend them, we do so by means of ethopoeia, and similarly if we want to compress, as **Hermogenes** showed by means of the fable of the apes. What does he say in the passage contained in his *Progymnasmata (see above, p. 75)?* **[195,4]** ". . . then fashion a speech also for the old ape"; for example, "Living together in a city will be the cause of many evils for us; for we shall grow softer in some way. One's way of life and soft living naturally weaken the mind as well as the body. Then, lack of the necessities of life follows for those collected in a city, and from that famine results. Nor will we have means of safety; if men already lay hands on us when we are widely scattered, how will they not do so more easily when we are shut in a city? Worst of all, as a group we shall be wholly wiped out, leaving no seed of our race." This is how a fable is extended by etho-

---

[76] John draws on some compendium of mythology; cf. Apollodorus, *Bibliotheca* 3.169.

poeia. Clearly it often occurs in narratives and refutations and encomion. Also in common-place, in creating a vivid impression of
the subject, we sometimes attribute words to those who have been
wronged, thus creating pathos. The same thing can be said in the
case of ecphrasis, since ethopoeia is also found there often. For
these two exercises[77] occur, as I said, within those previously
treated. Ethopoeia has been put first, and ecphrasis follows, as requiring greater skill; for it is more difficult than ethopoeia. Sometimes they also occur in thesis and in introduction of a law, and
since they come close to being complete hypotheses, they well perform the purpose of the progymnasmata.

You should know that under this genus—I am speaking about
ethopoeia—fall panegyrical and **[196]** and protreptic and epistulary
species. First of all, then, one should keep in mind what sort of persons the speaker and the addressee are, and their age at the time and
the occasion and the place and their fortune and the proposed material about which the speeches are going to be spoken. Then one
should try to speak appropriately; for different words are appropriate to different ages, not the same to an older and to a young man,
but in the speech of a younger man we should combine simplicity
and self-restraint, in that of an older man knowledge and experience, and different words will, because of their nature, be suitable
for a woman and a man, and because of their lot in life for a slave
and a free man and because of their occupation for a soldier and a
farmer and because of their state of mind for a lover and a shy person, and because of origin the words of a Laconian will be "few and
clear,"[78] and those of a man of Attica garrulous. We say that
Herodotus often spoke like a barbarian, although writing in Greek,
because he has imitated their speech. Speeches also need to fit the
places and occasions; for they are not the same in a military camp
and in a civilian assembly, nor in time of peace and in war, nor when
spoken by victors and vanquished, and in all the other situations
that befall persons. Moreover, each subject has an appropriate style
of expression (*hermêneia*). We shall master this if we do not speak
of great things in a lowly way nor about small things in a lofty way
nor about paltry things in a solemn way nor about awesome things
in an off-hand way nor about shameful things boldly nor about pitiful things excessively, but give what is appropriate to each, aiming

---

[77] I.e., ethopoeia and ecphrasis. "As I said" is apparently a reference to the beginning of this chapter, though ecphrasis is not mentioned there.

[78] Cf. *Iliad* 3.213, of the speech of Menelaus.

at the same time at [197] what fits the person and his way of life and the time and the fortune and each of the things mentioned earlier.

Since, then, there are various differences among persons and subjects—for we are either criticizing something or exhorting or dissuading or praising or seeking forgiveness or something else of this sort—it is necessary in each case to use the appropriate topics. When exhorting we shall say that what we urge be done is possible and easy and honorable and appropriate, that it is advantageous, that it is just, that it is pious, and the latter in two ways, toward the gods and toward the dead. And that we are not the only ones, nor the first, to do it, and that even if we are the first, it is much better to begin good works, and that when done they do not incur regret. One should also mention any previous benefits of the speaker toward the one who is being urged and if the latter was benefited at any time by having been persuaded by the speaker.

The treatment is the same if we are seeking something for ourselves, and when dissuading we construct arguments from the opposite topics. But if we are praising, we shall use the reason that what has been done was necessary and common to all, and that it was unintentional.[79] Intelligent people are least disturbed at unintentional actions. If it was done willingly, one should say that he was the cause by himself; for people are less distressed by self-motivation, having suffered misfortunes from their own actions. One should say that there is a greater evil than this, which many others have been happy to put up with. In addition, that if it is annoying in the short run, still it is both fine and honorable. Then, that it is beneficial, and that nothing is gained from grief at things already done. [198] And pity has great power for consolation, especially when one is making a speech about loss of a dear one; for the aggrieved are inclined to resist those thinking they have suffered nothing very bad and, as it were, to become angry, in addition to their grief, at those consoling them, but they accept comfort more willingly from those grieving with them, as from relatives. Thus, after lamentations one should continue the speech with advice. But whenever we seek forgiveness, we shall take our starting points from the following topics: first, that what was done was unintentional, whether through ignorance or chance or necessity. If it was intentional, one should say that it was a pious act, that it was the usual thing, that it was advantageous. One should construct the argument

---

[79] John is speaking of explanations in encomia of actions open to criticism; cf. Theon, above, p. 52.

from what topics are available; for all do not fit all prosopopoeias[80] or ethopoeias that fall under the same species of rhetoric. This exercise is useful for invention in ethical and pathetical speeches; for it makes the speech lively and presents the character of the speaker to the greatest extent.

Someone[81] might say that, if ethopoeia is concerned with the kind of action and the quality of the speaker, since complete hypotheses are concerned with a particular action and with the quality of the speaker, clearly ethopoeias and complete hypotheses are the same. And we reply, that ethopoeias are not divided into headings as are complete hypotheses, nor do they contain antitheses[82] nor the other parts of a political speech, and they are not spoken in lawcourts or assemblies, but ethopoeia is included **[199]** within complete hypotheses; so in all respects one should draw a line between them.

Some others say that if many ethopoeia are protreptic—for example, what words an aged war hero would probably say when sending his son to war—and since protreptic speeches are deliberative, deliberations are then ethopoeias. Now we say that these critics have spoken credibly and cleverly but not truly. For the opposite is not true. A protrepic ethopoeia, having some characteristic features of exhortation, is one thing and an actual exhortation is another. An ethopoeia is delimited by some few arguments from past, present, and future time, while exhortation, as an hypothesis dealing with acknowledged particulars, takes its amplification from final headings. In order to make the explanation clearer, we shall restate what is being said. Protrepic speeches are deliberative, yes, but on agreed upon subjects. For one who exhorts makes the hearer more zealous for some agreed upon action and no one is speaking against it, whereas the deliberative speaker is dealing with a subject that has two sides to it, of which he maintains one. The relationship of a protreptic ethopoeia to a complete exhortation is that an ethopoeia is included in the exhortation as a part, and the part is not the same as the whole. One can take as an example the protrepic

[80] In a passage omitted here (201,12ff. ed. Rabe) John explains the differences between prosopopoeia, ethopoeia, and eidolopoeia as stated by Aphthonius. Scholia to Aristeides' speech *On the Four* (vol. 3, p. 674 ed. Dindorf) quote Sopatros as saying that Aristeides' personification of "the Four" should be called ethopoeia, not eidolopoeia, since he represents them as alive; cf. Rabe's ed. of Aphthonius, p. 64.

[81] One of the "eristical sophists" of p. 182 above?

[82] I.e., objections to be refuted.

speeches of Aristeides, which he addressed to the athletes contending in the Olympic games.[83] These are wholes and contain a complete hypothesis. They are divided into final headings of the just, advantageous, honorable, possible. As a result, the protreptic ethopoeia has a trace and a likeness and **[200]** a similarity to a part of an exhortation, but is not an exhortation.

Practice in ethopoeia is most useful everywhere; for it does not contribute to only one species of rhetoric, but to all. Everywhere, as it happens, we form characters and attribute speeches to persons. Wherefore, they have thought it worthwhile to exercise us in the form of the ethopoeia since we shall have need of it in any speech.

***

[208,4] You will elaborate the characterization in a style that is clear: The style (*kharaktêr*), he is saying, of speeches of characterization should confirm to the nature of the supposed persons and subjects. A style without contrivance fits ethopoeias; for the speaker will say what is acknowledged universally in a scattered fashion, in short phrases and without connectives. And it ought to be wholly consistent with the character and the subject. **Concise** (*syntomos*): Vigorous, forceful; for that is the style of commonly accepted ideas and what each person knows. Speaking concisely is characteristic of both those who are happy and those who mourn, as is adding one thing to another in few words, which Aphthonius makes clear by saying *syntomos*. **Fresh:** (*anthêros*), i.e., extemporaneous. **Pure:** i.e., ranging at will, free, clear. For he will not seem to have suffered anything if he takes trouble about the beauty of his language in such circumstances. **Free from any inversion and figure.** "Inversion" means metaphorical diction; for the diction ought to fit the subjects. As a result, we admire what Isocrates said so aptly in his *Helen* (10.59), "As streaming gold he (i.e., Zeus) coupled with Danaë"; for the word "streaming," being even and smooth in pronunciation, **[209]** imitates the flow of the gold; for it is soft in sound, like gentle streams. An ethopoeia should avoid metaphorical language and varied figures, by which I mean periods and the like. The expression should be mostly in short phrases and not be filled out in periods. Over all, through the style of expression the speech should be proper to those supposed to be speaking, so that pathetic things are expressed pathetically, painful things epideictically, ethical things ethically, and each of the others similarly.

[83] The speeches are not extant.

***

[215]   12. ON ECPHRASIS

Some, indifferently, put ecphrasis after common-place,[84] some after ethopoeia. There is use for it in proofs and in introductory statements; for to describe a place or some part of a subject, such as a plague or war or occasion and the like, is necessary. Thus ecphrasis contributes to declamation.

You should know that the best treatment of ecphrases includes considering in each part of the description the reasons why the thing described takes the form it does or has a particular placement. You will draw these reasons from considering what results from the things described being as they are. You will be helped by getting to know the ecphrases of famous sophists. There are many by Epagathus and Callinicus and Prohaeresius and Himerius, the most learned of the wise, and others.[85] And the *Eikones* of Philistratus contain nothing other than ecphrasis.[86]

Ecphrases are most useful for all three species of rhetoric; for in encomia you will describe the places, harbors, stoas, and such things built by men; in judicial speeches, similarly, the places with which the trial is concerned and which you are impelled to make known to the judges. Much the same in deliberations; for in deliberative speeches we often must describe what we are talking about in order to be more persuasive.

[216]   You should know this too, that fable resembles ecphrasis to the extent that we describe some animal; for example, what the lion looked like or the ape that was wearing a lion skin. There is a difference, however, because fable gives a description in few words, ecphrasis in many. A description would not be the chief thing in a fable, whereas in an ecphrasis it is the one characteristic thing.

***

[223,18] In composing an ecphrasis one should use a relaxed style and adorn it with different figures. The style (*kharaktêr*), he is saying, that fits ecphrases in the exercise of the young is sweet

---

[84] No extant work does this.

[85] Athenian sophists of the third and fourth centuries after Christ, known from Eunapius and the *Suda*. Only Himerius, however, is known from extant speeches. None of these is wholly an ecphrasis but many contain ecphrastic passages.

[86] Philostratus' *Eikones* (c. A.D. 200) purports to describe works of art in a collection at Naples.

(*hêdus*) and relaxed, without periods and enthymemes; for the latter are assigned to things that are intense. One who wants to abound in a relaxed style should run away from anything rough, and practice what is simple. Clash of sounds and contentious syntax and rattling iambics **[224]** are characteristic of roughness: clash of sound (*synkrousmos*) as in *Pelops skêptron krouei* and other such combinations of many sounds; contentious syntax (*enagônios syntaxis*) as "If, on some new subject . . ." (Demosthenes 4.1) and in dilemmas and all the varied things that are suitable for intensity; and rattling iambics (*iambokrotos*) as in "*Dêlón gar ésti toís Olýnthioís* . . ." (Demosthenes 1.5). Such things as that ought to be avoided even in tightened passages. It is not frequent hiatus, as some think, that makes the plain style, but clarity; for example, *Achillea epothei he Hellas* or *Klytaimnêstra Agamemnona apekteine*.[87] Narrative construction is relaxed; for example, Thucydides' "Cylon was an Olympic victor"(1.126); here, they say, "the lion broke into laughter,"[88] so fitting was the narrative to the relaxed style. Also Herodotus' "Croesus was . . ." (1.6) and Xenophon's "Cyrus was . . ."[89] Repetition of similar endings (*homoiokatalêkton*), when sparsely used, has grace; for example, Thucydides' *Phainetai gar hê nun Hellas* **kaloumenê** *ou pala bebaiôs* **oikoumenê** (1.2) and *ethaumaze* **to** **plêthos; ** *ou gar êidei* **to pathos** (3.113), and Plato's *ô lôiste Pôle, hina proseipô* **se** *kata* **se** (*Gorgias* 467b). But one must avoid excess. The simple style also uses poetic freedom, describing the gods descending from heaven and ascending and engaging in dialogue—the source of Herodotus' description of the gods as kings of Egypt (2.144)—and inventing dreams and oracles.

Theon (above, p. 47) says that the virtues of ecphrasis are clarity and a vivid impression of all but seeing what is described. Vividness is what is very evident and presents itself to the eyes. For if the language is clear and vivid, **[225]** what is said is changed from being heard to being seen; for the language inscribes what is described in the eyes of the spectators and paints the truth in the imagination.

***

Aphthonius' ecphrasis of the acropolis of Alexandria (i.e., the Serapeum) is the most obscure of his compositions. John clarifies some pas-

---

[87] Object, verb, subject; subject, object, verb.
[88] Apparently a proverb; cf. John Siceliotes 504,5 ed. Walz, and Scholia to Thucydides ad loc.
[89] Probably the simple language of the opening of the *Anabasis* is meant, though this phrase does not occur there.

sages, but misleads the reader in others. What sources, if any, he was drawing on is unclear.

[226,5] Citadels, then, have been built in cities . . . : "Then" (*ara*) instead of "everywhere" (*pantelôs*). The prooemion is in the simple style because of the connective *de*. Aphthonius took his start from a thought characteristic of prooemia, which shows that his enthusiasm is reasonable. One should begin in this way so that the speech is not, as it were, lacking a "head" and does not immediately start the description with nothing preceding. **They are not more fortified themselves with buildings than they fortify their cities.** Going back to what he said above, that citadels have been built for the common safety, he now says that these are more a fortification for the buildings (in the city?) than the buildings (on the citadel?) are fortifications of them. **[227]** Some say that "they are fortified" and "they fortify" is the figure epidiorthosis (correction), but I call it a judgment and . . . (?) and a proposition. It would be epidiorthosis if he said "they are fortified, or rather they fortify." As it is, they should be called what we said.

***

[227,9] For here there is a road and there an entrance way. The straight road lying in front of the acropolis, he says, is, on the one hand, the road to those who live on the acropolis and on the other hand an entrance to the acropolis itself. **On another side, flights of steps have been constructed.** On the entrance, that is, of the acropolis. "Have been constructed"[90] instead of "have been dug from below to above," that is "brought up from level ground to the height." **Always increasing, leading from the lesser . . . :** Clearly, from the low to the high, which he made clear from the word "have been constructed." **For the limit of a number is the end that reaches perfect measure.** "Perfect," that is final. Clearly, he is speaking of the decade, since ten is the limit and end of the monad.[91] **[228] Enclosed by gates of moderate height . . . :** "Moderate" (*metriais*) instead of "small." "Hedged round" (*periergomenon*) has also been written,[92] the word meaning

---

[90] *Prosanespasthêsan,* a rare word; literally "have been drawn up beside."

[91] John apparently understands Aphthonius to be noting that 100 steps, specified in the text, represent ten decades of ten monads, having some philosophical significance; but there were in fact 200 steps. See above, p. 119, n. 90.

[92] We need not conclude that John had more than one mss.; the reference can come from an earlier commentary.

the same thing (as "enclosed"). **On the columns stands the Oecus, fronted by many smaller columns.** "Stands on" instead of "has been stationed" above the columns; it is elevated. "Fronted" instead of "having before it, put in front and as it were, showing it." **And when compared . . . :** Put next to each other, because of each having a different color, one being judged against another. **Around the dome is fixed a great memorial of things that are.** By "things that are" he means either the deeds of divine history—for the hemisphere in it is explained variously—or the four elements from which everything comes to be; I mean fire and water and earth and air. **Its figure is rather like that of a war machine.** A four-sided square. The (logical) order of words is "The figure of a war machine is rather similar." **And as for their measure . . . :** Clearly, the number of the decade.[93] **Offering an opportunity of knowledge . . . :** "Offering" (*epairontes*) instead **[229]** of (*five synonyms are suggested.*) **Different parts were done differently.** Clearly, some of the workmanship has been differently done. **One part has a representation of the contests of Perseus.** Perseus killed the Medousa and for that reason has been honored with not a few statues. **The beginnings of things have been carved around the top of the column.** He means the four elements: for fire and water and earth and air have been represented by allegorical figures on the top of the column. **A structure (divided into two parts) . . . :** The hemisphere of the sky. **Divided into two parts for gates, that are named for the ancient gods.** There are eight gates; for eight was the number of the ancient gods among the Egyptians, among the Greeks twelve. **Two stone obelisks rise up.** He means pyramids. For these are like high obelisks. **And a fountain considered better than that of the Peisistratids. . . :** That is, in water; the Peisistratus built a fountain having hot water. **On one side there is a place resembling . . . :** Topical, but to be read emotionally. **[230] Which has become the name of the place . . . :** That is, Stadion. **On another side. . . :** This too is topical, instead of "thus" (*hôde*). **Because of the amount** (*parenthêkê*) **. . . :** The excess, the addition, the distraction.

13. ON THESIS

After practicing the young in the judicial species of rhetoric up through encomion, we come next to the deliberative species; for it is most necessary for the young man to be practiced in thesis for de-

[93] I.e., 10 x 10?

liberative hypotheses. We say this not because the deliberative species has no need of encomia—for encomion is common to all species—but because thesis occurs more in deliberative hypotheses.

Before giving a line by line exegesis we must say where thesis got its name. Well then, the word *thesthai* ("to put") indicates different things, but among others it means "to define." Here then, since, as it were, we are defining the nature of the thing, thesis has taken its name from that. But others say (it is so called) from defining what one should do; for (the thesis) "one should marry" makes it clear it is necessary to marry; and among the grammarians such statements are called "thetic."[94] And **Sopatros** says that it is called thesis from our proposing (*tithesthai*) and, so to speak, expressing the opinion that something is good or bad.

***

[240,5] Then you will use the final headings: legal, just, advantageous, possible. These are called "final" (*telika*) because they are comprehensive of many thoughts; for they grasp many thoughts. Or they are said to be final because each of the others is referred to them as to a root.[95]

Now legal is what seems so to the laws. The just is divided into the legal and the similarly named just and the customary. The just and the legal are the most weighty of all arguments, and the legal is prior to the just as being a non-artistic proof;[96] for non-artistic proofs are stronger than artistic proofs. The legal is, then, a non-artistic proof. The just is derived from previous thoughts and from widely-accepted beliefs providing a counter-statement. Widely-accepted beliefs are not all the same. Some think it is good to eat their parents,[97] others to burn them; among the Athenians it is actionable not to feed or assist them. The advantageous, again, is naturally prior to the possible—for first we consider if something is advantageous, then, if so, whether it is possible—**[241]** and has included the possible in itself; for necessarily the possible is included in the advantageous, not the advantageous in the possible; for if it is

[94] As a grammatical term, *thetikos* means positive as contrasted with negative. Otherwise, it can mean propositional, in thesis-form, or apposite; cf. above, pp. 156 and 170.

[95] Probably the term *telika* refers to the purpose or end of the arguments.

[96] I.e., the law is used as a basis of argument, but not invented by the speaker's art; cf. Aristotle, *Rhetoric* 1.15.3–12.

[97] Among the Massagetae, according to Herodotus 1.216; cf. Aristotle, *Topics* 2.11.

deemed possible to kill someone or to rob a temple when the priests are not on their guard, this does not imply that it is also advantageous. If someone says that it is useless to consider the advantage when something is impossible, we shall say that even if there is no possibility, the advantage is always considered. For we should plan which is good for ourselves, even if we cannot effect it. The possible comes after the advantageous; for whenever we want to do something or whenever we are making plans about something, first we consider if it is lawful; for when we are living under laws, it is necessary to consider this first. But when something seems legal and just and advantageous, then one should examine how we can do it.

The topic of legality is expanded by considering the intent of the lawgiver and the circumstantial factors and other laws. We expand it also from consideration of the persons and the facts; from persons, by asking who is the one that introduced the law, (for example,) to fight or to help (someone) and when and whom and how; from facts, why it is necessary to fight or help, and why it is necessary to engage in politics or to philosophize or to farm. The just is understood in three ways: just by nature, by custom, by enactment. Let us propose the thesis Whether one should marry. We argue from nature when we say that by nature we have a desire to marry, from custom when we say that it is a long established tradition, and from enactment that "Since the laws punish adulterers, [242] it is clear that they think marriage to be a most honorable thing." Advantage relies on conjectural arguments; for it is established from what will result. Two lines of argument are available, either that it rids us from evils or that it provides good things, and the advantageous consists of both. It is examined in terms of the mind and the body and externals. If someone wants to expand it, one should scrutinize it in terms of fortune and way of life and opportunities and age; for example, whether this is being attributed to a rich man or a poor man or a soldier or farmer in such and such a way, and is advantageous to a young man and an old man and each of the other ages of life, and in happiness and grief, and in peace and in war. All in all, the heading should be examined in terms of all the differences that occur among people. Argument about the possible is also taken from three sources: from mind, from body, from externals. Some things we establish by means of the mind; for example, whether a philosopher should engage in politics; for you will say that it is possible to engage in politics in an intelligent way. Some by the body; for example, whether one should beget children. Some by externals; for example, whether a rich man should be tyrant; for power in this case comes from money. But whenever the thing is hard to establish and we cannot clearly introduce the heading of the possible, one should combine the necessary with it, saying that even if the thing was not easy, still it was necessary to do it, as in the thesis "Whether those suffering from the plague should change their residence";[98] for moving is unpleasant to the weak. You will say that it is possible for them to be carried in carriages and on pack animals, and even if the thing is not very easy, it is nevertheless necessary; for [243] the plague impels it. This is how this heading should be managed in the case of difficult things; with easy ones one should consider not only possibility but facility. Among those who are happy one should examine not only the possibility but the ease of doing something. This is an extension of the possible, when you say not only that the thing is possible but that it is without toil, as Isocrates in the *Philippus* (5.57) did, saying "That it is not impossible to bring these cities together is, I think, clear to you; that you will also do this easily, I think to make you understand from many examples."

Up to this point we have been following Aphthonius' teaching, but we thought it necessary to add the teachings of **Theon** and of **Sopatros** in order that treatment of thesis may be more detailed. Now Theon lists the topics of thesis as follows:

John here inserts quotation of Theon, above, pp. 56–59. There follows then a long quotation from Sopatros' lost treatise on progymnasmata.

[247,12] **Sopatros,** drawing a distinction between encomion and thesis, speaks as follows: "In encomion there is praise of a person, in thesis praise of an action; for we praise (or blame) something as good or bad. That praise when occurring in a thesis is praise of an action is made clear by the argument; for we construct the proof entirely from consideration of what is naturally good, and the good by nature is the goal of encomion and thesis; for example, (in an encomion,) that Achilles is naturally good, being descended from Zeus and Aeacus and Peleus and taught by Cheiron and having done this and that. In thesis the same argument is constructed in treating (such themes as) whether one should teach rhetoric, whether one

[98] Compare the declamation theme, "The Scythians, having falling ill, debate whether to move," cited repeatedly in Apsines' rhetorical handbook.

should sail on the sea; for we say the recommended action is good, being just and legal and advantageous and possible. But these are not set out as complete headings—for in progymnasmata there are no whole headings—; rather, taking from these headings epicheiremes that are illustrative of the just [248] and legal and advantageous and possible, we arrange for the young man to get practice by taking from us a taste of these headings in the treatment of theses.

"It is necessary to add something about the division of a thesis. One part is, as I said, the construction of an argument in the thesis that something is good by nature, and this is established by a variety of epicheiremes. Let the thesis be whether one should practice physical exercise. Now after one or two prooemia, and having set out the proposition, you will use epicheiremes drawn from the topic of the just, and you will divide these into three parts: just to gods, to men, to the dead. Now first, we shall use the argument from nature, saying that 'Our bodily strength is a gift of nature. It is, therefore, quite good and not at all out of place to have used existing advantages in games established by gods and other such gatherings. We shall thus contribute to the success of festivals.' Then, argument from the lesser: 'To have made use of offerings[99] is to have displayed ambition from fortune and external sources, but to have sought honor by the body is to have used one's own advantages.' Then the epicheireme relating to men: 'Since it is just for each man's strength to be known, and to what extent each surpassed his neighbor, it is also just for our natural advantages not to be hidden.' Further, if there are games for the dead, we shall honor them by our natural advantages. Since epicheiremes from justice are, as I said, divided into three, justice toward gods is called being reverent, that toward men, living and dead, is called by one word, pious. You will find many up to now who have maintained this usage [249] of words. We say 'He has acted piously' when someone gives something appropriate to some one, just as one who does not honor his parents is called impious and burial of the dead is called a pious act, this honor being justice for the dead.

"After this you will put an epicheireme from legality, saying that 'No law and no government hinders anyone from trying to show his natural assets, but the unwritten laws and custom among Greeks and barbarians wisely teach that people should exercise and not destroy their physique by neglect.' Then the epicheireme from the advantageous; this concerns when the action produces a profit or in-

[99] I.e., to become known by making costly offerings to the gods.

crease from outside, not from inborn nature: 'Physical exercise will enhance the body, produce health, create beauty.' Then from the purpose, which is an extension of advantage, saying that 'We become respected through exercise and we seem manly, and being well spoken of by many is a prize of exercise for men.' Then by argument from the possible, saying that 'To exercise within one's ability is both easy and not tiresome.'

"You should know that we shall use applicable epicheiremes, not all possible ones; for thesis, by itself, teaches how to choose epicheiremes, in order that through practice in thesis we may be readied for the invention of epicheiremes in debates. After the epicheiremes that are applicable for the thesis at hand, you will confirm the argument with examples; for rhetorical demonstration is enthymematic and paradeigmatic, and **[250]** I have often said that an epicheireme is an enthymeme, because the judge or hearer has to add in his mind either the conclusion or one of the premises.[100] When what was left out is added, an enthymeme becomes a complete and dialectical syllogism. If you call a syllogism rhetorical, using the adjective 'rhetorical,' you are saying that it lacks the conclusion or one of the premises, and that is what is properly called an enthymeme.

"But let us return to examples. 'It was because of exercise that Heracles became famous, powerful, celebrated, immortal; Minos similarly, Rhadamanthys too; all these inhabit the Elysian Field after death.' Then you will use one antithesis, so that those who are being exercised may have some experience and conception of the use of these. 'But exercise,' he says, 'is wearisome to men.' You will always discover an antithesis in theses by taking the refutation (*enstasis*) from difficulties incident to the action under discussion. The solutions will usually be comparative, saying that 'One should not overlook many good things because of one difficulty, but one should persist and bear it patiently for the advantage of the benefits,' and so on. Then, as in a conclusion, you will say, 'And so it is possible to honor exercise and to use the activity.'

"You will refute a thesis in the same way that you confirm it, using epicheiremes from the opposites; **[251]** for rhetoric has starting points for each side of the question; but it has not been customary to refute theses; for it is wrong to accustom the young to entertain thoughts opposed to the good.

---

[100] The explanation is poorly expressed. Probably, like Minucian, Apsines, and others, Sopatros regarded an epicheireme as a general term for logical argument, including both enthymemes and examples.

"As for the possible objection to thesis on the ground that it has headings and is a complete hypothesis, I say that these are not headings but epicheiremes connected with the heading. A heading is confirmed by many, different epicheiremes, so often the heading suffices for the whole hypothesis. Since the subject in hypotheses refers to specifics and the person and action involved are particulars, the heading probably is a particular question and has been confirmed from various epicheiremes invented and spoken from the circumstances. In thesis, nothing of this sort is the case. The headings are not in question,[101] but the subject being set out on its own, we are primarily concerned with displaying what is naturally good by this means, not having to deal with any objection arising from the headings; but composing an interpretation and, so to speak, a rough sketch of the headings, and preparing a choice of epicheiremes, we practice the exercise in this way. Further, the heading (in a complete hypothesis), containing the question that has already been defined and first providing us with a perception of the question in it, is either refuted or confirmed on the basis of all the circumstances, but in thesis there are no circumstances, no person, no place, no time, no other things like that. So **[252]** how is it possible for headings to be spoken in a thesis, where there is no question at issue, and everything is devoted to what is good? Except that it is possible for those dragging their long beards in rhetoric to ask, fond of a quarrel as they are, and to nit-pick about the existence of headings in thesis."

The quotation from Sopatros ends at this point. John then returns to Theon without identifying him and quotes at length his discussion of theses on theoretical subjects (above, pp. 59–61). Finally, John adds a short passage from Hermogenes on single and double theses.

***

14. ON INTRODUCTION OF A LAW

[261,16] Once the young have been practiced in these exercises, taking them to what is more difficult, Aphthonius logically considered last an exercise that is close to complete hypotheses.

You should know that fable resembles introduction of a law in that also in a fable we require students not to speak ill of parents and not to dishonor gods. It differs in that in fable we offer advice

[101] He probably means that definition of the question at issue, or stasis, central to a judicial hypothesis, does not enter into defending a thesis.

solely through the subject, but here there is enforcement by law, and there we impart the moral as generally agreed upon, whereas here we debate first about whether the law has been ratified.

***

The End

Index

For quotations from and references to Greek poets, historians, orators, and historical figures before B.C. 300 and to mythological figures, see the full indices in the editions of Patillon, Rabe, and Felton.

For discussion of each progymnasma, see the sub-headings in the Table of Contents, above, pp. v–vii.

ethos, 13, 67, 85, 164
exergasia, 8, 71, 77

final headings, 79, 81, 87, 106, 121,
153, 171, 176, 201, 216, 217, 222

glaphyros, 161
Gorgias, 132
Gregory of Nazianzus, 90, 95
(n. 20)

habroteros, 161
Hegesias, 14
hellenismos, 97 (n. 23), 137 (n. 24)
Hermagoras, 55 (n. 175)
Himerius, 218
historia, historiography, 1, 4 (n. 12),
32, 52, 67–69, 75, 109–10, 159,
184, 189, 191
homonymy, 51, 62, 63
hyperbaton, 31
hypothesis, xiv, 3, 5, 120–21, 151,
153, 206–7
hyptiotês, 158

invective, 43, 50, 56, 111–13, 149,
154, 158–59, 210–11

letter writing, 47, 48, 166
Libanius, xii, 2, 73, 89, 93 (n. 13),
97 (n. 26), 98 (n. 27), 99 (n. 35),
101 (n. 41), 106 (n. 54), 112
(n. 64), 116, 121 (n. 99), 131,
154 (n. 62)

makhomenon, 146
Menander Rhetor, 49 (n. 152), 159
(n. 85), 174
metalepsis, 17, 19
metaphor, 18, 70, 217
metaphrasis, 70 (n. 207)

Palaiphatus, 42
parabolê, 195
parakatêgorêma, 152
paraphrase, xi, 6, 12, 70, 98
pathos, 67, 164
periokhê, 152
periphrase, 100

Philodemus, 147 (n. 44)
Plato, xi, 3 (n. 4), 9, 11, 13, 17, 18,
24, 42, 52, 59, 60, 76, 84, 97,
133, 142, 156 (n. 66),
219
pleonasm, 22, 62, 63
Plutarch, 18 (n. 75), 49 (n. 152), 69,
99 (n. 33), 164
pompikos, 163
Porphyry, 91, 94, 160
Priscian, ix, 73, 74
Prohaeresius, 218
promythion, 96, 135
prooemion, 4, 23, 26, 44, 51, 56, 62,
79, 80, 106, 108, 142, 150–51,
156, 164, 169, 170, 204
propemptikos, 210
prosody, 62
prosopopoeia, 4, 8, 11, 47, 49, 55,
84, 115, 165, 216
prosphônêtikos, 154, 208 (n. 65)
psogos. See invective
psychagôgia, 135 (n. 18), 177

Quintilian, ix, x, 1, 2, 6 (n. 18), 29
(n. 107), 60 (n. 182), 66, 67, 70,
131 (n. 5)

semnos (semnotês), 161, 163
Sextus Empiricus, 174 (n. 4), 182
(n. 20)
Siricius, xii, 144
sminthiakos, 155
Sopatros, 173, 174, 178, 190 (n. 32),
197, 202, 206, 216 (n. 80), 222,
224–28
Stoicism, 1 (n. 2), 152 (n. 57)
style, 14, 24, 27, 30–31, 47, 62–64,
84, 86, 95, 136, 154, 157, 161,
164, 166, 168, 172, 217,
218–19
synkrousmos, 219
Syrianus, 159 (n. 83), 160 (n. 86)

telika kephalia. See final headings
Theano, 16
Theodorus of Gadara, 1, 55, 131
(n. 5)
thetikos, 156, 170, 222 (n. 94)

virtues of narration, 29–33, 97,
137–38, 185
vividness, 45, 86, 187, 219. *See also*
diatypôsis, enargeia

Zeno of Citium, 60

9 781589 830615